THE KADAMBAS OF GOA
&
THEIR INSCRIPTIONS

THE KADAMBAS OF GOA
&
THEIR INSCRIPTIONS

DR. S. L. Shantakumari
Professor of Ancient Indian History
& Epigraphy (Rtd.)
Karnatak University, Dharwad

AGAM KALA PRAKASHAN
DELHI

First Published 2015

ISBN : 978 -81-7320-146-2

Published by:
Dr. Agam Prasad, M.A., Ph.D., Diploma in Museology
For **Agam Kala Prakashan**
34, Central Market, Ashok Vihar
Delhi - 110 052
Tel.: 91-11-27212195, 65688806-7
Fax: 91-11-27212195
Email: agambooks@gmail.com, agambook@yahoo.com
www.agamkala.com

Composed by:
Aman Printographics
Delhi - 110 052
Mobile: 9891395309

Printed by:
Balajee Imaging Systems
Wazirpur Village, Ashok Vihar
Delhi-110 052

Printed in India

Dedicated To

My Mentor
Revered
Professor Shrinivas Ritti

FOREWORD

I have pleasure in writing a few words of appreciation by way of Foreword to this book 'The Kadambas of Goa and their Inscriptions' produced by my erstwhile colleague Dr. Leela Shantakumari, formerly Professor and Head of the Department of Ancient Indian History and Epigraphy, Karnatak University, Dharwad. Ever since the beginning of her research career as Research Assistant way back in 1966 in the Department, she has evinced keen interest in Epigraphical studies and has pursued them with utter zeal and devotion. She has taught also for several years this subject to the post graduate students.

'The Kadambas of Goa and their inscriptions' is the outcome of Dr.Shantakumari's long experience in the field and the abiding interest in the subject. Procuring a Senior Fellowship from the Indian Council of Historical Research, New Delhi, she has conducted extensive field work in the area concerned and has herself collected large number of new inscriptions, the study of which have brought authenticity and originality to the work.

Study of the minor dynasties like the present one in question, has its own merits. They enhance the study of regional history, which, in turn, enriches the study of national history. National history is painted on a wider canvas where many minor details have to be furnished to make the narration complete. In the process there is a possibility of the missing of essential details which may create a lacuna in the narration itself. Hence, the need for in depth study of regional history which augments and strengthens the study of national history. The present work, I suppose, fulfills this need to a considerable extent in relation to history of South India in general and particularly of that of Karnataka. I congratulate Dr. Shantakumari for her successful endeavour in this direction.

The work is divided into several chapters dealing with the sources, the origin and genealogy of the family, the political history and social, economic and religious conditions. A useful appendix is added at the end which contains texts of the many hitherto unknown inscriptions. In the more recent times such a study is characterised as a conventional one with less importance to the study of society and the social life. The author has touched upon these points adequately and gives due importance to the study of chronological and genealogical studies also. In my opinion this is necessary also since genealogy and chronology prepare the necessary frame work for the study of the kingdom or period. The political history provides the necessary foundation for the study of any other aspect of history.

Dr. Shantakumari's is a modest attempt in this direction which she has achieved amidst several handicaps including major health hazards. I am sure that the academic community will whole heartily welcome this useful addition to the study of the history of Karnataka which needs to be strengthened off and on by such studies.

Dr. Shrinivas Ritti
Prof. of Ancient Indian History
and Epigraphy (Retd.)
Karnatak University, Dharwad.

ACKNOWLEDGEMENTS

The epigraphical and archaeological material discovered by me during the course of my survey in the Kalghatgi region of Dharwad district in Karnataka State prompted me to select this topic viz., the Kadambas of Goa for my project work. The Kadambas of Goa were the feudatories of the Chālukyas of Kalyāṇa who ruled between 10th and 13th centiries A.D. having Goa as their capital. The contribution of the Kadambas to political, social, economic, religious and cultural aspects is note worthy.

I express my sincere gratitude to the Indian Council of Historical Research, New Delhi, for providing me financial assistance through offering a Senior Fellowship, after considering my request.

Prof. S.H. Ritti, former Professor of Anceient Indian History & Epigraphy, Karnatak University, Dharwad,who has been a source of inspiration to me in carrying out this work. I am grateful to him for his constant help, encouragement and guidance in completing this work and also in deciphering the inscriptions discovered by me.

My thanks are due to the Chief Epigraphist, Archaeological survey of India, Mysore, and his staff, for allowing me to make use their Library.

I remember with gratitude the help rendered by Dr. V. Shivananda, Director of Archaeology, (Retd.) Archaeological

Survey of India, New Delhi for his help in providing the copies of Portuguese records, photographs and also the xerox copies of inscriptions which were essential for this work.

I am thankful to the Superintending Archaeologist, Dharwad Circle, Dharwad, and also Dy. Director, Directorate of Archaeology and Museums, Karnataka Government, Dharwad, for their help in consulting their Library.

My thanks are due to Dr. S.V. Padigar, Professor of Ancient Indian History and Epigraphy, (Retd.) Karnatak University, Dharwad, for his help in carrying out this project.

I am thankful to the Librarian, Karnatak Uuniversity, Dharwad and also the Director, Kannada Reasearch Institute Karnatak University, Dharwad, for helping me in consulting their Libraries.

I am grateful to Fr. Jacob, Chairman, Good News Education Society, Kalaghatgi, who helped me during the course of my field work for which I am deeply indebted to him.

I am grateful to Mr. C.R. Kadkol, for his constant help in the course of my survey and also in the preparation of the computer copy of the work.

In this connection I remember the help rendered by, Mr. Shankar Kalghatgi of Mishrikoti, Sri Kallappa of Kamadhenu, late Mr. Chickmath and also late Sri Shankar Chougle, of Kannada Reseaarch Institute, Karnatak University, Dharwad, for their constant help at the time of my survey, for which I am thankful to them.

I specially thank to Dr. Agam Prasad, proprietor, Agam Kala Prakashan, for publishing the book with in such a short span of time and I impeccable Manner.

S. L. Shantakumari

PREFACE

For me the publication of this dissertation is a dream come true. While going through the large number of inscriptions of different dynasties in connection with a research project undertaken by the Department of Ancient Indian History and Epigraphy, Karnatak University, Dharwad of which I was an accredited member, I came across quite a few interesting inscriptions belonging to the later Kadamba families like the Kadambas of Goa and Haṇgal and other smaller families who functioned as the feudatories of the Chālukyas of Kalyāṇa. Of them, I was particularly attracted by the inscriptions of the Kadambas of Goa who played a vital role in the political and cultural life of the people in the coastal as well as adjoining upland in the medieval period of the History of Karnataka. Technically, Goa has nothing to do with Karnataka in the present day, but it was a very pleasant thing to discover that it was a part and parcel of ancient Karnataka. I was particularly fascinated by the lengthy poetic compositions contained in quite a few inscriptions discovered in Goa and the adjoining regions of Dharwad and Belgaum districts of Karnataka. Looking into the rich material contained in these inscriptions, it occurred to me that it is worthwhile taking up a research project dealing with this subject. While probing into the problem I noticed that the region covered by the activities of these rulers contain a large number of inscriptions strewn over the vast area. I was certain that these unpublished inscriptions would provide rich material for the study. Collection of such inscriptions of course would involve field work i.e., the process going in search of inscriptions and copying them. The idea was thrilling, but also discouraging considering the travel in the interior villages, thick forest areas and other hazards it involved. Yet the urge did not subside. Encouraged by my Professor and senior colleagues, I ventured upon the project and started prelimnery work.

I approached the Indian Council of Historical Research, New Delhi, for financial assistance and luckily for me they offered Senior Research Fellowship for a period of two years, which highly encouraged me and boosted my spirits. I am glad that the result of hard labour has borne fruit today.

It is well known that after the disintigration of the kingdom of the erstwhile Kadambas of Banavasi the scions of this family migrated to different regions and continued to hold subordinate positions under different rulers of the land. It is very interesting that it is the only family which survived the longest period in the history of south India. There are indications that some families even crossed the Karnataka borders and settled in different regions. Most prominent among such families were the Kadambas of Goa and the Kadambas of Hangal. Right from the days of the Chālukyas of Kalyāṇa to the end of the Sēuṇas, they took active part in the political and cultural activities under their masters.

The Kadambas of Goa as they are called, because of their affiliation to their titulary deity, the famous Saptakōtīśvara, who even today claims large number of devotes from Goa and other regions around. As the study shows, they started their career in 10th cent. A.D. as subordinate chiefs under the Kalyāṇa Chālukya king Taila II. The first member of the family was Shashṭha I. The last one was known as Shashṭha III functioning under Sēuṇa Mahadēva. Like all other political entities of the day they also succumbed to the onslaughts of the Muslim invasions at the end of the 13th century. Geographically speaking, their activities covered the whole of present Goa, the north-western part of Dharwad district covering primarily Kalghatgi and Hubli taluks and the adjoining parts of Belgaum district covering Khanapur and Bailhongal taluks.

The story as gleaned mainly from the inscriptions, many of which are discovered for the first time. As narrated below they shaped the destiny of their over lords through actively taking part in their warfare and conquests in an effort to establish supremacy over others. They encouraged different religions rooted in the land and were responsible for the rise of famous religious luminaries and institutions. Art and architrecture flourished in the period and their contribtion was in no way small.

I am happy that I am able to place before the community of scholars my findings in the study of this early medieval family in the history of Karnataka. The special feature of this dissertation is the presentation of the text of as many as 34 inscriptions, most of which were discovered by me in course of my field work.

Dharwad
24.9.2013 **S.L. Shantakumari**

CONTENTS

CHAPTER - I

INTRODUCTION

The purpose of this present dissertation is to study in depth, the contributions of the Kadambas of Goa to the history and culture of Karnataka. The Kadambas of Goa were ruling over a vast tract covering the present day Goa and the districts of Belgaum, Dharwad and parts of North Kanara districts of the Karnataka State. These chiefs held this position under the Chālukyas of Kalyāṇa, who held sway over the vast region between Narmadā and Tungabhadrā including Goa in the West and Andhra Pradesh in the East. It can be said that the study of the Chālukyas of Kalyāṇa is nothing but a study of the history of ancient *Dakshiṇāpatha* and the study of feudatory families under them, who governed their respective provinces. These and similar other chiefs are generally known in history as the feudatory families for the reason that they functioned as subordinates to the ruling monarchs. Though subordinates to the imperial dynasty, they exercised the supreme power over their own regions and possessed certain rights which fell but little short of complete independence.

One interesting feature of the political and administrative system in medieval Karnataka was a sort of decentralization, where the administrative power was delegated to the local chiefs who were entrusted with the over all administration of their own regions.

This was indeed necessary because of the vastness of the empire and difficulty in controlling the remote regions by the central authority. Competent men were appointed in such position and in course of time this system became hereditary and the successive generations of chiefs held sway over such regions. In course of time, as said earlier, they functioned almost as independent rulers, though owing allegiance to the ruling king. Many of them, by dint of their ability became quite powerful and even indispensable to the ruling monarch. By their military strength and administrative skill, they weighed considerable influence on the ruling king and even became a source of his strength. Many such subordinate chiefs have been described as the right hand (*dakshiṇa-bhuja-daṇḍa*) of the ruler. Enjoying full freedom in their respective regions, they considerably contributed to the political, social and cultural development of that region and also continued almost all aspects of the traditions of their masters. These studies have been helpful in understanding the over all history of a particular period and ruling dynasty.

The structure of the administration of such feudatory chieftains was almost comparable to the administration of the kingdom itself. They ran almost a parallel government in their territory with all ingredients of an independent kingdom. For example, like his master, Jayakēśi I had assumed the titles as *Koṇkaṇādhīśa*[1] and *Koṇkaṇa-chakravarti*[2] (the lord of Koṇkaṇa). He has been described in inscriptions as *Paśchima-samudrādhīśvara*[3] i.e., the lord of western ocean.

They had their own administrative machinery with several officers at different levels. There is a reference to the *mantriparishad* of Gūvala II which is said to be consisting of the *mukhya-svīkaraṇa, pratihastaka*, three ministers, *saṇdhivigrahika, rāja-paurōhita* and others.[4] They were expected to be learned in *Śāstrās*, grammar, logic, polity and philosophy.[5] Some times even an ordinary person of merit was also raised to the highest office in the state. An inscription gives an interesting information that Jayakēśi I appointed Chchhadama, an Arab merchant as his *pradhāna*,[6] obviously because of his experience in the trade and navigation.

Like their liege lords they also divided their regions into different districts or *vishayas* and these *vishayas* were further divided. For example, Palasige-12000, Konkaṇa-900, Kāvaḍidvīpa-savalakka, Vēlugrāme-70, Kadroḷḷi-30, Utsugrāme-30, Sabbi-30, Kontakuḷi-30, Uṇakal-30, Poḷala-gunḍe-30, Māvaḷḷi-12 and Tambūr-12 and so on. The lowest unit of administration was the village, managed by the *Ūroḍeya* or *Gāvuṇḍa* etc. Some of these rulers issued their own coins. For example, we come across the names of the coins like *Ganga-gadyāṇa*[7] and *Bhairava-gadyāṇa*[8] issued by these chiefs. They also encouraged education and gave importance to art and architecture also.

They built up their own army which safeguarded the interest of their own region and also helped the ruling king in times of need. There are instances to show how the feudatory chiefs stood by their masters in times of need. For example, we notice below how Shashṭhadēva II of this family helped his over lord Sōmēśvara I in subduing the recalcitrant chiefs of North and South Koṇkaṇ regions ably.[9] Similarly Jayakēśi I of this family accompanied Vikramāditya VI in his expedition against the Chōḷa king.[10] It is also said that Jayakēśi I negotiated a treaty of friendship between Vikramāditya VI and the Chōḷa king Vīrarājēṇdra,[11] which also earned for him the title *Rāyapitāmaha*.[12] Jayakēśi I assisted Vikramāditya VI in the latter's fight with his elder brother Sōmēśvara II. Similarly, Jayakēśi III stood by Sōmēśvara IV in his difficult days.

The feudatory chiefs performed judicial functions also. For example, in a case, when the jewellary of god Narasimha was misappropriated by one Vaishṇava Padmanābha, Jayakēśi III punished the brāhmaṇa by withdrawing lands granted to him and gave the equivalent amount of the stolen ornaments by selling the land, to the god Narasimha.[13]

The relationship between the liege lord and the feudatory were generally cordial. The chiefs earned the favour of their overlords through their ability and sincerity. Many times this type of relationship resulted in matrimonial alliance with the royal family. The marriage between Vikramāditya VI and the daughter of Jayakēśi I and also of the daughter of Vikramāditya VI, with Jayakēśi II are the best examples in this regard.[14]

There are also instances when the feudatory chiefs rose against their masters and tried to assert their own independence. Jayakēśi II, for example, tried to become an independent ruler by flouting the authority of Vikramāditya VI, though in vain.

Thus, in general, the feudatory families have contributed to the growth of political, social, religious and cultural institutions in their own region and worked for the welfare of the people. It can be said that the study of the history of Karnataka will not be complete without the study of the history of the feudatory families.

We may explain here in brief the import of the term feudatory in the context of our study. This term feudalism is used by different scholars with different connotations. Indeed, in the medieval European context, it denoted a peculiar system of landlordism which gave rise to a class of influential landlords, who wielded enormous control over the tenants of land and occupied a highly prestigious place in the society and political set up. They held an absolute ownership of large tracts of land and even maintained relations with the ruling monarch. This type of feudalism does not certainly apply to the Indian context.

A theory has been propounded by certain scholars that feudalism developed from the practice of giving grant of lands to the Brāhmaṇas (*Brahmadēyas*). This practice came in vogue particularly from the Gupta period and continued for centuries downwards. The principle behind this was to donate lands to the Brāhmaṇas, engaged in religious and educational activities. According to some scholars, such donees became in course of time big landlords and thus became feudal lords also. But this contention is not correct because land grants were normally given to the Brāhmaṇas for particular functions like pursuit of religious and educational activities. For this purpose *agrahāra* was created and land related to that area was distributed among many learned people, for their maintenance. Further, engaged as they were in religious and educational activities, their exercising administrative authority was too remote. There were separate officers like the *gāvuṇḍas* for looking after the administration of such regions. It could be wrong, therefore, to hold that land grants or creations of *Brahmadēyas* gave rise to feudalism in our country. In fact, the expression feudalism itself does not suit our political context. What came into existence were the families with the power to govern a particular region, under a ruling king. The rise of such families was the outcome of political necessity of delegating powers to the subordinates to secure the safety of the whole kingdom by entrusting the responsibility to different chiefs. Thus, it is proper to call such families as subordinate families, rather than feudatory families.[15]

Such subordinate chiefs were normally known as *sāmantas* and *mahāmaṇḍalēśvaras* meaning the subordinate chiefs and the master of a region respectively depending upon the position they enjoyed. Some times they were called *mahāsāmanta* and *mahāmaṇḍalēśvara.*

In the history of Karnataka, such subordinate families came into existence particularly from the days of the Chālukyas of Bādāmi and this institution grew from strength to strength in the successive kingdoms. Thus, we find such famous subordinate families as Raṭṭas of Saundatti, Kadambas of Goa and the Kadambas of Hāngal, Guttas of Guttavoḷal, the Sindas, the Śilāhāras, the Pāṇḍyas and the like. Many of these families have been subjected to detailed study by earlier scholars like J.F. Fleet in his *Dynasties of Canarese Districts,* G.M. Moraes in his *The Kadamba Kula* and as a part of dynastic history by scholars like A.S. Altekar, in his *Rāshṭrakūṭas and Their Times,* William Coelho in his *Hoysaḷa Vaṁsa*, Shrinivaṣ H.Ritti in his *The Sēuṇas*, B.R.Gopal in his *Chālukyās of Kalyāṇa and the Kalachūris*. Dinakar Desai has produced a whole volume exclusively for the study of such subordinate families in his The *Mahāmaṇḍalēśvaras Under the Chālukyas of Kalyāṇa.* Similarly, B.R.Gopal has exclusively studied some subordinate families in his work *Minor Dynasties of South India (Karnataka).* Both Dr. G. M. Moraes and Dr. B. R.Gopal have studied this particular family of the Kaḍambas of Goa, which is a subject of our study, in some details. Nevertheless, the study is undertaken in view of the availability of the considerable fresh material in the form of inscriptions, which necessitate a reappraisal of the contribution and the role of this family in the history of Karnataka.

REFERENCES AND NOTES

1. *EI.*, XIII, p.303.
2. *JBBRAS.*, IX, p. 297.
3. *Ibid.*
4. *Kadamba Kula*, App.III. No.1.
5. *Goa Gazatteer*, p.117.
6. *Kadamba Kula*, pp.396 ff.
7. *Unpublished inscription.*
8. *EI.*, XXX, pp.71 ff.
9. *Ibid.*, XIII, pp.302 ff -
   vāridhi mēredappi Kavitappavōl-ōvade baṁda chōḷanaṁ Vāridhīśan-appa Jayakēśi-nripaṁ Chaladiṁ turuuṁbi.
10. *Ibid.*, p.303.
11. *JBBRAS.* IX, p.242; and also EI., XXVI, pp.306 ff. The record says -
    Chālukya- Chōḷa- bhūpālau Kānchyāṁ-mitrẹ vidhāḥ-yaḥ||
12 *Ibid.*
13. *Ibid.*, p.281, and also KI., V, No.63.
14. *EI.*, XIII, pp.308 ff.
15. For discussion on this subject see Dr. Zakia Khanum Ansari - *Some Feudatory Families of Medieval Karnataka – A. Study,* Sri Hari Prakashana, Dharwad, 1998, pp.137 ff.

CHAPTER - II

THE SOURCES

For the study of the history of any ruling dynasty or feudatory family in the early period of history of Karnāṭaka, inscriptions form the main source. This is the case with the history of ancient India also in general. We all know that the practice of writing inscriptions in India goes to as far back as the 3rd century B.C. (we do not include here the writings of the Indus Valley period, as a final conclusion about which is yet to be reached). This practice was commenced by the most famous of the Indian emperors, Maurya Aśōka. To communicate to the people of his own days and those of posterity he chose a novel way of recording his thoughts, ideas and teachings, on the most permanent material i.e., stone. His idea in choosing this media was to preserve, the writings which could be a guideline to the people of several centuries later. His anticipation, indeed, came true and even today, 2400 years after he wrote, we can see, read and understand his thoughts and ideas.

Whether his ideas and thoughts are followed or appreciated today, or not the students of history are ever beholden to him for starting this method of preparing written documents. Luckily for us, the succeeding generations of rulers who followed him for centuries together followed this practice of writing on stones for the use of posterity. Aśōkan inscriptions or edicts are a class by themselves. None of the succeeding rulers followed or practiced what he said and preached. Yet at least they followed the practice of putting on record the events that took place during their periods. That is how from that day downwards we get thousands and thousands of inscriptions belonging to different ruling dynasties and periods which serve as the most important sources for our study of history to day.

In course of time the rulers introduced the system of recording the events and other details on copper plates also. So much so a lot of material is available today for our study. There are other metals like silver and gold which were used, though rarely for writing inscriptions.

It is also well known that there are other sources of studies like archaeological artifacts, built up structures which are generally called monuments, coins issued by different rulers in different periods and also literature. But, for the study of the history, particularly of the early period, these can be described as only secondary as compared to the inscriptions. They, at best, augment the information supplied by the inscriptions. It is not necessary to go into detail about the utility or the merits and demerits of the inscriptions, which are well known; suffice it to say that in the absence of other notable sources, the inscriptions alone come to our help in knowing the past.

Coming to the period under study it is to be noted that it is only the inscriptions which happen to be the most important sources for the period ruled over by the Chālukyas of Kalyāṇa and the largest number of inscriptions came to be written in this period. They provide ample material for the study of the period and also for the study of the Kadambas of Goa. The Kadambas of Goa were the subordinates of the Chālukyas and therefore, their history is interwoven with those of the Chālukyas. So the inscriptions of the Chālukyas are essential for the study of the Kadambas of Goa. With this background we review here some of the more important inscriptions which supply the useful information regarding the dynasty.

The copper-plate inscription from Kire-Halasige [1] dated 1186-87 A.D. gives a detailed genealogical account of the family up to eight generations. Interestingly, it commences with the mythical account of the family stating that the originator Jayanta Trilōchana-Kadamba "was born from the drops of the sweat, which flowed from the forehead of Śiva to the root of a Kadamba tree, when he conquered the demon Tripura." The same information is supplied by the Panjim copper-plate of Jayakēśi I.[2] This mythical part of the genealogy is imagined obviously to ascribe a hoary antiquity to the family. The Halasi inscription also speaks of the relationship with the Chālukyas of Kalyāṇa and it states that Jayakēśi of this family was married to Maiḷaladēvi, the daughter of Chālukya Permāḍi i.e., Vikramāditya VI and the sister of Sōmēśvara III.[3]

The copper plate inscription of Tribhuvanamalla[4] also narrates the mythical genealogy but in a different way. It states that the first member of the family viz., Trilōchana Kadamba was born out of *vīra-rasa* of lord Śiva, when he destroyed Tripura. This account is different in certain respects from the familiar version. In this inscription we find that Trilōchana Kadamba is stated to have sprung up on the earth under a Kadamba tree. The present inscription mentions Tribhuvanamalla, as the grandson of Shashṭha. This Tribhuvanamalla is identified with Gūhalla or Gūvaladēva, the son of Jayakēśi-I. Another interesting aspect in the inscription is the stipulation laid down for the enjoyment of the endowment by the Brāhmaṇa donees.

An inscription from Narēndra[5] dated 1125 A.D. is a lengthy record running through 115 lines. It also refers to the story of the sweat of Śiva falling on the ground from where sprang the originator of the Kadamba family. The inscription also gives a vivid description of the military exploits of the Kadamba chief Chaṭṭayyadēva, who is credited with the conquests of islands like Kāvaḍi-dvīpa, Laṁkā and Gōve and also refers to Jayakēśi's marriage with Maiḷaladēvi, the daughter of Vikramāditya VI. The inscription provides abundant material for the study of the family. It supplies the interesting information that Chaṭṭayyadēva employed the services of boats across the sea to reach Laṁkā. It says that Shashṭha built a bridge of ships upto Laṁkā. Another inscription from Narēṇdra, dated 1126 A.D.[6] is useful for the study of historical geography of the region as it mentions many geographical and administrative divisions prevailing in the kingdom.

A stone inscription from Halasi is an interesting record.[7] Actually, it contains two records, written one after the other, dated in 1169 A.D. and 1172 A.D. respectively. One inscription was composed by Nāgavarma and written by Madhusūdana Sūri, who held the office of *Dharmmādhikaraṇa* or a judge. The second one was composed by Dēvaśrma and written by

Yajñēśvara Sūri. Interestingly, these two inscriptions were engraved on stone by Śankarārya, the disciple of Matēśa. It also gives the genealogy of the Kadamba chiefs down to Śivachitta Permāḍi. The Halasi inscription also refers to grants made to the temples of Varāha and Nṛsiṁha at Halasige. It is dated 1186-87 A.D. The text of the inscription is stated to have been composed by Gangādhara Sūri, who is described as *divyādhyaksha tulādhāri*.[8]

An inscription of Jayakēśi I of 1054 A.D.[9] is worth mentioning here. It refers to an officer named Aṇṇayya *dharma-maṇtri*, who was serving (Bī)Vīravarmadēva of the Kadamba family. Here Vīravarma is identified with Jayakēśi I by Dr. K.V. Ramesh, the editor of the record. Another inscription worthy of mention in this connection is the Courtorim grant of Vīravarmadēva.[10] It mentions him as the son (probably the second son) of Shashṭha II. Almost all the Kadamba inscriptions refer to Jayakēśi I as the successor of Shashṭha II. But this grant is important as it brings to light a new chief of the family.

An inscription from Kittūr[11] belonging to Jayakēśi III and dated 1201 A.D. is interesting from the point of view of the judjcial system in ancient days. It refers to a dispute regarding a land, between the heads of two religious institutions. In the absence of other tangible evidences, the dispute was settled by invoking the divine power *Divya*. Through this method, the contestants were asked to hold a heated piece of iron to prove their claim. One of the contestants underwent this successfully and won the case.

The Gaṇadevi inscription of Shashṭha II dated 1042 A.D.[12] is important as it happens to be the first Kadamba record found in Gujarat. After giving the genealogical account of the origin of the family, it mentions the early members of the family, and describes the exploits of Shashṭha II and also his conquests of Siṁhala, Pārāsika and Kanaka-dvīpa through naval force. The main purpose of the inscription is to record the construction of a *maṇḍapikā* or a pavilion by Shashṭhadēva at the market place near Gaṇadēvi. It mentions the name of the composer of the record as Chaṇdra Sūri of *Sāligrāma gōtra*, which is mentioned for the first time in an inscription of Gujarat. It was incised by Sarvadēva.

The Sadāśivagaḍ plates[13] of Vijayāditya are also important as it is the only inscription which throws welcome light on the independent rule of Vijayāḍitya. The latter is generally known as *Vishṇu-chitta*. But, here he is called *Vishṇu-dāsa,* both of which, of course, mean the devotee of god Vishṇu.

The Asoge plates[14] of Jayakēśi II is interesting as it supplies information on the genealogy of the family and also refers to the extension of the reign period of Jayakēśi II. The Goa plates of Shashṭhadēva[15] may be mentioned here as it introduces certain Kāmadēva as the establisher of Shaṣhṭhadēva.

A short inscription from Degave[16] is highly interesting. It mentions Kamalādēvi, the wife of Śivachitta Parmāḍidēva. She was the daughter of Kāmadēva and Chaṭṭaladēvi. The interest of the inscription lies in the fact that it mentions the artists Tippōja and his son *Pratāpa Sūtradhāri* Bāgōja who constructed the temples of Śrī Kamala-Ṇārāyaṇa and Śrī Mahālakshmī at Degave at the orders of (*niyamadim*) Kamalādēvi. They were the son and grand son of Holōja, who is described in the inscription as an expert in the construction of temples as well as carving sculptures. The inscription extols him as incomparable in both architecture and sculpture (*prāsāda-lakshaṇa pratimā-lakshaṇa pravīṇar-appa*).

Tippaṇōja i.e., Tippōja was an expert not only in architecture but even in *Bharat-āgama-śāstra*, music, dance, arts and also composing poetry (*kalā-pariṇateyoḷ-varṇṇa-kaviteyoḷ*).

The inscription from Mishrikoṭi[17] belonging to Jayakerśi II gives an interesting information that his queen Maiḷaladēvi, who was the daughter of Chālukya Vikramāditya VI, was in charge of admninistration of the division of Kundūru-nāḍu, a part of Palasige division in Kuntaḷa-dēśa.

The inscription from Muttage,[18] dated 1076 A.D. is important as it happens to be the earliest known inscription of Guvaladēva III. The date of this inscription reflects clearly on the date of the commencement of the rule of the Chālukya king Vikramāditya VI also.

A hero-stone dated 1267 A.D.[19] is worthy of mention here as it throws new light on the date of Shashthadēva III. The latest known date of Shashthadēva III was supposed to be 1264 A.D.[20] But this hero-stone indicates that he was in power even in 1267 A.D.

An inscription from Māvaḷḷi[21] is interesting as it introduces Padmaladēvi, who was the elder (*piriyaḷu*) sister of Jayakēśi II, and was given in marriage to Hākiballadēva. Another inscription from Tambūr [22] is also interesting as it refers to the elder sister (*agraje*) Sāvitri, of Permāḍidēva who was given in marriage to Gangidēva (*Gangiḍevaṇg-ittaru*).

An interesting feature of the inscriptions of this family lies in their literary value. A good number of inscriptions of this family, while recording historical facts, are written in highly literary style, using different metres and other embellishments, suitable for a *Kāvya*. Though most of them are eulogies, they contain highly imaginative descriptions of the personalities like the kings, queens and subordinates. They also describe the scenic beauty of useful historical information. Interestingly, some of them at least, record the name of the composer also. Thus, these inscriptions add to the literary output of the period in adding new names of poets, to the history of Kannada literature.

Copper plate grants of the period are mostly composed in Sanskrit, while a good number of stone inscriptions are found composed in chaste literary style, in Kannada. The copper plate of Shashṭha II,[23] for example, is a good example of Sanskrit composition. The inscription begins with obeisance to the god Saptakōtīśvara and narrates the genealogy and the greatness of the successive rulers of the family. The text of the grant was composed by Chaṭṭaṇārya. It was written by Nārāyaṇa, the son of Durgaṇa.

The inscription from Muttagi[24] referred to earlier is a fine piece of poetry in 37 lines. It begins with the *praśasti* of Vikrāmaditya VI and introduces Gūvaladēva as governing from Gōvage i.e., Goa. It then describes his subordinate Singa and his sons. The whole inscription is composed in verses of different metres. It is composed by a poet called Jayadēva. He describes this poem as *Śrāvyaṁ, Navyaṁ, Manōharaṁ*, (as pleasing to hear, new and attractive).

The inscription from Kamadhenu[25] dated 1171 A.D. belonging to Śivachitta Permāḍidēva is again a fine composition. It gives the *praśasti* of this chief Śivachitta Permāḍi and describes Palasige-12000 division. It describes the subordinate chiefs also. The whole inscription makes a very pleasing reading, though, unfortunately it does not disclose the name of the poet.

An inscription from Tambūr[26] is also a good Kannada composition by Kannapayya, who calls himself *Paramakavi*. It contains verses in praise of this subordinate of the Kadamba chief. Unfortunately, the inscription is damaged in some places.

An inscription from Budarsingi[27] of Kadamba Chaṭṭayyadēva dated 1257 A.D. is worthy of mention here. It refers to the construction of the temple called Kapilasiddha Mallikārjuna, by the famous Śaiva saint Siddharāma at Sonnalige i.e., the modern Sholāpūr. Here, Sonnalige is described as *abhinava Śriśaila-yōga-ramaṇiya-kshētra*. He is said to have constructed *Ashṭha-shashṭhi-tīrtha-Siddha-taṭāka.* It is worth noting in this context is that an inscription dated 1264 A.D. from Koṭṭagi (Kotabagi) puts on record a *vachana* or saying of the famous *Vīraśaiva* saint Śiddharāma.[28] This *vachana* is found in later inscriptions also.

An inscription of Jayakēśi II dated 1144 A.D. from Halyal[29] in North Kanara district is worth mentioning here. Its main interest lies in the usual description of the *Mahājanas* of the place, who were stated to be experts in all arts and sciences, thorough in all languages like *Sanskrit, Apabhramsa* and *Paiśāchi* and experts in composing works in different styles of writing like *Gauḍa, Vaidarbha* and *Pānchāla*. This inscription is a true reflection on the religious, social and educational conditions of the period.

Another important aspect of these inscriptions is the script used in them. Most of them are written in a very attractive hand on dressed and polished stones. A comparative study helps in studying the development of Kannada script in the period.

Another interesting characteristic feature of the Kadamba inscriptions is the *Kaliyuga* era in their records. Sometimes both the *Śaka* and *Kaliyuga era*[30] are used. Often the regnal years of the chiefs are also mentioned besides these *eras*.[31] Some times the dates are given in chronogram also.[32]

There are a number of memorial stones in the form of hero-stones and sati-stones found in the villages as well as in the middle of the forest area of both Goa and Kadamba territory in Karnataka. Hero-stones were erected in the name of those who sacrificed their lives for a good cause like saving the cows from raiders, fighting against thieves, or boundary disputes or for the sake of their masters etc. For example an inscription from Tambur[33] refers to the death of a hero named Koṇḍala Basavayya-nāyaka, while rescuing cows from raiders. A record from Bailandur,[34] Yallapur taluk refers to the death of a hero (name lost) while opposing thieves. Another inscription from Bailandur [35] refers to the death of a hero when one Jayakēśi attacked the place. The Dodwad inscription dated 1206 A.D.[36] is interesting as it refers to one Lahaḍa, who was a servant (*ḍingariga*) of Jayakēsi III. Another fragmentary record [37] refers to the death of one Vijayama-sāhaṇi son of Rāya-sāhaṇi Sōḍapa, who was a *ḍingariga* of Vajradēva. Another hero-stone from Tambur [38] refers to the death of a hero (name lost) when Sāteyanahaḷḷi was attacked by enemies. His sister Malliyabbe Nāyakiti erected the stone. A hero-stone from Tambur[39] is interesting as it refers to a hero (name lost) who fought against one Māyidēva, with the permission of his master Permāḍi. It is said that he put to death the soldiers and also their horses. The devotion to their overlords and the country was so much that they never bothered for their won lives. According to them, both victory and defeat brought them Lakshmi.

Another interesting feature is the large number of sati-stones found in some villages and also in the middle of the forest region in the Kalghatgi area. Some of the sculptures contain the figure of a single lady, with raised right hand and some stones contain more than one figure of a lady. On some stones, they are shown along with the hero. Occasionally, a pillar with raised decorated right hand attached to it are found in the area under study. Some of the sati-stones are beautifully carved with all the sacred symbols on their person including flowers in their dressed hair. In some places the sati-stones are even worshipped as a deity.

To this category belong the *Nishadhi*-stones. They were erected in the name of the Jaina devotees who ended their lives by the rite of *Sallēkhana.* These types of inscriptions add much new information for the religious and cultural study of the period.

The literary sources for the study of the history of the Kadambas of Goa are not many. There are only two works worth mentioning here. One is the famous *Vikramāṇkadēva-charita* of Bilhaṇa[40] which narrates the history of the Chālukyas of Kalyāṇa, particularly Vikramāditya VI. The work contains references to the Kadamba chiefs of Goa who were not merely the subordinates of the Chālukyas, but were their close allies and even participated in many battles fought by the Chālukyas with the Chōḷas and other contemporary rulers. In one place it tells us that after defeating the Chōḷa king, Vikramāditya VI spent some time in Banavāsi-maṇḍala which obviously was governed by Kadamba Jayakēśi. It is also known that Jayakēśi helped that king in establishing good relationship with the Chōḷas.

Dvyāśraya-kāvya[41] of Hēmachaṁdra is another Sanskrit work which gives some interesting details regarding the relationship of the Kadambas with the Chālukyas of Anahilawāḍa. The author of this work viz., Hēmachaṁdra, flourished in the court of Jayasiṁha Siddharāja and his successor Kumarapāla. He was a Jaina scholar, who wrote both in Prākrit and Sanskrit. The famous work of this poet is *Kumarapālā-charita*. The *kāvya,* in twenty-eight chapters, describes the rulers of Anahilawāḍa dynasty, particularly, Kumarapāla. Interestingly, the first twenty chapters are in Sanskrit while the next eight are in Prakrit. This Prakrit part is called *Dvyāśraya-kāvya*, because of its being in two languages and because of another interesting fact that by one interpretation it explains the rules of grammar and by another interpretation it narrates the story of Chālukya chiefs.

The work indicates that the Kadambas of Goa had contacts with those chiefs for generations. In one place it is stated that a king of Banavāsidēśa offered Mūlarāja of this family precious gifts and in this context makes an interesting statement that in the country of that king much gold was found. In another context the work tells us that the king Karṇa, the successor of Mūlarāja was enamoured by the beauty of a daughter of Jayakēśi, the king of Chandrāpura. The name of the daughter was Mayanalladēvi and the narration states that he married this princess also. This event is confirmed by other sources also. The work states that the famous Kumārapāla of this family was the son of Karṇa and Mayanalladēvi. Thus, *Dvyāśraya-kāvya* supplies interesting informatioin about the relatioinship between the Kadambas of Goa and the Chālukyas of Anahilawāḍa.

It is well known that the Kadambas of Goa issued coins in their own names and some of them have been discovered also. The inscriptions mentioned above refers to some new types of coins like *Bhairava-gadyana*, *Brihad-Bhairava-gadyāṇa*, and *Bhairava-nishka*[42] and *Ganga-gadyāṇa*[43] etc. It is known that the coins do disclose interesting information though in brief, the names and titles of rulers mentioned on the coins help us in identifying the rulers mentioned in inscriptions. Many times, the coins disclose the new names and titles unknown to inscriptions. Further, coins also throw light on the economic conditions of the Period. It is also to be noted that inscriptions themselves mention a number of coins which were in currency in the period under study. Many times it is possible to co-relate these coins with those actually discovered. A detailed study of such coins is made in an appropriate chapter in this work.

As seen from the above description, the inscriptions happen to be the primary or almost the only source for the study of the history of Kadambas of Goa. Most of them are in Kannada language, but some at least particularly the copper plates are in Sanskrit. Apart from supplying vital information regarding the political history of the region they speak of the development of language and literature in the period. They also give copious information regarding the religious, economic and social conditions of the period. An attempt is made in the following pages to give a detailed account of these aspects of the history of the Kadambas of Goa, by utilizing and scrutinizing all the available material.

REFERENCES AND NOTES

1. *JBBRAS.*, IX, pp.241 ff.
2. *KK..*, App.No.II
3. *JBBRAS.*, IX, p. 245
4. *EI.*, XXX, pp. 29 ff.
5. *Ibid.*, XIII, p..304
6. *Ibid.*, p.320
7. *JBBRAS.*, IX, p.281; KI., V, No.63
8. *JBBRAS.*, IX, p.245.

9. *EI.*, XXXVII, pp.284 ff.
10. *GG.*, p.98
11. *JBBRAS.*, IX, pp.304 ff
12. *IIBS.*, pp.65 ff
13. *EI.*, XXIX, pp.29 ff.
14. *Ibid.*, XXVI, pp.304 ff.
15. *IA.*, XIV, pp.288 ff.
16. *JBBRAS.*, IX, p.294 ff.
17. From personal collection
18. *Karnataka Bharati*,Karnatak Unmiversity, Dharwad, XX, 1988, pp.83 ff.
19. Ritti S.H. "*Inscriptions from Śaravati Valley*" JKU., (Soc. Sc.), Vol.III, 1967, pp.3 ff.
20. *ARSIE.*, No.447 of 1926
21. From personal collection
22. *Ibid.*
23. *IA.*, XIV, pp.289 ff.
24. *Karnataka Bharati*, Vol .XX, pt. III, pp.283 ff. 1988, KUD
25. *SII.*, XX, No. 252
26. From Personal collection
27. *EI.*, XXXVI, PP. 164 ff.
28. *SII.*, XV, No. 195
29. Un-published
30. *KI.*, V, No. 68
31. Ibid.
32. Ibid., No. 63
33. From Personal Collection
34. *Ibid.*
35. *Ibid.*
36. Doddawad plates of Jayakēśi III A.D. 1209, JKU. , (1975), pp. 146 ff.

37. Un-published
38. From Personal ollection
39. *Ibid.*
40. Buhler, Vikramānkadēva Charita, pp. 34 ff.; KK., p.182
41. *IA.*, IV, pp.233 ff.
42. *EI.*, XXX, pp. 71 ff.
43. Ritti S.H. "An Inscription From Kadarolli, JKU., (Soc.Sc.), Vol. IV, April 1968, pp.6, ff.

CHAPTER - III

TERRITORY OF THE KADAMBAS OF GOA

We have now seen that the Kadaṁbas of Goa were a prominent ruling subordinate family and ruled over fairly a long period from 11th to 13th centuries and over a vast region covering most of the North Western part of Karnataka including Goa. Though the inscriptions claim hoary antiquity and legendary origin they came to prominence during the days of the Chālukyas of Kalyāṇa and they weilded considerable influence over these monarchs under whom they functioned as subordinates. They continued to hold on to their power even after the end of the Chālukyas, when Kalachuris and the Śeuṇas successively came to power and ruled over the region.

The inscriptions of the Kadambas of Goa mention many administrative divisions, big and small, a study of which helps us to assess the territory they governed. More prominent among them were Konkaṇa-900, Palasige-12000 and *Gōpakarāshṭra*. Aṁong these, Palasige-12000 was the biggest. Palasige is identified with modern Halsi in Khānāpur taluk of Belgaum district. As regards the numerical suffix to the name of the division, there have been considerable discussions about the significance of such numbers. But it can very well be concluded that these figures broadly represent the number of villages incorporated in a division.[1] It is worth noting that Palasige was a provincial headquarters even during the time of the early Kadambas of Banavāsi.

In a conventional way, Palasige division is described in a record from Dharwad as being a part of *Kuntaḷadēśa* and a land of plenty.[2] The record describes *Kuntaḷadēśa* thus -

Sakal-ōrbbī-nuta tat-payōdhi-vṛita -Jaṁbū-dvīpa-bhūpēṁdrarum |
dra-kanat-kāṁchaṇa-māḷeyant-esedu-tōrkkuṁ mērur-ā bhūdharā |
ntaka dig-bhāgadoḷ-oppi-tōrppa Bharata -Śri-līleg-ā lōla ma |
staka-vinyasta-sukuṁtaḷām-bol-esed-irkkum Kumtaḷ-ōrbbī-taḷam ||

Further, the record describes Palasige as –

Janatā-sukha-niḷayaṁ-taj
jana-padadoḷutōrkku-negaḷdaṁ Palasige-dēśaṁ |
vanaja-viḷasam grāma-nagara-kharbaḍa
maḍamba paṭṭaṇa-nichayaṁ |||

As the very name indicates, Palasige occupied an extensive area covering 12000 villages in the southern part of Belgaum district and the adjoining Northern and North Western parts of Dharwad district.

One of the major sub-divisions in this division was Kundūru-500.[3] The head quarters of this division, viz., Kundūru is identified with modern Narēṇdra, about eight kilometres to the North of Dharwad. Interestingly, Dharwad which is a prominent district headquarters today, was a place in Kundūru division with the headquarters at Narēṇdra, which is now a small suburban village nearby. There are two Goa Kadaṁba inscriptions in Narēṇdra,[4] which supply a highly useful information regarding this division. One of these inscriptions extols Kundūru in eulogistic terms and describes it as a chief town of the five hundred division within Palasige-12000.[5] It also mentions other villages like Mareyavāḍa[6] i.e., modern Marēvāḍ near Dharwad and two other villages also near Dharwad viz., Navilūru[7] and Kauvalageri[8] which are now a part of Dharwad, under the same name. Sāvaṇanapalli[9] was another village included in this division. Anilāpura[10] i.e., modern Alṇāvar, also near Dharwad was included in this division. Mention may be made of the following villages, among other villages, which were the part of Kundūru-500: Amminabhāvi,[11] Beḷavaḍigēri,[12] Kanakāpura,[13] Koṭṭabāgi[14] i.e., modern Kotabagi in Dharwad district, Taḍakōḍa,[15] Narēndrapura,[16] Dārwaḍa,[17] Halguṇḍi,[18] Jērigevāḍa,[19] Bhōgūru,[20] Nuggiyahaḷḷi,[21] Sattiyūru,[22] Nīrasāgara,[23] Huppavaḷḷi[24] (all around Dharwad), Bommanahaḷḷi,[25] Mallanahaḷḷi,[26] Haḷḷaṁgere,[27] Savaṇanapaḷḷi,[28] were included in this division.

Mārajavāḍi-nāḍu[29] or Mahārājavāḍi-nāḍu was an important sub-division of Kundūru-500 in Palasige-nāḍu. Within Mārājavāḍi-nāḍu was situated the sub-division Mugunda-30.[30] It is the modern Mugad in Dharwad district. Its head-quarters Mūguṇda is the same as Mugad, a village, about fifteen kilometres to the west of Dharwad. Mugada, Koḷnūru,[31] and Nigadi,[32] were in Mugunda-30.

Pullambi-70[33] i.e., the modern Hullambi in Kalghatgi taluk, was also a village belonging to Mārajavāḍi-nāḍu. This Hullambi was the head-quarters of Pullambi-70. Kittur-30[34] was also a part of this division. The village Muttage,[35] Sigigaṭṭi,[36] and Maṇiguṇḍage[37] were a part of Hullambi. Mūguṇda-30[38] was another small division in Mārajavāḍi-nāḍu.

Kāḷagiri Kaṁpaṇa[39] is said to be a part of Palasi-dēśa i.e., Palasige-12000. It cannot be asserted, however, in which sub-division it was situated. Sindavaḷḷi[40] and Bhalika[41] are stated to be included in this division.

Dēgāve Kaṁpaṇa,[42] was also a part of Palasige-12000. Dēgāve, the present Degaon is near Halasi. Sīgeri[43] is a village included in this division. Vēlugrāme-70,[44] is mentioned in inscriptions, as being under the Kadambas. Vēlugrāme, the modern Belgaum, obviously was a part of Palasige-12000. Kiru-Saṁpagāḍi,[45] was a part of this sub-division. Sampagāḍi, is the modern Sampagaon is in Belgaum district. The inscriptions of Śivachitta Vīra-Permāḍidēva[46] indicates that the villages Kuṇilagere, Sēḍibiḍa, Polavase, Lokkiguṇḍi, Hānuṁgal, Māruḍige, Gaṅgādhara and Parabige were also situated in this sub-division. It is, however, difficult to locate some of them on the modern map.

An inscription from Narendra[47] stated above, mentions a few divisions like Hānuṁgal-500, Haive-500, Kontakuḷi-30, Utsugrāme-30, Poḷalgunde-30, Kadroḷḷi-30, Uṇkal-30 and Sabbi-30, apart from Konkan-900, as administrative divisions of the Kadambas of Goa. Hānuṁgal-500 was a division comprised of 500 villages, having Pānuṁgal as its head-quarters. Pānuṁgal is the present Hangal in Haveri district. Haive-500 was a division comprised of 500 villages. It is said that it was the coastal tract in North Kanara district and also a few villages of the North of South Kanara district. Kontakuḷi-30 comprised of 30 villages was in Western part of Shiggaon and southern part of Kalghatgi taluks. Utsugrāme-30, consisted of thirty villages having Uchagaon (in Belgaum distrrict), as a principal town. Hoḷalgunde-30, comprised of 30 villages in Saundatti and Bailhongal taluks. Kadroḷḷi-30 is near Belgaum district including Bailhongal taluk. Uṇukal-30 i.e., modern Unkal is originally a separate village. Uṇkal-30 was a division consisting of 30 villages having Uṇkal as its principal town. It was in Palasige-nāḍu and presently, it is a part of Hubli- Dharwad city. Similarly, Sabbi-30, was also included in Palasige. Sabbi viz., modern Chhabbi is also in Dharwad district. Inscriptions indicate that villages like Beṭdur, Nūlvi, Kaṭanūr and Budarsingi, all around the present Hubli, were a part of Chhabbi-30.

Another division of 500 villages was Māvaḷe-500.[48] Its head-quarters Māvaḷe is the same as Mavalli in Kalghatgi taluk of Dharwad district. Māvaḷḷi-12, Tammiyūru-12 were a part of this Māvaḷe-500.[49] Other villages which were included in Māvaḷe-500 were Kōṭe-Kiruvaatti, Kaggavige, Nelkuṇda, Kalukaṇḍi, Bharaṇipura, Chandāvura, Huligōḍu. Bharaṇipur-12 and Huligōḍu-12 were also a part of this Māvaḷe division. This Bharaṇipura is the same as modern Bammigatti in Kalghatgi taluk. Tammiyūru-12 included within itself the villages Kerewāḍa, Sēḍambige and Handinira.

Konkaṇa-900[50] was another prominent region under the Kadambas of Goa. It was, originally, under the Śilāhāras of Kolhāpur and it was wrested from them by Kadamba Shashṭhadēva II and some inscriptions of him and his successors mention that they were ruling over Konkaṇa-900. This region consisted mainly, of the present district of Ratnagiri. Of course, we do not get any inscriptions of the Kadambas in this region. Yet the consistent claim of the Kadambas over this region shows that it was a part of the Kadamba territory. Technically, the present Goa region, to the South of this region, was a part of Konkaṇa-900. Because of its political importance it was considered as a separate region and named Gōpaka-rāshṭra or Gōpaka-dvīpa-vishaya[51] also known as Goa-diva-dēśa. Other villages in this division were Palagrāma and Kichakhanḍi. Gōvage or Gove was the head-quarters of this division and also the capital of the whole territory of the Kadambas of Goa. An inscription from Kadroḷḷi dated 1098 A.D. mentions that Gūvaladēva III of this family was ruling over Palasige-12000 from his capital at Gōve.[52] The capital Gōve is identified with Velha-Goa.[53] Another village Morambika[54] is identified with Morambi near the present day Panaji. Panaji itself was a part of this division. It was known as Panjhanakhani.[55]

Shaṭshashṭhi-dēśa,[56] probably, meaning a dēśa of sixty-six villages, was a part of this division. This Shaṭshaṣhṭhi is equated with Salseṭṭe, a taluk head-quarters in Goa. Raigrāma was another village in this division. Raigrāma, Kuḍatari and Maṭhagrāma were other villages in this division. Maṭhagrāma is identified with Madgaon in Goa.[57]

Gaḍivōre grant of Shashṭhadēva II,[58] mentions a Panāsadēśa, which appears to be situated in Gōva-divā-vishaya. This has been identified with Palāsikā or Halasi, the headquarters of Palasige-12000.[59] But looking to the villages situated in this division, it appears that it was different from Halasi. Dr.Thosar identifies this village with Panasi in Goa.[60] The Gaḍivōre inscription says that Ajjagāve-kaṁpaṇa was a part of this division.[61] This Ajjagāve is identified with Ajgaon which is close to Panasi mentioned above. Dr.Thosar identifies Gaḍivōre with Gandaulim in Tiswādi taluk of Goa.[62]

Many inscriptions of the Kadambas of Goa claim that they ruled over Kāvaḍi-dvīpa also.[63] This region broadly representing northern Konkaṇa, which was originally under the Śilāhāras. It seems that Kadamba Shashṭhadēva II, obviously with the support of Chālukya Vikramāditya wrested it from them and the successors of Shashṭhadēva also claimed their authority over that region.

REFERENCES AND NOTES

1. Ritti S.H. *The Sēuṇas*, p. 328.
2. *KI.,* V, No.68.
3. *EI.*, XIII, p. 307.
4. *Ibid.,* pp. 298 ff.
5. *Ibid.,* p. 308.
6. *Ibid.*, p. 321.
7. *Ibid.*, p. 309.
8. *Ibid.*
9. *Ibid.*, p. 308.
10. *SII.,* XI, (II), No. 178.
11. *Ibid.,* No. 121, and also SII., XV, No. 232.
12. *Ibid.,* XV, No. 228.
13. *Ibid.*, XI (II), No. 154.
14. *Ibid.,* XV, No. 195.
15. *Ibid.,* No. 232.
16. *Ibid.*
17. *Ibid.*
18. *EI.*, XIII, p. 321.
19. *SII.*, XV, No. 230.
20. *Ibid.*, No. 16.
21. *Ibid.*, No. 233.
22. *Ibid.*
23. *Ibid.*
24. *Ibid.*, No. 232, and 233.
25. *Ibid.*, No. 233.
26. *KK.*, p. 411.
27. *KI.*, V. No. 68.

28. *EI.,* XIII, P. 308.
29. *SII.,* XI, (II), No. 211.
30. *Ibid.*

    - *Palasige pannirchchāsidoḷage Mahārajwāḍi-nāḍ-embudu bhū-lalan- ālapanaṁ-adakkaṁ Tilakav-enippudu Mūgunda-Muvatt-endu*

31. *Ibid.,* XI, No. 128.
32. Ibid., No. 160.
33. *KI.,* V, No. 32.
34. From personal collection.
35. *Ibid.*
36. *Ibid.*
37. *KI.,* V, No. 68.
38. *SII.,* XI, (II), No. 211.
39. *KI.,* V, No. 63.
40. *Ibid.*
41. *Ibid.*
42. JBBRAS., IX, p. 291.
43. Ibid., p. 310.
44. *EI.,* XIII, p. 320.
45. *SII.,* XV, No. 229.
46. *KI.,* V, No. 64.
47. *EI.,* XIII, p. 320.
48. From personal collection.
49. *Ibid.*
50. *SII.,* XI, (II), No. 121.
51. Thosar H.S. *Historical Geography of Maharashtra and Goa,* p. 383.
52. Ritti S.H. *An inscription from Kadarolli*, JKU., (Soc. Sc.), p.178 ff.
53. Thosar H.S. *Op.Cit.*, p. 383.

54. *EI.*, XXX, p. 75.
55. *Ibid.*
56. *Ibid.*
57. *Ibid.*
58. *EI.*, XXXIV, p. 106.
59. *Ibid.*
60. Thosar H.S., *Op.Cit.*p.383.
61. *EI.*, XXXIV, p. 106.
62. Thosar H.S., *Op.Cit.*
63. *EI.*, XIII, p. 300.

CHAPTER – IV

THE ORIGIN AND GENEALOGY

The Kadambas are so designated because they ruled over the North Western part of Karnāṭaka, initially with Chandrāpura or modern Chāndōre, in Goa territory as their capital. Later on, it was shifted to Gōpaka i.e. Goa and hence they are called as the Kadambas of Goa.

These Kadambas were an off-shoot of the main Kadamba family which ruled in Karnāṭaka between 4th-6th centuries A.D. Interestingly, the inscriptions of these Kadambas, who were known as the early Kadambas, do not give any details of their origin where as the inscriptions of their off-shoots, mainly the later Kadambas known as the Kadambas of Hāṇgal and the Kadambas of Goa, ascribe mythical origin to the family. There are different versions of the story. But, the gist of these stories is that the first member of this family was known as Trilōchana Kadamba or Mukkaṇṇa i.e., the Tri-eyed Kadamba, who is supposed to have been born from the sweat of the god Śiva, which fell under a Kadamba tree, at the time of slaying of the demon Tripura by god Śiva. It should be noted that though these versions differ in details, all of them point to the Kadamba tree at the place of their origin. This fact is best narrated in the famous Tāḷagunda inscription of Śāntivarma where it states that without any mythical association that the family came to be called Kadambas, because of the lone Kadamba tree situated near their house.[1] This fact has been utilized for ascribing a mythical origin to the family by the later inscriptions. For example, an inscription from Halasi[2] states that Trilōchana Kadamba was born under the Kadamba tree where a drop of sweat from the fore-head of Śiva fell down, at the time of conquering the demon Tripura. From him was born Jayanta. In that family were born many kings, who performed the Aśvamēdha sacrifice eighteen times. In that family was born Shashṭhadēva, who, according to many inscriptions was the first historical person of the family.

There are a few inscriptions which give a detailed genealogy of the family up to the ruler to whom the inscriptions belong. A coordinated study of these genealogies helps us in creating an acceptable genealogy of the family.

In this respect the Marcella plates[3] of Shashṭha II are worthy of consideration. They do not mention the usual Trilōchana Kadamba but give some names which appear to be historical but belonging to a period earlier than the regular member of the family like Shashṭha-I. These plates give the genealogy of the fmily as fallows:

Kaṇṭakāchāryā Nāyavyadēvi
i
Nāgavarma = Māḷavyadēvi
i
Guhalladēvā = Gauravyadēvi
i
Shashṭhadēva

The Gaṇadēvi[4] record of Ṡhashṭhadēva II mentions Trilōchana Kadamba as the earliest member of the family who was followed by Shashṭha I and he was followed by Nāgavarma, Gūvaladēva and Shashṭhadēva II respectively.

The Goa plates of Shashṭhadēva II[5] dated in the Kaliyuga era 4348 also gives the genealogical account of the family from Tryaksha till Shashṭhadēva III. The account is as follows –

Three eyed Jayanta
i
Gūhalla
i
Shashṭha
i
Jayakēśin
i
Vijayārka
i
Jayakēśin=m.Maiḷaladēvi
i

Permāḍi | Vijayāditya
i
Jayakēśi =m.Mahādēvi
i
Tribhuvanamalla=m. Māṇikadēvi
i

Shashṭhsa | Sister=m.Kāmadēva

The Gāḍivore grant [6] begins with Trilōchanna Kadamba and says that many rulers were born in this family. They are mentioned as follows –

Gūhala (I)
i
Shashṭha (I)
i
Jayakēśin (I)
i
Vijayāditya (I)
i
Jayakēśin(II)=m.Maiḷaladēvi,daughter of Vikramāditya VI
i

Permāḍi

Vijayāditya (II)
i
Jayakēśin III
i
Tribhuvanamalla
i
Shashṭha (III)

The Asoge plates of Jayakēśi II[7] dated 1134 A.D. also mentions Trilōchana Kadamba as born of the sweat of Śiva. Then it mentions Jayakēśi, was born in this family. Thus the names of successors are as follows –

Trilōchana Kadamba
I
Jayakēśin (I)
i
Vijayāditya
i
Jayakēśin (II)

The Halasi plates[8] of Jayakēśin III equate Trilōchana Kadamba with Jayanta, where as the others call Jayanta as the son of Trilōchana Kadamba. The plates then states that in the family several kings were born, who performed eighteen Aśvamēdha sacrifices. In that family was born Shashṭhadēva and his successors. The genealogy given is as follows –

Jayanta or Triloōchana Kadamba
i
Shashṭhadēva
i
Jayakēśi
i
Vijayāditya
I
Jayakēśin (II)=Maiḷaladevi
I

Permādi | Vijayāditya or Vijayārkadēva
| Jayakēśi (III)

The Dodwād plates[9] of Tribhuvanamalla also equate Trilōchana Kadamba with Jayanta. They then mention –

Gūhalla I
i
Shashṭha II
i
Jayakēśi I
i
Vijayāditya I

i

Jayakēśi IĪ=m. Maiḷaladēvi d/o Vikramāditya VI

i

Permāḍidēva | Vijayāditya II

i

Jayakēśi III=m. Mahādēvi

i

Tribhuvanamalla

The Dēgave inscription[10] dated 1174 A.D. also equates Trilōchana Kadamba with Jayaṇta, like Halasi plates. This inscription also mentions many successors of Jayaṇta, who performed eighteen Aśvamēdha sacrifices. In that family was born Shashṭhadēva. Then the names of the successors are given as below –

Gūhalladēva

i

Shashsṭhadēva

i

Jayakēśidēva

I

Vijayāditya

i

Jayaakēśi (II)=m.Maiḷaladēvi d/o Vikramāditya VI

i

Śivachitta Permāḍī=m.Kamalādēvi d/o Kāmadēva of Pāṇḍyā family

Thus, it can be seen that by and large most of the inscriptions indicate that Shashṭha was the first historical figure in the family. However, the Marcella plates[11] mention some names as mentioned above, which appear to be historical. They are –

Kaṇṭakāchārya
i
Nāgavarma
i
Gūhalladēva
i
Shashṭha

Of these, the names like Kaṇṭakāchārya and Nāgavarma do not appear in other inscriptions.

Dr. G.M. Moraes thinks that these chiefs and their successors, Gūhalladēva etc. were the contemporaries of the early ruling members of the Chālukyās of Kalyāṇa family and possibly, they became their subordinates. Both Kaṇṭakāchārya and Nāgavarma's son Gūhalladēva are described as an ally of the kings (reigning dynasties) "extending to the sea." Dr.Moraes considers that these rulers were the Southern Śilāhāras of Koṇkaṇ.[12] Gūvaladēva's son Shashṭhadēva is supposed to have joined the early Kalyāṇa Chālukya rulers in putting down the Rāshṭrakūṭas. It is to be noted that the existence of these chiefs and the incidents ascribed to them are not corroborated by other inscriptions. A large number of Kadamba inscriptions begin their genealogy with Shashṭhha I, though some times the order of the names is changed.

The copper plate grant of Vīravarmadēva dated Śaka 971[13] (1049 A.D.) is the first known grant of the Goa Kadamba king Vīravarmadēva, who is described as the son of Shashṭha II. His name is not found in the genealogies mentioned in other records of the family. The other records say that Shashṭha II was succeeded by Jayakēśi I. But it is made known to us from this grant for the first time that Vīravarmadēva, the elder brother of Jayakēśi-I succeeded the king Shashṭhadēva II.

Taking into consideration, the genealogical accounts given in several inscriptions, we have formulated the following genealogical table for facilitating the study of the political history of the family, and it is as follows. –

Shashṭha I=m. Nāvavyadēvi
(c.998-1013A.D.)
i
Nāgavarma=m. Malavyadēvi
i
Gūvaladēva I
(c.980-1005A.D.)
i
Shashṭhadēva II=m. Akkadēvi
(c.1006 A.D.- 1072 A.D.)
i

Gūvaladēva II (c.1038 A.D.) | Vīravarmadēva (c.1046-1054 A.D.) | Jayakēśi I (c.1050 – 1078 A.D)

Children of Jayakēśi I: Gūvaladēva III (1076-1125 A.D.) | Vijayāditya=m Chaṭṭaladēvi (c.1081-1104 A.D.) | Mayanalladēvi | Another daughter (name not known)

Children of Vijayāditya: Padmaladēvi | Jayakēśi II m Maiḷaladēvi (1125-1147AD) | Udayarmadēva | Tribhuvanamalla

Children of Jayakēśi II: Sāvitri | Permāḍidēva (Śivachitta) =m.Kamalādēvi (1147-1186 A.D.) | Vijayāditya II (Vishṇuchitta) (c.1147-1187 A.D.) = m.Lakshmidēvi and Hampādēvi

Son of Vijayāditya II: Jayakēśi-IIĪ=m.Mahādēvi (c.1187-1225 A.D).

Children of Jayakēśi III: Vajradēva (1215-1225-26 A.D.) | Tribhuvanamalla=m.Maṇikadēvi (c.1226-7-1246-47A.D.)

Children of Tribhuvanamalla: Shashṭha-III (c.1246-1267 A.D.) | Sister=m. Kāmadēva

REFERENCES AND NOTES

1. *EC.*, VII, Sk. 117.
2. *JBBRAS.*, IX, pp.241 ff.
3. *Kadamba Kula., App.III, No.1.*
4. *IIBS.,* Vol.I, pp.64, ff.
5. *IA.*, XIV, p.288 ff (L.23) – *Shashṭh-bhūpāl-pratishṭh-adhishṭito-bhavat.*
6. *EI., XXXIV,* pp.105 ff.
7. *Ibid., X XXVI,* pp.304 ff.
8. *JBBRAS.*, IX, p.241 ff.
9. Gurav R.N. *"Doḍwad plates of Jayakēśi III, A.D.1209"* JKU., XI, (1975). pp. 146 ff,
10. *JBBRAS.,* IX., pp.287 ff.
11. KK., APP. III, No.1.
12. *Ibid. p.168.*
13. *GG.*, p.98.

CHAPTER – V

RULERS

SHASHṬHA-I (c.998 – 1013 A.D)

As it is well known, the Kadambas of Goa were a branch of the earlier Kadambas, viz., the Kadambas of Banavāsi, who ruled between 4th – 6th centuries A.D. from Banavāsi. With the rise of the Chālukyas of Bādāmi, the Kadambas lost their power. But some members of the family had scattered in certain areas, perhaps, in some subordinate position. However, they became prominent with the rise of the Chālukyas of Kalyāṇa, in the late 10th century A.D. These chiefs accepted the suzerainty of the Chālukyas and started governing their own regions as the subordinates or the *Mahāmaṇḍalēśvaras* of the latter. Prominent among them were the Kadambas of Hānagal, who had retained their base in Banavāsi and the Kadambas of Goa, who governed that region from Chaṇḍrāpura and Gōpakapaṭṭaṇa. Like the early Kadambas these chiefs also called themselves *Banavāsi -puravarādhīśvara* and bore other titles borne by the early Kadambas. The lion was their royal crest which appears on the copper-plates and also on coins. They carried *vānara-dhvaja*. Their family god was Śiva under the name *Sapta-kōtīśvaradēva* and the goddess *Chāmuṇḍā*. As noted above, they claim their origin to the mythical person viz., Trilōchana Kadamba and his son Jayanta.

Most of the inscriptions start the genealogy with Shashṭhadēva, who was the subordinate of the Kalyāṇa Chālukya king Taila II.[1] However, the Marcella plates give the account of the family starting with Kaṇṭakāchārya.[2] This Kaṇṭakāchārya is identified by scholars with Shashṭha and thus call him Shashṭha I. Even the Gaṇadēvi inscription of Shashṭha II mentions his name as Shashṭha.[3] The name Kanṭakāchārya is indeed unusual in the family of the Kadambas. Really speaking no historical information is available regarding him. Only it is said that his fame had spread beyond the seas.[4] The record refers to Shashṭha I as *Jhampaṇāchārya*.[5] But the exact import of this word has not been clear. He was also called as *chaturbhuja*.[6] He is considered to have arrived with the Chālukyas, who were just then rising to power. He was known for heroism and the inscriptions say that he had installed many distressed rulers on throne.[7] It is also said that Āvarasa II, a South Silāhāra chief rendered military service to a prince (name not given) ruling at Chaṇdrāpura and it is said that it may be Kaṇṭakāchārya of Goa.[8]

A point to be noted here is that his name is omitted in the later records of the family.

Shashṭha's wife was Nāyavyadēvi and his son was Nāgavarma.

NAGAVARMA

Nāgavarma is described only in a general way as a famous ruler.[9] The inscription describes him as learned and that he had studied all scriptures, Vedas, political science, literature and science. He has been described as Bṛihaspati, Viśvakarma, pure like Vyāsa and handsome like cupid. But his name is also omitted in the later records of the family. His wife was Mālavyadēvi and son was Guhalladēva.

GŪVALADĒVA-I (c.980 –1005 A.D.)

The history proper of the Kadambas can be said to have to started from the next ruler Gūvaladēva who can be designated Gūvalla–I, the son of Nāgavarma, mentioned above. He was also called Gūvala, Gōvala, Gūhalla. He is described in a general way as a great hero and a famous ruler respected by the other kings, in the Marcella plates, dated 1038 A.D. of his son Shashṭhadēva II.[10] Ascribing as usual, twenty-five years to every generation, the date of this Gūvaladēva can be tentatively fixed as 988 A.D. Taila II, the first Kalyāna Chālukya king was ruling at that time. The Dēgave inscription[11] says that he could suppress the enemies easily. It compares him to Aṛjuna and Śiva in valour and in the art of warfare. It says that he brought the kingdom under the royal umbrella, by protecting it from the enemies. He has been described as the one who put an end to wicked and cruel enemies. The inscription says

Lōka-chakshur-Gūhalladēvaḥ prasarat-pratāpaḥ yat-tējasā
vairi-tamaschamānāmuddāma-Bhīmāsu guhāusu-vāsaḥ ||

The Dodwād inscription dated 1209 A.D. describes him as *Panchānana* and Aṛjuna in valour.[12] The inscription says–

Tataḥ-khyyātō bhavattēshu Panchānana-parākramaḥ |
Gūhalla-nṛipatiḥ śrīmān-Āṛjuno-Pāṇḍavēshṭhi-vayah ||

The Marcella plates credit him with killing a fierce tiger by his fists.[13] The Dēgāve[14] and Gaṇadēvi[15] inscriptions mentioned above also refer to this incident. Thus he became famous in the world as *vyāghramāri* .[16] The interest shown by him in hunting is referred to in the inscription thus –

sva-śaurya-simhasya balaṁ didrukshuḥ vyāghrān-anēka
mṛagayāsu nighnanyō | vyāghramārīty- abhavat-prasiddhaḥ ||

It is also said that he was an ally of king extending up to the sea. Dr. G.M. Moraes identifies him with Śilāhāra of Koṇkan region, up to the west coast, with Goa as his capital.[17]

The *Gazetteer of Goa*[18] narrates an incident relating to him which is referred to in an inscription of Jayakēśi I. It says that once Gūvaladēva was on a pilgrimage through sea, to the famous Sōmanātha at Prabhāsa–Paṭṭaṇa in Saurāshṭra, in a ship from his capital Chaṇḍrāpura. On the way, the mast of the ship was broken and he was forced to take shelter at Goa, the nearest port, where he received help from a rich Arab merchant (Tājjīka) Madhumat or Mohammad, who, (as stated, in the record as a resident of Haṇjamāna-nagara or a settlement of Arab traders in Goa), not only entertained the king, but also gave him much wealth. This Gūhalla is considered as Gūhala II by Dr.Moraes[19] in his *Kadamba Kula* whereas Dr.B.R.Gopal and Dr.Dikshit consider him to be Gūhalla I only.[20]

SHASHṬHADĒVA-II (c.1006 -1072 A.D.)

Gūhalldēva II's son Shashṭhadēva was also called Chaṭṭa, Chaṭṭayya. He can be designated Shashṭha II, born of the queen Gauravyadēvi,[21] who succeeded his father to the throne. He was ambitious and had the credit of bringing name and fame to the family and also the credit of acquiring Laṁkā i.e., Goa permanently, goes to him.

It may be noted that the original name of the king as said earlier, appears to be Chaṭṭa or Chaṭṭayya, and it is Sanskritised as Shashṭha, which means the sixth. An inscription explains the significance of this term saying that the king was called Shashtha, because he was the sixth in the line of the Pāṇḍavas who were five.[22] The term Chaṭṭayya figures in quite a few Kannada inscriptions.[23] In Kannada, this term Chaṭṭa stands for wise, famous, great and so on.

Though he has a few inscriptions to his credit, the inscriptions of his successors supply ample material on him. The Gaṇadēvi inscription of Shashṭhadēva II[24] describe him as being respected by all the rulers and that his kingdom had extended up to the ocean.

He was pious, learned and well versed in *Purāṇas* and *Smṛitis* and a sole resort of virtues. He had studied various systems of logic and was a poet among the poets.[25] As said earlier he was pious and is stated to have visited Sōmanātha at Prabhāsa in Saurāshtra, Gōkarṇa and Kolhapur, where he worshipped the gods Mahākālēśvara and Mahālakshmi[26] respectively. He is stated to have crossed the ocean and worshipped Rāmēśvara. Probably this refers to his visit to the famous Rāmēśvaram through sea. He visited Sthāṇaka i.e., modern Thane near Bombay and made several donations. He not only offered worship but also distributed wealth and even arranged for a common man to worship the god in an abundant way by reducing the price of camphor in the place.[27] The inscription refers to his performance of *Tulāpurusha* in countless quantities and made grants to the brāhmanas on a lavish scale. The record also refers to his performance of sacrifices as many as there are and made grants to worthy people on a large scale.[28] His period can be tentatively fixed as 1007-8 to 1072 A.D., when the Chālukyā king Irivabeḍanga Satyāśraya was ruling. He was the contemporary of Jayasiṁha II, Sōmēśvara I and Sōmēśvara II of the Chālukyas of Kalyāṇa family and ruled over Koṇkana-900 for nearly forty-five years.[29]

The earliest record of this king found so far, is from Gudikatti, dated 1051-52 A.D.[30] belonging to Sōmēśvara I. While referring to an earlier grant made in 1007-08 A.D., it mentions Jayasiṁha II as the ruler and Chaṭṭayya as his subordinate. The latest known date of Shashṭhadēva II is from Nūlvi[31] which refers to him as ruling Konkaṇa-900 while his son Jayakēśi I was governing along with his wife Boppādēvi, the territories viz., Palasige-12000, Kundūru-500 and Sabbi-30 divisions, besides Konkaṇa-900 in 1072 A.D. This indicates that Shashṭhadēva was alive in 1072 A.D.

It may be added in this connection that Shashṭhadēva was ruling jointly with his elder son Gūvala II and Jayakēśi I in the early and the later parts of his reign respectively. The Savaivare plates of Gūvala II dated 1038 A.D.[32] indicate the rule of Shashṭha with his son Gūvala on the date specified. The Nūlvi record dated 1072 A.D. mentioned above refers to the joint rule of Shashṭhadēva and Jayakēśi I and it is known that Jayakēśi I was already in power in 1050 A.D. The Gaṇadēvi inscription of Shashṭhadēva himself indicates his rule in 1042 A.D.[33] From these records it was surmised that Gūvala II associated himself with his father Shashṭha II in administration by 1038 A.D. The early death of Gūvala II or some unknown reason, might have made Shashṭha II to shoulder the responsibility of the administration alone till he passed on the responsibility to his another son Jayakēśi I, who was ruling the kingdom by about 1050 A.D. Though Shashṭha II passed on the responsibility to Jayakēśi I, he himself continued to rule till 1072 A.D., and from this it can be said that he ruled over Konkaṇa-900 and Palasige-12000 for a long period of nearly forty-five years. The Curtorim copper plate of Vīravarmadēva dated 1049 A.D.[34] is worth mentioning here as it brings a change in the genealogical account of the family. The record says that Vīravarmadēva was the son of Shashṭhadēva (probably the second son). It mentions Vīravarmadēva as a *Mahāmaṇḍalēśvara* who made grants of land in Tundukapura in Kuḍatarikā-agrahāra of Chhatśathi-dēśa i.e., modern Salsette or Shatshasthi ragion of Goa, in the presence of the god Malege-Bhairava. The council of ministers consisting of two *pradhānas* viz., Gōvinda and Mādhavārya and Malapārya, the *sandhivigrahi,* made the grant when Vīravarmadēva was ruling from Gōpaka, to a learned brahmana named Mādhavārya who was the son of Shashṭhadēva and grandson of Mādhava, who belonged to Kauśika gōtra. It was exempted from all taxes. This indicates that Vīravarma was ruling independently in 1049 A.D., from Gōve. There is a reference to Vīravarmadēva in another stone inscription dated 1054 A.D.[35] from Goa which is at present preserved in the Museum at Goa. This inscription refers to one Aṇṇayya, the *dharma mantri* of Panjaṇakhaṇi i.e., modern Panaji. He is said to be meditating at the feet of Vīravarmadēva who is also described as *Mahāmaṇḍalēśvara.* The record refers to this Aṇṇayya as Vīravarmadēva's servant (*sannahaṁ bhritya*) and exemplary lieutenant *(ādarśa baṇṭaṁ)* of Jayakēśi. Jayakēśi here is referred to without any royal titles. From this it can be surmised that he had joined hands with his brother Vīravarmadēva as *yuvarāja* in administration. From these two records it can be surmised that it was not Shashṭha II who was ruling alone in the gap period (1049 and 1054 A.D.). But it was Vīravarmadēva who was incharge of the administration during this period.

Shashṭhadēva has been described as brave and valarous *(sahaja-vivardhita-vīra-vrittiḥ)*.[36] The inscription says that he could control the elephants in rut and tie them to the posts.[37] He has been described as a great warrior and conqueror. The Gaṇadēvi record[38] refers to his conquests of countries like Saurāshṭra, Kalinga, Māḷava, Mahārāshṭra, Āndhra, Vindhya and Kānchi and his defeat of the rulers of Śri Laṁkā, Parāsika and Kāvaḍidvīpa and says that he arrived at Prabhāsa with his fleet. The Narēndra inscription[39] of Jayakēśi II also mentions these countries. The conquests of the countries mentioned above may be conventional or Shashṭhadēva might have accompanied his overlords Jayasiṁha and Sōmēśvara I in their expeditions to these countries. It is known that Sōmēśvara I had conquered northern Silahāras and later on by taking advantage of the disturbed condition in Siṁhaḷa kingdom, Shashṭhadēva occupied southern Silahāra's territory and conquered Goa permanently. Aparājita, the Silahāra chief is said to have inflicted a defeat on Gūvala II which might have made his son Shashṭhadēva to take revange on Chittarāja the successor of Aparājita.[40] Hence he might have tried to annex south Konkana i.e., Konkaṇa-900. The Narēndra inscription describes the exploits of Shashṭhadēva in a vivid manner.

As mentioned earlier he is credited with the conquest of Śrī Laṁka. An inscription from Degave[41] dated 1174 A.D.

fancies in a figurative way that unlike Śrī Rāma of Rāmayaṇa who struggled hard to conquer Laṁka by building a bridge across the sea and facing many other difficulties, this king Shashṭhadēva easily overpowered Laṁka without under going any impediments.

nā sētu-bandhō na-chadūrga-rōdhō na
vānarānīkapati-prayāsaḥ |
nō-va-sumitr-ātmaja-saṁbhramō-bhūl-
Laṁkāpatis-tasya tatāpi vasyaḥ ||

Dr. G.M. Moraes[42] and Dr.B.R.Gopal[43] however, consider that Laṁka conquered by Shashṭha was not Śrī Laṁka but southern part of Goa, which was ruled over by the Goa Silahāras who called themselves as *Siṁhalēśvaras*[44] or the lords of the Siṁhaḷa, metaphorically applied to the island of Goa.

The Narendra inscription[45] gives an interesting incident in connectioin with shashṭhadēva. It describes his visit to Saurashṭra with a big entourage from Goa by sea as far as Saurashṭra. As conjectured by Dr. Moraes, it was obviously his visit to the famous temple of Sōmanātha.[46] The record says –

. . . . . keregaḷ kaṇg-oppamaṁ-māḍe neṭṭane-bahitraṁgaḷa-
mēle-Gōve-veras-aṁbhō-rāsiyoḷ-līleyim-vanādhīśaṁ-naḍedaṁ
Mahā-mahimeyiṁ Saurashṭra-dēśaṁbaraṁ ||

It may be recalled here that his father Gūvladēva had also undertaken such a voyage. The inscription says that after conquering Kāvaḍi-dvīpa and other islands Chaṭṭayya built a bridge of ships upto Laṁka and claimed tribute among brim barbarians.[47]

Kavaḍi-dvīpamum-ādiy-āge palavum dvīpangalam koṇḍu Laṁ |
ke-varaṁ taḷta bahitra-saṁtatigaḷ-indaṁ sētuvaṁ-kaṭṭi ka |
ppavan-ugrāsuraralli bēḍe polaruṁ . . . .

The same inscription refers to his visit to Saurāshṭra for the worship of god Sōmanātha and performance of *Tulāpurusha* and *Aśvamēdha* sacrifices and grants made to the worthy on a lavish scale. This made the king Mummuni of Thāneya, the successor of Chittarāja who had heard about Shashṭhadēva, come to him, meet him, with great respect and affection and take him to his place and bestow on him his daughter with much pomp and also give him five lakhs of gold *(suvarṇṇaman-aidu-lakkamaṁ)* and bestow on him the title *chāga-jaga-jhampaḷāchārya.*[48]

The conquests and voyages of Shashṭha indicate that he had maintained a good army and navy. The Gaṇadēvi record[49] says that he even surpassed the ancient kings like Bali, Karṇa, Yudhishṭhira and others. Further it says that he was surrounded by learned men and he performed his *Suvarṇa-tulā* ceremony. The Panjim copper plate of Jayakēśi I[50] gives an interesting note in this connection. It beautifully describes that the roads that led to the capital of Shashṭha were filled with people either going to the capital or returning from his capital. The record says that the roads were full with travellers who were coming to him from all directions (i.e., eastern and western oceans and from Sētu to Himālaya) for wealth, and others used to go away from the capital, with their desire fullfilled, without leaving place for others.

The capital Chandrāpura was an important maritime centre during this period. In this connection a reference may be made to the trade contact between the port of Gaṇadēvi with east African coast. The Gaṇadēvi[51] (in Surat district of Gujarat state) inscription of Shashṭha, mentioned above refers to the construction of *Maṇḍpikā* or Pavilion in a market place near Gaṇadēvi port, while he was on his pilgrimage to Sōmanātha. The record says that it was for the *Śānthyarthaṁ Jīvalōkasya.*[52] This indicates that he had maintained friendly relationship with the Lāṭa king.

Thus, it is clear from this that the Kadamba chiefs came to limelight with Shashṭhadēva and occupied a prominent place in contemporary history, even by establishing friendly relationship with the rulers of the land viz., the Chālukyas of Kalyāṇa. Akkādēvi was the queen of Shashṭhadēva II. The Marcella plates eulogise her and compare her prowess to the lustre of the Sun.

The genealogical account given in inscriptions do refer to his two sons viz., Gūvaladēva II and Jayakēśi I and it was believed that he was succeeded by his son Jayakēśi I on the throne as his elder son Gūvaladēva II had a very short reign period. But interestingly the Curtorim grant of Vīravarmadēva mentioned above refers to him as the son of Shashṭhadēva II and it was Vīravarmadēva who succeeded Shashṭhadēva and ruled for about eight years and after whom Jayakēśī I became the ruler of the dynasty.

GŪVALADĒVA II (c.1038 A.D.)

Gūvaladēva II was born of Akkādēvi, the queen of Shashṭhadēva.[53] The Marcella Plates describe him in general terms as a hero subduing the Malaya kings. He is described as having brought the "whole world under his umbrella". He received honour and respect from other rulers.[54] The inscription seems to state that he had very competent ministers, whose qualities are described in the same inscription. The plates further state that Gūhala granted the village Savai Pāṭhaka situated in the division of Vēraka to

Nārāyaṇa Paṭṭavardhaṇa, son of Āditya, on the shore of the ocean of Gōkarṇa. His elder brother was Gōvardhaṇa. The genealogy of this Nārāyaṇa is given in detail. He appears to have held an important office (*purōdhā*) during the rule of Gūvala. The grant was made, says the inscription, with the consent of all the ministers of the state.

Nārāyana was the son of Āditya and had a brother called Gōvardhaṇa. Gōvardhaṇa was well versed in *Purāṇas, Sāśtras* and the *Āgamas* and was the *purōdhā* of the king. It is said that he passed on the post of *purōdhā,* due to old age, to his younger brother Nārāyaṇa who continued during the days of Vīravarmadēva also and he is described as highly learned in all the *Śāstras, Āgamas* and *Purāṇas* and was called Paṭṭavardhaṇa. Gūhala was highly pleased with them.

Gūvala is said to have made Chaṇdrāpura as his capital and ruled over the whole of Konkana. The Marcella plates mention several officers with their designations like Chhadama and Ḍēvaṇa, designated *mukhya svīkaraṇa*, Shashṭharāja as *adhyaksha*, Gōviṇda as *Pratihastaka*, Sriyamai Demapai, and Mādhava as *pradhānas*, Khallapai as *Mohalla*, Mallapai as *Saṇdhivigrahika,* Gōvardhaṇa as *Purōdhā*. These are said to be the members of the *maṇtri-maṇḍala.*

There is only one date available for Gūvaladēva II and it is Śaka 960 i.e., 1038 A.D.[55] It appears that he had a very short rule. It is likely that he was associated with the administration even during his father's rule. It is even said that the donor of the Savai-vare plates i.e., Gūvala II was only a minor son of the king Shashṭha who had entrusted the administration of his kingdom to this son during his pilgrimage to Sōmanātha at Kathewar.[56]

VĪRAVARMADĒVA (c.1049-1054 A.D)

The Goa Gazatteer[57] refers to the Curtorim grant, which mentions Vīravarmadēva and the date of the record is said to be 1049 A.D. wherein he is called a *mahāmanḍalēśvara*. He is also described as the son (probably the second son) of Shashṭhadēva and was ruling over Gōpaka. On the basis of this, it is held that he was the son of Shashṭhadēva II. An inscription of Jayakēśi I from old Goa[58] also mentions one Bī(Vī)ravarmadēva, as a Kadamba chief. His subordinate officer Aṇṇayya has been highly eulogized in the inscription, as a trusted lieutenant of Vīravarmadēva and also of Jayakēśi I. The record is dated 1054 A.D. In this connection Dr.K.V. Ramesh, the editor of the record opines that the epithets borne by Vīravarmadēva, in the absence of any other rulers of Kadambas of Goa bearing that name and the date of the inscription all suggest the likelyhood of Vīravarmadēva "being none other than Jayakēśi I himself." But the mention of both Vīravarmadēva and Jayakēśi in separate contexts indicates that the two were different and Jayakēśi is mentioned here without any royal titles. It is quite likely, therefore, that Vīravarma was the brother of Jayakēśi, with whom he must have been associated in the administration of the kingdom.

Aṇṇayya the subordinate chief seems to have occupied a very important position in the kingdom. The high sounding titles, like *Karṇāṭaka-kula-kamala-mārthaṇḍaṁ,* suggest that he played a decisive role in the affairs of the kingdom including warfare. His titles *Paḍavaḷa-rāja-bhujaṁga-vainateya.* i.e., *garuḍa* to the serpent viz., the king of the west, indicates that he played an important role in the conquest of the Āḷupas and the Śilāhāras by Jayakēśi I. This chief, described as *Darma-manṭri,* was in charge of the administration of Panjanakhaṇi, which is the modern Panaji, capital of the present Goa State. This Vīravarmadēva appears to have been in power between 1049-1054 A.D.

A point worthy of mention here is the Courtorim grant of Vīravarmadēva[59] and its contents. It is the first known inscription of Vīravarmadēva. It refers to a grant of land made by Vīravarmadēva in Tuṇḍakapura identified with modern Goa-Vella in Kudatarik-āgrahāra (identified with Curtorim) and the country named Chhaṭsaṭhi i.e., modern Salsette taluk of Goa, to a learned brāhmaṇa named Mādhavarāya son of Shashṭhadēva and grandson of Mādhava, who belonged to *Kauśika gōtra*, free from all taxes, in the presence of the god Malege-Bhairava, and his council of ministers Gōvinda and Mādhavārāya and Maḷapārya, who was *saṇdhivigrahika* or minister for war and peace.[60] The record is dated 1049 A.D. This indicates that Vīravarmadēva was the ruler at the time of the issue of the record. Another record from Goa referred to above indicates that Aṇṇayya was serving both Jayakēśi and Vīravarmadēva which indicates that both were ruling jointly. A point of interest here is the fact that the name of Vīravarmadēva is not found in any genealogical list given in the inscriptions found so far. But this inscription refers to him as the second son of Shashṭhadēva II. Hence it can be said that he succeeded his father and was ruling from Gōpaka, before Jayakēśi I. He was ruling jointly with his brother Jayakēśi I for some time, before Jayakēśi I started his rule independently. It is even said that it was Vīravarmadēva who shifted the capital from Chaṇdrāpura to Goa.[61]

JAYAKĒŚI I (c.1050 - 1078 A.D.)

Jayakēśi I succeeded his brother Vīravarmadēva.[62] The earliest known date of him which is Śaka 973, Naṇdana corresponding to 1051-52 A.D. comes from Guḍikaṭṭi inscription[63] in Belgaum district, Karnataka State. If the Kadamba kingdom came to lime light, during the days of Shashṭhadēva II, it rose to further prominence during the time of Jayakēśi I. Like his father, he was also governing Konkaṇa-900 and Palasige-12000, from Gōpakapaṭṭaṇa. Gōpakapaṭṭaṇa or Goa being a strategic harbour on the west coast facilitated Jayakēśi to build up a strong navy. The harbour also helped the development of trade through sea. Jayakēśi I was very active and soon earned the good will of the ruling kings like Sōmēśvara I and also his successors Sōmēśvara II and Vikramāditya VI. It appears that the Kadamba chiefs tried to establish friendly relationship with the neighboring rulers viz., Chālukyas of Gujarat and their own masters, viz., the Chālukyas of Kalyāṇa. This was achieved by effecting matrimonial alliance with them. For example, Jayakēśi strengthened this alliance by giving his own daughter in marriage to Vikramāditya VI.[64] *Dvyāśrayakāvya*[65] tells us that he struck a similar alliance with Karṇa, the Chālukya king of Anahilawāḍa. In this *kāvya*, Jayakēśi is described as the lord of Chandrāpura.

Inscriptions claim that Jayakēśi I achieved victory over the Chōḷas, Pallavas, Pāṇḍyas, Paramāras and the Lāṭa kings.[66] He was a terror to the ruler of Sri Laṁka. In a figurative way his Paṇaji plates state that the lord of Laṁkā was spending sleepless nights on account of the fear of Jayakēśi I, who had over spread the sea with his fleet. Though these claims appear to be tall, it is quite likely that he assisted the Chālukya rulers in their expeditions against the enemy rulers. The Narēṇdra inscription[67] emphatically states that he subdued Kīrtirāja of Banavāsi and gave the credit to his lord Permāḍi i.e.,Vikramāditya VI. This Kīrtirāja was obviously the Kīrtivarma of the Kadamba family of Hāngal.[68]

The Dēgāve inscription[69] tells us that he killed the king of Kāpardikadvīpa, who is supposed to be Śilāhāra Mummuni. Jayakēśi is also said to have defeated Kāmadēva,[70] who was probably same as Kāmadēva of Hānagal Kadamba family. That Jayakēśi's position was quite strong in contemporary politics is indicated by a statement that he established the Chālukya king in his kingdom. Probably, he might have helped his son-in-law viz.,Vikramāditya VI in acquiring the throne from his brother Sōmēśvara II. The Kirē-Halasige plates[71] refer to Jayakēśi I as the one who brought friendship between the Chōḷa king (Vīrarājēṇdra) and Vikramāditya VI which brought him the name like *Rāya-pitāmaha.* The Narēndra inscription[72] speaks of Jayakēśi as the performer of many sacrifices. He was a great conquerer and was proud of his army. The record says that he had great strength of arm and strength of foot soldiers *(tōḷ-valamum padāti-balamum pirid-umṭ-enag-endu garvvadiṁd-āḷvara chakra -).*

The Paṇaji plates[73] introduce an Arab family, which appears to have attained prominence obviously at Goa. It mentions a person named Aliyama, belonging to Tājiya i.e., Arab family, coming from Vaimūlyapura. His son was Madhumada whose navy was his wealth and the latter's son was Sadhano whose might protected the realm of Kēśirāja which made him equal to Kēśirāja. This Sadhano, it is said, was an ally of Kēśirāja, who seems to have been an officer, under Jayakēśi I. This Kēśirāja is stated to have granted a village called Laghumōraṁbika full of trees and creepers situated in Gōpakadvīpa. It is further stated that the grant was made with the consent of the ministers.

The Goa Gazetteer[74] refers to a grant of Jayakēśi dated 1073 A.D. and states that the Arab minister Chȟaddama, built a mosque at Gōpaka and made certain grants to it. A

Portuguese charter mentions Sadhano, a minister of Jayakēśi I. He can be identified with Sadhano of the Paṇaji plates. The charter states that under the administration of this minister, the trade activities in Goa increased and it became a prosperous city. Pleased with his services, Jayakēśi is said to have invested him with full powers in administration. He is stated to have established a charitable institution meant for the maintenance of the poor and the helpless people. He also made provision for the upkeep and effective management of the institution by levying taxes on the merchant ships, coming from foreign countries and also on the local trading ships. Interestingly, the charter states that provision was made even for the funeral of the dead and the performance of their obeseques.[75]

The trade activity from Gōpakapaṭṭaṇa under Jayakēśi I was in a flourishing condition. It is said that it had trade contacts with no less than fourteen countries, such as Kaḍan, Srytem (Sumatra), Bomgalla, Pusta (Pulikat), Chanda (Chōḷa), Panḍya, Keral, Lat, Gurjar, Zungavar etc.[76]

Jayakēśi was a contemporary of Sōmēśvara II and Vikramāditya VI, in the early years of the latter. The inscriptions of his successor Gūvala III appear from 1076 A.D. It is reasonable, therefore, to presume that his rule ended in 1076 A.D. Many inscriptions of Jayakēśi do not mention the overlord at all. It indicates that Jayakēśi had grown quite powerful and even claimed to be ruling independently.

Dvyāśraya-kāvya[77] of Hēmachandra narrates the relationship of Jayakēśi I with the Chālukyas of Anahilawāḍa. It is said that the king Karṇa of this family who was enamoured by the beauty of Mayanalladēvi, the daughter of Jayakēśi I married her. A story recorded in *Prabandha Chintāmaṇi* [78] narrates that he died a tragic death due to a promise he had made to his parrot. The story, however, has no historicity about it.

The inscriptions mention Gūvaladēva and Vijayāditya as the sons of Jayakēśi I. He had two daughters. One was Mayanalladēvi who was given in marriage to Karṇa of Anahilawāḍa and the name and other details of another daughter is not known.

GŪVALADĒVA-III (c.1075-76 - 1125 A.D.)

Jayakēśi I was succeeded by his son Gūvaladēva III. Most of the genealogies given in the Kadamba inscriptions do not mention this king. But the Narendra inscription very clearly states that Gūvaladēva was born to Jayakēśi I, "just as lion was born".[79] The Alṇāvar inscription[80] also confirms this statement. He also bore the title *Trībhuvanamalla.*[81] Some writers consider *Trībhuvanamalla* as different from Gūvaladēva. But the Mugad inscription clearly mentions him as *Trībhuvanamalla* Gūvaladēva, showing that *Trībhuvanamalla* was his title.[82] He seems to have assumed the title Śivachitta-Permāḍi.[83] It is also said that he was the first ruler of the Kadambas to call himself *Gōpaka-puravarādhīśvara,*[84] i.e., the lord of Gōpakapura.

Gūvaladēva has more than twenty-one inscriptions to his credit. The earliest of them is from Muttage, dated 1077 A.D.[85] and the latest inscription of him found so far is from Mugad dated 1125 A.D.[86] There are different dates given by scholars like Dr. B.R.Gopal and others with regard to the ascendency of Gūvala III to the throne. But the finding of Muttagi inscription dated 1077 A.D. indicates that Gūvala might have succeeded his father by about 1075-76 A.D. The inscriptions of Gūvala III show that his rule extended over a vast region in addition to Konkaṇa-900 and Palasige-12000 divisions and it seems that he established his authority over Kāvaḍidvīpa also. The dominion claimed by Gūvala is the largest ever claimed by the rulers of Kadambas of Goa. For example, an inscription from Alṇāvar,[87] dated 1081 A.D. mentions the following tracts as being ruled by Gūvaladēva. They are –

> *Koṇkaṇa-ombhainūru, Palasige-pannischhāsira, Kundūru-inūru, Kādaravaḷḷi-eraḍu-mūvattu, Kontakuḷi-mūvattu-and Kavaḍi-dvīpa-savalakka.*

Inscriptions indicate that there was some rupture of relationship between Vikramāditya VI and Gūvaladēva. An inscription from Naregal[88] dated 1104-05 A.D., of Achūgi II of the Sinda family of Yalburga states that Achūgi took over Goa and also Konkana at the instance of Vikramāditya VI. An inscription from Kalkēri[89] also states that Anantapālayya, the famous *daṇḍanāyaka* of Vikramāditya VI was governing Palasige-12000 under Vikramāditya VI. However, inscriptions also indicate that Gūvaladēva III continued the authority over the region. For example, the inscriptions from Mukkal[90] and Nigadi dated 1111-12A.D.[91] refer to Gūvala's rule over *Koṅkaṇa-maṇḍala*. This indicates that Vikramāditya VI decided to put down Gūvaladēva, who appears to have behaved in a high handed manner. That Palasige continued to be under Gūvaladēva is clear from the fact that Vikramāditya VI gave Palasige-12000 as dowry to Gūvala's nephew Jayakēśi II at the time of the latter's marriage with the daughter of Vikramāditya VI.[92] Obviously, Vikramāditya did not want to continue the hostility with Gūvaladēva, who was the prominent subordinate in the Konkaṇ region. He, therefore, followed a policy of friendship by giving his daughter Maiḷaladēvi in marriage to Gūvaladēva's nephew

Jayakēśi II. The Mukkal inscription referred to above mentions a Hāngal Kadamba chief Śāntivarma as ruling over Pānumgal-500 along with Gūvaladēva.[93] Another inscription dated 1103 A.D.[94] from the same place, mentions another Hāngal Kadamba chief Taila, who was obviously the son of Śāṇtivarma ruling with Gūvala. Mention of these chiefs in the inscription of Gūvaladēva is highly unusual. The reason seems to be that Mukkal was on the borders of the regions of both the Kadamba families.

The inscriptions speak of three capitals of the period of Gūvaladēva III, viz., Chandrāpura, Aṇilāpura and Gōpaka or Gove. If Kadroḷḷi and Tersikoppa inscriptions mention Chandrāpura as capital, the inscriptions from Aḷnāvar and Saṇgamēśvara mention Aṇilāpura as his capital. The copper plate grant of Tribhuvanamalla refers to Gōpaka as his capital.

Chandrāpura is identified with Chāndor in Salseṭṭe, Goa which was the earliest capital of the Kadambas of Goa. The Marcella plates[95] and a record of Jayakēśi I from Velha-Goa mention Chandrāpura as the capital of Gūvaladēva III. An undated record from Kādaravaḷḷi[96] also refers to Chaṇḍrāpura as the capital. *Dvyāśraya-kāvya* of Hēmachaṇdra also refers to Chandrāpura as the capital of Jayakēśi I.[97] The records of Jayakēśi I and Gūvaladēva III mention Aṇilāpura i.e., modern Aḷnāvar as the capital.[98] A record from Sēḍaṁbi dated 1062–63 A.D.[99] mentions Jayakēśi I as ruling from Aṇilāpura. Similarly a record from Saṅgamēśvar dated 1082-83 A.D.[100] says that Gūvaladēva III was ruling Palasige-12000 and Konkaṇa-900 from his capital Aṇilāpura. An inscription from Kadroḷḷi mentions Gūvaladēva as ruling from his capital Gove.[101]

Goa became the permanent capital from the days of Vīravarmadēva and continued during the days of Jayakēśi I. The Halsi record[102] and Paṇaji plates referred to above, mention Gōpakapaṭṭaṇa i.e., Goa as the capital of Jayakēśi I, which grew to prominance as a commercial centre and through which sea-trade was carried on.

Another event worthy of mention here is the marriage that took place between the nephew of Gūvala III and Maiḷaladēvi the daughter of Permāḍi or the Chālukya *chakrēśvara* viz., Vikramāditya VI and Malayavatidēvi[103] by about 1104 A.D. An inscription from Kanakūr mentions the grant of the village Kanakūr in Kundūru-500 by Jayakēśi II to the temple of Sōmanātha in Saurāshṭra after receiving it from Vikramāditya VI.[104]

The latest known date of Gūvaladēva III is 1125 A.D.[105] He was in power between 1076 and 1125 A.D. i.e. for nearly 49 years. As he had no issues and as his younger brother Vijayāditya appears to have predeceased him, Jayakēśi II the son of Vijayāditya had to shoulder the responsibility of the government after Gūvaladēva III.

VIJAYĀ DITYA I (c.1081-1104 A.D.)

Vijayāditya, also called Vijayārka was the son of Jayakēśi I.[106] There are no inscriptions of Vijayāditya except one i.e., from Kanakūr dated 1104 A.D which refers to a grant made by him to a person named Purushōttama Bhaṭṭōpādhyāya.[107] But the inscriptions of his successors describe him as a great warrior. From this it can be surmised that he associated himself with administration at least for some time. The inscriptions describe him as a good administrator, "through whose might no tale of woe was heard upon the earth."[108] Further the record refers to his successful naval expeditions to several islands.[109] Perhaps he might have helped his brother Gūvaladēva III in recovering some parts of North Konkaṇa from Anantadēva.[110] The Doḍwāḍ inscription describes him as a swordsman.[111] He is also described as a "torch for the jewels of the land of the Konkaṇa."[112]

The description of Vijayāditya in the records appear to be conventional without any historical value. His wife was Chaṭṭaladēvi.[113]

As there are no further details about this ruler found so far, it can be said that he might have died early which made his brother Gūvaladēva III to pass on the kingdom to his nephew Jayakēśi II.

JAYAKĒŚI II (c.1125 – 1147 A.D.)

Jayakēśi II succeeded his uncle Gūvaḷadēva III by about 1125 A.D. He might have ruled jointly with his uncle Gūvaladēva III as there is a reference to Jayakēśi II in an inscription from Kanakūr.[114] He was one of the prominent rulers of the family. He was a feudatory of Chālukya Vikramāditya VI,[115] and his period also coincided with the rule of Sōmēśvara III and his son Jagadēkamalla II. The inscriptions reveal that the power of the Kadambas reached the acme of its glory during Jayakēśi II.

The period of Jayakēṣi II was an eventful one. The inscriptions indicate that the territory of the Kadambas extended to the maximum extent in his period. An inscription from Narēndra[116] mentions the territories that were under the control of Kadambas of Goa in 1125 A.D. Thy were Konkaṇ-900, Palasige-12000, Uṇakaḷ-30, Sabbi-30, Kontakuḷi-30, Hāngal-500, Utsugrāme, Kadaravaḷḷi-30, Poḷalagunda-30, Velugrāme-70, Haive-500, and Kavaḍi-dvīpa-savalakka. These comprised of some parts of Belgaum (including

Belgaum), Dharwad and North Kanara districts . But some of the territories except Konkaṇa-900 and Palasige were changing hands in the later period.

An important development in this period was the rise of the Hoysaḷa Vishṇ̃uvardhaṇa and other feudatories of Vikramāditya VI. Vishṇ̃uvardhaṇa was an ambitious chief. He tried to expand his territory beyond Tungabhadrā in the north, which earned the displeasure of Vikramāditya VI. He encouraged him to an extent in the beginning but when he was found to be highly unruly Vikramāditya VI curbed his power through his trusted general Sinda Āchugi II.[117] Perhaps, Jayakēśi II was also encouraged by the aggressive activities of Vishṇ̃uvardhaṇa, and himself tried to assert and declared himself *Konkaṇa-chakravarti.*[118] Vikramāditya curbed his power by sending Āchugi II. The inscriptions claim that he conquered Goa and seized Konkaṇa.[119] But soon Jayakēśi II is found ruling over these territories. It indicates that he was reinstated to power, perhaps on account of him being the son-in-law of Vikramāditya VI. Jayaskēśi II also came into conflict with Vishṇ̃uvardhaṇa, who appears to have marched up to Halasi and he is said to have occupied it for some time.

Jayakēśi came into conflict with Silāhāra Aparāditya also and Aparāditya was thoroughly defeated. An inscription from Narēṇdra[120] refers to him as governing Kavaḍi-dvīpa-savalakka. An inscription from Vaḍavāḷi dated 1127 A.D. of Aparāditya[121] is worthy of notice here. It describes, the calamity in a graphic way and says that a demon named *Chittūka*, invaded the kingdom and the feudatories sided with him. Dharma was lost, the elders were oppressed, the subjects became exhausted and the country's prosperity was at an end. Still undaunted Aparāditya fought single handed and put to flight the enemy who was forced to take shelter with the *Mllechchās*. The demon *Chittūka* of the record has been identified with Jayakēśi II. The Śilāhāra chief Gaṇḍarāditya of Kolhapur appears to have come to the help of Aparāditya.[122]

Jayakēśi II kept up his aggressive activities during the time of the next Chālukya ruler Sōmēśvara III. But, Sōmēśvara sent his general Permāḍi I, the son of Āchugi II, who forced Jayakēśi II to accept Chālukya supremacy.[123] With all these skirmishes with the Chālukya kings, Jayakēśi II continued to rule over a vast territory up to the year 1146-47 A.D.

Jayakēśi II was a good administrator. He was assisted by his ministers and generals. For example, an inscription from Tambūr[124] refers to a minister who has been described as *Mantribhūshaṇa* and *sandhivigrahi*. Some of them who were in the service of Vikramāditya VI were serving under him. For example, Lakshmaṇarāja,[125] an officer under Vikramāditya was sent to accompany Maiḷaladēvi to the Kadamba kingdom after her marriage with Jayakēśsi II. Lakshmaṇarāja has been mentioned as *Mahāpradhāna antaḥpurādhyaksha, pasāyita* and *Maneverggaḍe.* Not only Lakshmaṇarāja but even his grandson Siṅgarasa served Jayakēśi II.[126] He is also described as *mahāpradhāna antaḥpurādhyaksha, pasāyita* and *maneverggaḍe.*

Gōpaka-paṭṭaṇa or Gōve was the capital of the Kadambas of Goa during his period also. For instance, the Tambūr[127] and Kurḍikēri[128] inscriptions and many other records refer to Gōva as the capital. There are a few inscriptions which refer to the other capitals of the family, in the early years i.e., during the days of Shashṭhādēva II and Gūvaladēva II as mentioned above. Chandrāpura was their capital. The inscription from Narēndra dated 1126 A.D.[129] describe Kundūru as the capital of Jayakēśi II. An inscription from Siddāpura dated 1135 A.D.[130] and an inscription from Mādanabhāvi[131] dated 1138 A.D. mentions Bhōgāpura as his capital. Saṁpagāḍi was another capital of the Kadambas during the days of Vijayāditya II.[132] But Gōva continued to be the permanent capital of the Kadambas during Jayakēśi II and even during the period of successive rulers.

An interesting event connected with Jayakēśi II is his marriage with Maiḷaladēvi, the daughter of Vikramāditya VI. Vikramāditya VI who was pleased with the heroic qualities of Jayakēśi I, who also had given his daughter in marriage to Vikramāditya VI, thought of doing good to him. An inscription says that he gave his daughter in marriage to Jayakēśi II,[133] the nephew of Gūvaladēva III. Another inscription from Tambūr[134] also refers to the marriage of Jayakēśi II with Maiḷaladēvi and the presents like hoards of elephants, horses, choicest articles, chariots and golden ornaments along with Palasige country bestowed on him by Vikramāditya VI. The inscription mentions Jayakēśi II as the beloved (*nechchina-aḷiya*) son-in-law of Vikramāditya VI.

Jayakēśi II was pious. His religious attitude can be seen in the grants made by him to the temples mentioned in inscriptions. Almost all the inscriptions speak of the grants made by him for the maintenance of the temples. To name a few – the village Kanakūr was granted for burning incense to the god Sōmanātha of Saurashṭra, at the time of his marriage with Maiḷaladēvi.[135] The Narēndra inscription refers to the grants made by him and Maiḷaladēvi to the temple of Śankaradēva of the place.[136] The Asōge plates dated 1123 A.D.[137] refer to the grants made for the maintenance of the god Gaḷagēśvara at Baḷoge. The Mādanabhāvi inscription[138] refers to his observing religious rites on Mondays (*Sōmavārada-vāriy-āgirdda-vṟat-ōdyāpaṇa samayadoḷu*).

The kingdom witnessed the cultural development also during his period. Being learned he patronized education. People of the period used to take interest in learning. *Agrahāras* were created for this purpose. The *agrahāras* were managed by the *Mahājanas* who were learned. For example an inscription from Beṭdūr[139] refers to the *agrahāra* managed by the 62 *Mahājanas.* The Halyal inscription dated 1144 A.D.[140] refers to the *Mahājanas* of the place. This inscription describes the *Mahājanas* as truthful, engaged in the performance of *Agnishṭōma* and other sacrifices, and having mastery over Manu's *Dharmaśāstra,* and *Vyākaraṇa.* They are extolled as being bereft of evils like hypocrisy, anger, avarice, jealousy etc. They were also poets, reciters,. debaters, speakers, enjoying the recital of literary pieces composed in easy and difficult styles of Sanskrit, *Apabhraṁśa* and *Paiśāchika* language which were with sweet and gentle constructions in various styles, such as *Gauḍi, Vaidarbhi* and *Paiśāchi* etc. This indicates the interest shown by the learned in literary compositions of various styles and different languages.

There are references to the architects also. For example, an inscription from Tambūr[141] refers to Jatōja and his sons Kēta and Mudda, who built Nakara Jinālaya of the place.

As noted earlier Jayakēśi II had an elder sister named Padmaladēvi[142] (*tan-mahēśvaranim piriyaḷu Padmaladēviya*), married to Hākiballa son of Māvulidēva of the Hāngal Kadaṁba family and two younger brothers viz., Udayamadēva[143] and Trībhuvanamalla.[144]

Permāḍidēva and Vijayāditya were the two sons of Jayakēśi II. He appears to have also had a daughter named

Sāvitri. An inscription of Jayakēśi II from Tambūr[145] refers to Sāvitri the elder sister of Permāḍidēva. She was given in marriage to Gaṇgidēva, son of Taila-nṛipa. Though it is hard to identify him it can be said that he might be Taila II of the Hāngal Kadaṁba family.

MAIḶALADĒVI

Maiḷaladēvi, as mentioned above, was the daughter of Vikramāditya VI and Malayamatidēvi.[146] A number of inscriptions pertaining to the Goa Kadambas speak of her. She has been described as *Chālukya Chakriya-magaḷu* in an inscription from Tambūr.[147] She was given in marriage to Jayakēśi II. The Narēndra inscription[148] says that Vikramāditrya VI performed the marriage not only on a grand scale but also bestowed on his son-in-law, with heaps of gold, elephants and horses which surpassed śakra's fiercy elephant and the greatness of *uchchaissravas.* Another inscription from Tambūr[149] mentioned above refers to this marriage and says that Vikramāditya gave Jayakēśi II hoards of gold, elephants, horses, jewellary along with Palasige. The celebratioin of the marriage and customs followed by Vikramāditya mentioned in the Narēndra inscription, remind us of the customs and traditions followed in these days also. Vikramāditrya VI not only bestowed territory and wealth on Jayakēśi II but also commissioned a general named Lakshmarasa to accompany his daughter, who became the *maneverggaḍe* of Maiḷaladēvi.[150] Later on his grandson Singarasa also continued as the *maneverggaḍe* of Maiḷaladēvi.

Maiḷaladēvi was the most celebrated queen of the Goa Kadamba family and was a woman of outstanding quality. The ability of Maiḷaladēvi made her take part in the administration of the kingdom. For instance, the inscriptions speak of her rule from different capitals. The Narēndra inscription mentioned above, states that she was ruling from Kundūru[152] i.e., modern Narēndra. Another inscription from Siddāpura mentions that Bōgur was her capital.[153] An inscription from Goḷihaḷḷi[154] refers to her as ruling from Gōve along with her husband Jayakēśi II. An inscription from Kurḍikēri[155] dated 1126 A.D. refers to Jayakēśi II as ruling from Gōve and Maiḷaladēvi as ruling her own tracts from Kundūru. The Mishrikōṭi inscription[156] dated 1136 A.D. mentions Maiḷaladēvi as ruling from Kundūru and her husband from Goa. From this, it becomes clear that she was ruling either jointly with her husband or son Permāḍidēva or ruling independently. It is worth mentioning an inscription from Narēndra[157] which mentions Maiḷaladēvi as ruling over a vast territory consisting of Konkaṇa-900, Palasige-12000, Kavaḍi-dvīpa-savalakka, Kontakuḷi-30, Haive-500, Poḷalgunda-30, Pānuṁgal-500, Uṇakal-30, Sabbi-30, Utsugrāme-30, Kādaravaḷḷi-30, and Vēlugrāme-70. The inscriptions from Narēndra,[158] Mishrikōṭi,[159] Belvantara[160] dated 1149 A.D. and Ugnikēri[161] describe the personality, liberality, beauty and ability of the queen.

Maiḷaladēvi had two sons viz., Permāḍi and Vijayāditya[162] who were generally known as Śivachitta and Vishṇuchitta. The inscription from Tambūr[163] stated above mentions Sāvitri, who was given in marriage to Gangidēva (perhaps of the Hāngal Kadamba family) as the elder sister of Permāḍidēva.[164] Maiḷaladēvi was generous in religious attitude. She was a devotee of Lord Śankara.[165] The Gūgikaṭṭi inscription[166] states that she established an image of Kēśava there. There are references to grants made by her to the Jaina temples also.

Maiḷaladēvi commanded respect of all. She used to take part in the activities of her sons. For instance when Permāḍi granted the village Sindavaḷḷi to a temple he obtained the permission of his mother.[167] It is mentioned in the same inscription that her younger son Vijayāditya visited the holy place of Palāsikā i.e., Halasi with his mother and Purōhitas and made grant of land to god Nṛsimha of the place in 1172 A.D. The Dēgāve inscription[168] dated 1174 A.D. is interesting. When Kamalādēvi, the queen of Permāḍi, who was very much impressed by the scholarship of the brāhmaṇas wanted to convert the village Dēgāve into an agrahāra asked the permission of her husband Permāḍidēva. Permāḍidēva gave permission to her after getting consent from his mother Maiḷaladēvi. This indicates the importance given to this senior queen of the family.

PERMĀḌIDĒVA (1147-48 -1185-86 A.D)

Jayakēśi II had two sons viz., Permāḍidēva and Vijayāditya from his queen Mailaḷadēvi.[169] In a poetic way, in an inscription from Kalkundi[170] they are described as Rāma and Lakshmaṇa and fruits of the same plant. They are also compared to Bhīma and Arjuna.

Permāḍidēva who was also called Perma, Permāḍi, Hemmāḍidēva succeeded his father Jayakēśi II in the year 1147-48 A.D. as indicated by the regnal years mentioned in his records. For instance a record from Bammigaṭṭi dated 1147 A.D. refers to first year of his rule.[171]

An inscription from Miśrikōṭi dated 1158 A.D. refers to his twelth regnal year.[172] The Gōḷihaḷḷi[173] and Sigigaṭṭi[174] records refer to the fourteenth and seventeenth year of his reign. His twenty-third and twenty-eighth regnal years are mentioned in Halasi[175] and Dēgāve[176] records.

There are more than thirty-five inscriptions of Permāḍidēva. Most of them are in Kannada language and some of them are in Sanskrit. The first reference to Permāḍidēva is found in an inscription of his father Jayakēśi II from Mādanabhāvi, dated 1127 A.D.[177] wherein he is described as *yuvarāja*. The earliest record mentioning him as functioning independently is dated 1142 A.D. and it comes from Hunsikaṭṭi,[178] Kalghatgi taluk of Dharwad district. In a highly eulogistic way this inscription ascribes his victory over the kings of Lāṭa, Draviḍa, Māḷava, Nēpāḷa, Gūrjara and Pāriyātra. This obviously is a conventional description. But it suggests that he participated in the expeditions of his over lord Chālukya Jagadēkamalla II.

The Halsi[179] record describes him as a monorach of outstanding ability, an abode of learning, prudence, sportiveness, of benevolence and of profoundity of high mindedness, of valour and bravery and of spotless fame.

When Permāḍidēva was governing, his younger brother Vijayāditya II was holding the position of *yuvarāja* and was assisting his brother in the administration of the kingdom. It is quite likely that both Permāḍidēva and Vijayāditya were ruling jointly for quite some time. A fragmentary record from Siddapura dated 1158 A.D.[180] is the earliest record to speak of their rule. It mentioins Vijayāditya as *yuvarāja.* Permāḍi was a feudatory of the Chālukyas of Kalyāṇa king.

Permāḍidēva, served under the Chālukya king Bhūlōkamalla Sōmēśvara III, Jagadēkamalla II and Taila III. An inscription from Belavantra[181] dated 1149 A.D. mentions him as feudatory of Jagadēkamalla. An inscription from Tambūr dated 1156 A.D.[182] refers to him as the feudatory of Trailōkyamalla i.e., Taila III. During the latter's period the Chālukya kingdom became weak and Kalachuri Bijjala usurped the Chālukya throne. This major change in the political scene gave an opportunity to Permāḍidēva to shake off the yoke of subordination and he started ruling as an independent ruler. This is indicated by the use of his regnal years in his inscriptions. He claimed himself to be the ruler of Konkaṇa and several adjoining regions and called himself as *Konkaṇa- Chakravarti.*[183]

The inscriptions also indicate Permāḍi's conflicts with the Silāhāra chiefs of Konkaṇa. But these skirmishes did not affect their authority over their respective territories. Permāḍidēva assumed the titlẹ *Malavaramāri*[184] i.e., the slayer of the Malavas or Sahyādri tribes. It is said that it refers to the subjugation of the hilly province of Veḷugrāma-70.

Permāḍidēva asserted independence after the suppression of the Chālukyas by the Kalachuris and called himself as *Konkaṇa chakravarti*. The Kalachuris could not divert their attention towards the Kadambas of Goa as they were busy in reducing the Sāntaras, Kadambas of Hangal and the Hoysaḷas. It was believed that he died without any issues and was succeeded by his brother Vijayaditya II by about 1180 A.D. But an inscription from Angaḍi gives as later date as 1192 A.D,[185] when Chālukya Sōmēśvara IV was ruling. This indicates that he had a long political career. It is even indicated that his brother Vijayāditya predeceased him and he continued to rule over the kingdom and that Jayakēśi III, the son of Vijayāditya succeeded Permāḍidēva. As an early inscription of his successor Jayakēśi III[186] is dated 1187-88 A.D. it can be said that Permāḍidēva ruled till 1185-86 A.D.

The inscriptions ascribe both Permāḍidēva and Vijayāditya with authority over large territories like Kavadidvīpa, Konkaṇa-900, Palasige-12000 and the like. The inscriptions of Permāḍidēva, Kamalādēvi and Vijayāditya indicate the all sided development in the territory during this period. As menioned earlier, Permāḍi had a sister named Sāvitri. An inscription from Tambur[187] refers to this fact and says that she was given in marriage to Gangidēva, son of Tailanripa, who has been identified with Taila of Hangal Kadamba family by Dr. B.R.Gopal.[188]

Permāḍidēva appears to have issued gold coins.[189] The gold coins dated Śaka 1072 (1150-51 A.D.), Śaka 1078-79 (1156-57 A.D.) Śaka 1083 (1161 A.D.), and Śaka 1096 (1174 A.D.) indicate the flourishing trade and commerce, during this period. The title of Permāḍidēva viz., *Malavaramāri,* is noticed on his coins along with the name of their family deity, Śri *Saptakōṭiśvara* on the obverse and a lion on the reverse of the coin . The title *Malage Bhairava* is also found on the coins of Jayakēśi I.

Permāḍidēva is stated to have married Kamalādēvi, who was born of Kāmabhūpa and Chaṭṭaladēvi.[190] She constructed the temples of Kamala-Nārāyaṇa and Śri Mahālakshmi in the *agrahāra* Dēgāve.[191] The inscriptions describe her as generous to a fault, her desire to grant equalled the wishes of the supplicants. She was responsible for the spread of learning among her subjects. It was, she who created the *agrahāra* Dēgāve after obtaining permission of her husband Permāḍidēva.[192] The *agrahāra* was granted to 30 brāhmaṇa families led by Vindhyāvāsi Bhaṭṭōpādhyāya who was proficient in a variety of subjects like the *Vēdas, Vēdāṇga, Nyāya, Mīmāṁsa, Sāṁkhya, Yōga, Vēdānta, Smṛiti, Itihāsa, Purāṇa* and Astronomy.

Interestingly, the inscription gives details of the highly talented architect named Tippōja of the period.[193] He is described as not only an expert in architecture, but also in *Bharatāgama* and literature. He was the son of Holōja, who was thorough in architecture and sculpture. Tippōja was assisted by his son Bagōja in the construction of the temples.

KAMALĀDĒVI

Kamalādēvi,as mentioned earlier, was the crowned queen (*prathama mahishi*) of Permāḍidēva.[194] The inscription mentions that she was the daughter of Kāmadēva and Chaṭṭaladēvi of the Pāṇḍya race.

Kamalādēvi was a devotee of Pārvati and Saptakōtīśvaradēva of Goa was her *ārādhya dēvata*. She encouraged the learned. The inscription from Dēgāve[195] mentioned above says that while she was in Gōpakapuri, she used to listen daily the *Purāṇas* and *Dharmaśāstras* read by the brāhmaṇas. Listening to the gift of land praised in the *purāṇas* and *Dharma-śāstras* and the greatness of the brāhmaṇas who were well acquainted with the *Vēdas, Vēdāngas*, learned in *Nyāya, Mimāmsa, Sānkhya, Yōga, Vēdānta, Smṛiti, Itihāsa, Purāṇa* and the followers of six duties etc., she thought of creating an *agrahāra* in Dēgāve and brought these learned brāhmaṇas from different places[196] to settle at Dēgāve. On the date specified, she made grant of *vṛittis* or shares to the brāhmaṇas of various *gōtras* led by one Vindhyāvāsi Bhaṭṭōpādhyāya. Grants were made to the god Kamala-Nārāyaṇa and goddess Mahālakshmi. Grants were also made for the study and teaching of *Śāstras* and *Vēdas* and also for *Bālaśikshā* i.e., primary education. Further, the record refers to one Gōvindadēva who was an expert in *Tarkka* (logic), *Tantra* (*śāktā* practices) and *Kavita* i.e., composing poetry who composed the record at the orders of the queen Kamalādēvi.

Kamalādēvi was also interested in arts. An inscription from Dēgāve of 12th century A.D[197] is worth mentioning here. It refers to construction of temples of Kamala-Nārāyaṇa and goddess Śri Mahālakshmi, complete with *maṇḍapa* (hall) and *Kaḷasa* (pot finial) by *sūtradhāri* or sculptor named Tippōja and his son *pratāpa-sūtradhāri* Bāgōja at the *agrahāra* Dēgāve at the orders (*niyāmadiṁ*) of the queen Kamalādēvi.

The inscription further gives the genealogy of the sculptor. According to it, Tippōja was the son of the *sūtradhāri* Hōlōja of Hūvinabāge, who was proficient in the features of the temples and images (*prāsāda-lakshaṇa* and *pratimā-lakshaṇa*). The inscription further refers to Tippōja as an expert in *Bharatāgama śāstra*, in composing poetry and also in charity.

VIJAYĀDITYA II (c.1147 – 1187-88 A.D.)

Vijayāditya was also called Vijayārka.[198] He was also called *Vishṇu-dāsa*,[199] *Vāṇibhūshaṇa* or *Sarasvati bhūshaṇa* by the favour of lord of Gōkarṇa.[200] It is noted above that Permāḍidēva and Vijayāditya were ruling jointly for some time. As mentioned earlier there is an early reference to Vijayāditya in an inscription from Mādanabhāvi dated 1127 A.D[201] wherein he is mentioned as *Kumāra* and his elder brother Permāḍi as *Yuvarāja-kumāra*. The Kalkuṇḍi inscription[202] refers to Permāḍi and Vijayāditya as ruling the country in the capacity as *adhirāja* and *yuvarāja*. The Kulavaḷḷi inscription[203] refers to him as *yuvarāja-kumāra*, while referring to the rule of Permāḍidēva. Interestingly, the Sadāśivagad plates of Vijayāditya dated Śaka 1107[204] (1185 A.D.) refer to the independent rule of Vijayāditya II. It appears to be the first and the only record of Vijayāditya found so far attributing an independent rule to him, disassociating from his brother Permāḍidēva. Inscriptions show that Vijayāditya actually participated in administration as well as warfare. He seems to have come into conflict with Kalachuri Āhavamalla, who probably tried to subdue him and reduce him to the position of subordination. The inscription of 1180 A.D.[205] refers to an attack by *Danḍanāyaka* Chanḍugidēva, a general of Kalachuri Āhavamalla. The record claims that this Chanḍugidēva burnt the territories of Vijayāditya. However, the Kalachuri regeme was a short lived one. With the revival of the Chālukya rule by Sōmēśvara IV, Vijayāditya appears to have supported him in his struggle for power. An inscription dated 1186 A.D.[206] states that Sōmēśvara was then ruling from the capital Gōvage i.e., Goa. Vijayāditya was also confronted by Vīra Ballaḷa of the Hoysaḷa family, which was another rising power, in the southern part of the Chālukya empire. The Hoysaḷa inscriptions claim that the king of Konkaṇa was subdued and that they extracted tribute from Vijayāditya, who was obviously Vijayāditya II.[207]

Taking advantage of the political disturbances, Kāmadēva of the Kadamba family of Hāngal forced Vijayāditya to accept his suzerainty.[208] The power of the Kadambas of Goa was weakened by the end of Vijayāditya's reign in 1188 A.D. Inscriptions associate both Permāḍidēva and Vijayāditya with authority over large territories like Kavadidvīpa, Konkaṇa-900, Palasige-12000 and the like.

An inscription from Halasi dated 1172 A.D.[209] refers to a grant of land in the village Bhalika situated in the Kāḷagiri Kaṁpaṇa to the temple of Nṛsiṁha at Halasi. Another grant made by him is mentioned in the Sadāśivagaḍ plates mentioned above.[210] It refers to the grant made by him to a virtuous brāhmaṇa named Gōvinda and for the goddess

Āryā Bhagavati. Gōvinda was well-versed in the science of Astronomy. His genealogy is given in the record.

The Doḍwād inscription dated 1209 A.D.[211] describe him as an expert in several fine arts and science of war-fare. His mastery over vocal as well as instrumental music like *vīna, hadduka* and *jalataranga* are extolled. He had mastery over various weapons such as spear, sword, bow, lance etc. The Kire-Halasigi plates also describe him as interested in *gīta, vādya, kavitva* etc.[212]

Though he was the devotee of Vishṇu he also worshipped Śiva in the form of Gōkarṇēśvara.

Ineresting ly an inscription from Kāmadhēnu dated 1171 A.D.[213] of Permāḍidēva refers to one Kumāra Mallayya as a trusted servant *(gandhavāraṇa)* of Vijayārka, the younger brother of Permāḍi. The record says that this Mallayya struggled for the welfare of the kingdom of Vijayāditya. The record describes the heroic qualities of this chief. He was in no way inferior in the battle field. He was generous to the needy (*hēma-hasta).*

Vijayāditya II had two wives viz., Lakshmīdēvi and Haṁpādēvi. The Kire-Halasige[214] record describes Lakshmīdēvi as the crowned queen of Vijayāditya., It further describes her as virtuous, and learned. An inscription from Muttage dated 1192 A.D.[215] refers to her and also to a treasury officer (*Śri-karaṇa*) named Sankayya, with his twin brother Nārāyaṇadēva, who made grants to the god Brahmayadēva of Muttage. Her son was Jayakēśi III who succeeded his uncle Permāḍidēva in the year 1187-88 A.D.

Haṁpādēvi was also the queen of Vijayāditya. The Kulavaḷḷi record dated 1162 A.D.[216] describes her as *Piriyarasi* of *Yuvarājakumāra* Vijayādityadēva. The record mentions that she was ruling from her capital Saṁpagāḍi.

The record further says that she made grants for the worship and renovation of the temple Kūlakabbe in the village Kulavaḷḷi over which she was ruling (*tann-āḷikeya*) at the request of *Aravattokkalu* of the place in the presence of 64 families. This shows that she commanded a high position like Maiḷaladēvi and Kamalādēvi of the family.

JAYAKĒŚI III (c.1187 – 1225 A.D.)

Jayakēśi III, the son of Vijayāditya and Lakshmīdēvi succeeded to the throne in the year 1187-88 A.D., as learnt from his records and also on the basis of the regnal years mentioned in many inscriptions of his period.

There are nearly thirteen inscriptions of this king found so far. The earliest inscription of Jayakēśi III is from Muttage, dated 1192 A.D[217] which mentions his fifth regnal year. The latest record, which is also from Muttage[218] is dated 1223 A.D. and his son's reign commences from 1226-27 A.D. Hence it can be said that he had a reign of 39 years. Dr.Moraes, however, on the basis of the material available to him had concluded that he ruled for about twenty-five years.[219]

The political situation in the region was fast changing, when Jayakēśi III assumed power. The Kalachuris were loosing ground and the Chālukya king Sōmēśvara IV was staging a come back. Jayakēśi III accepted his over-lordship, though perhaps, nominally. An inscription from Dharwad[220] dated 1207 A.D. states that he was a *mahāmaṇḍalēśvara* under Trībhuvanamalla, who has to be identified with Sōmēśvara IV on the basis of the date.

Another important development was the rise of Sēuṇa Bhillama V and Hoysaḷa Ballāḷa II, who were vying with each other for supremacy over the Chālukya empire. Both of them challenged Sōmēśvara IV. Sōmēśvara on his part tried his best to save his empire, but in vain. The Kadambas, on their part did support the Chālukya king. But, finally Sōmēśvara IV had to seek shelter under the Kadambas themselves. This is indicated by an inscription of 1211 A.D. from Kaḍalewāda,[221] which states that Sōmēśvara IV was ruling from Gōve. Jayakēśi III is stated to be the subordinate of Sōmēśvara IV. Bhillama occupied the northern portion of the erst while Chalukya empire and Ballāḷa took possession of the southern portion.

With the rise of Sēuṇa Singhaṇa II, the grand son of Bhillama V, Jayakēśi seems to have come into trouble. Singhaṇa was a powerful king and soon he expanded his kingdom upto the river Tungabhadrā, subduing all the earstwhile subordinates of the Chālukyas.

An inscription from Mangani,[222] dated 1206 A.D. refers to Singhaṇa's conquests, when it is stated that he attacked Kadamba Jayakēśi of Goa. The inscription from Aṁbe[223] also mentions Kēśi, who is said to have been vanquished by Singhaṇa II. This Kēśi was obviously Jayakēśi III. Towards the end of his career, Jayakēśi III associated with his son Vajradēva, in administration, as *yuvarāja.* The Dharwad[224] inscription records this fact. It is said that this Vajradēva came into conflict with the enemies and died in the battle even when Jayakēśi was ruling. Consequently, the second son of Jayakēśi III viz., Tribhuvanamalla succeeded to the throne.

Mahādēvi[225] was the crowned queen of Jayakēśi III. The parntage or any other details about her are not known.

VAJRADĒVA (c1215-1225-26 A.D)

Vajradēva was the son of Jayakēśi III.[226] The inscriptions call Vajradēva as Vīra-vajradēva,[227] *Śrī Kadamba bhujabala*

Vajradēva,[228] and *Śri Kadamba Śivachitta Vīra Vajradēva*.[229] An inscription from Dharwad dated 1215 A.D.[230] of Chālukya Sōmēśvara IV gives the genealogical account of the family from Permāḍi to Vajradēva. According to the inscription – Jayakēśi III was the son of Vijayadēva , who was the brother of Permāḍi. Jayakēśi III's son was Vajradēva. The record describes Vajradeva thus-

Purūhutang-entu vajrāyudhav-atuḷa-balaṁ Rāmang-entu bāṇam |
Gīrijadhīsaṁge tējan pirid-enisida kanu Pāṇḍurājaṁge Pārtham |
Kiranaṁ Sūryaṁge puṭṭirddam avara teradi puṇyātmakam

The inscription also eulogises Vajradēva by saying that he was to king Jayakēśi like Vajrāyudha to Puruhūta i.e., Indra, arrow to Rāma, Tējas of Girijādhīśa, Arjuna of Pāṇḍurāja and Kiraṇa (rays) to Sūrya. Vajradēva has four records to his credit. They are dated in his second,[231] third,[232] Fourth[233] and Ninth[234] regnal years coresponding to 1215 A.D., 1216 A.D., 1218 A.D., and 1221 A.D., respectively. The ninth year of Vajradēva was the 16th year of his father Jayakēśi III which indicates that he was ruling jointly with his father from 1214-15 A.D.[235] There is an inscription from Muttagi dated 1222 A.D.[236] which was issued in the independent rule of Jayakēśi III in his 42nd regnal year. The earliest record of Tribhuvanamalla, the successor of Jayakēśi III, is dated in 1225-26 A.D.[237] From this it can be surmised that Vajradēva might have met his death by this time which made Tribhuvanamalla, another son of Jayakēśi III, to succeed him in 1225-26 A.D.

One or two inscriptions pertaining to the period of Vajradēva are worthy of mention here. His record dated 1216 A.D.[238] while referring to the grants made to the god Siddhēśvara, refers to a person named Bhairava, who died when a cart hit him, which made his father to construct a temple named Bhairavēśvara and make a grant of land to Chandrabhūshaṇadēva, the *āchārya* of the temple, after purchasing the land for ten *Lokki-gadyāṇas* from Īśvarabhaṭṭa of Hūli.

Another point to be noted here is the festival called *Pavitra-parva* celebrated in that place. It is interesting to note that people from different places like Kandamgallu, Nandagāve, Sonnaligeyapura (Sholapur), Vijayapura (Bijapura), Aihoḷe and Khēḍa visited the place on this occasion and participated in this festival.[239]

Another inscription refers to the death of one Vijaya Sāhaṇi, son of Rāya Sāhani who was a *ḍingariga* or a loyal attendant of Vajradēva in a fierce battle.[240] The reason for the battle is not known. The political conditions of the period might have been a cause for the early death of Vajradēva and succession of his brother Tribhuvanamalla.

TRIBHUVANAMALLA (c.1226-27 - 1246-47 A.D)

Jayakēśi III was succeeded by his second son Tribhuvanamalla in the year 1226-27 A.D. as learnt from the regnal years mentioned in his records. For example a hero-stone inscription from Bailandūr is dated in his eigth regnal year corresponding to 1223 A.D.[241] The Amminabhāvi inscription is dated in his 18th regnal year,[242] corresponding to 1243 A.D. These dates indicate that he commenced his rule in 1226-27 A.D. He is mentioned as *Śrī-Kadamba Śrī-Śivachitta-vīra-Tribhuvanamalla* in the records.

As noted earlier, Sēuṇa Singhaṇa II was the ruler in this period and he subdued all the subordinate chiefs of the erstwhile Chālukya rulers. Inscriptions of Singhaṇa show that his general Bīchaṇa[243] also called Bīchiseṭṭi thoroughly defeated the Kadambas who were obviously the Kadambas of Goa. Another chief of Singhaṇa, named Lakshmīdēva is also credited with the victory over the Kadambas.[244] Another chief named Ārya Mallisețți, is actually described as the governor of Konkaṇa.[245] His son Honnabommasețți is also said to have borne the title *Konkaṇa-chakravarti.*[246] All these indicate that Singhaṇa, through his generals overpowered all the subordinate chiefs of the Chālukyas and appointed his own officers to govern the respective regions. Kadamba Tribhuvanamalla's inscriptions do claim that he was ruling in as late as 1246-47 A.D. It must have been only nominal under the authority of the chiefs of the Sēuṇa king. A few hero-stones of Tribhuvanamalla found at Amminabhāvi, Bailandur and other places indicate that he opposed the enemies, who probably were the Sēuṇa generals. But his efforts to remain independent became futile. For instance, the Amminabhāvi inscription[247] describes a hero in glowing terms and says that he fought with some king under the orders of Tribhuvanamalla. Unfortunately, both the name of the enemy king and the name of this hero have been lost. But his efforts to remain independent became futile.

Goa inscription of Tribhuvanamalla's son Shashṭha III states that the queen of Tribhuvanamalla was Māṇikadēvi, to whom was born Shashṭha[248] i.e., Shashṭha III. Tribhuvanamalla had also a daughter, who was married to one Kāmadēva, the son of Lakshmīdēva. The identity of this Kāmadēva cannot be established.

SHASHṬHADĒVA III (c.1247-1267 A.D.)

Shashṭhadēva was also known as Shashṭha. His Goa plates call him Śivachitta Vīra-Shashṭhabhūpati.[249] Politically, his reign was not of much significance. The Kadamba territory by now was practically taken over by the Sēuṇa rulers, whose generals were administering the region. However, some of the inscriptions do claim that the Kadambas ruled in their traditional territory viz., Goa and Konkaṇa. As noted above his sister had married Kāmadēva who was also called Kāvadēva. He appears to have stood by Shashṭha in times of difficulty. The inscription calls him as the establisher of Shashṭha.[250]

An inscription from Kotabāgi,[251] Dharwad taluk and district, associates him with the Sēuṇa king Mahādēva. This means that he had accepted the sovereignty of the Sēuṇas. Inscriptions glorify him as a liberal and brave ruler. However, all such descriptions appear to be only conventional. Two hero-stones from Yalivaḷ[252] in Kundagoḷ taluk describe him as Chaṭṭayyadēva of Halasige-nāḍu and associate him with the Gutta chief Jōyidēva, who was a subordinate of the Sēuṇas. The hero-stone says that Jōyideva led a cattle raid at the instance of Chaṭṭayyadēva. The details of the incident are, howoever, not known, though it is stated that a hero (name lost) opposed Jōyidēva. Interestingly Shashṭha's Budarasisngi[253] inscription states that he made a grant to the temple of Kapilasidda Mallikārjuna at Sonnalige i.e., modern Sholapur. This place indeed was situated far away from the traditional territory of Shashṭha. It can only be surmised that Shashṭha visited the place on a piligrimage. It is worth noting that he made a grant of a village called Uchchangi which was situated in the Sabbi Kaṁpaṇa of Halasige-nāḍu which was governed by him (*tann-āḷva Halasige-nāḍu*).

That Shashṭha was an ardent devotee of the god Mallikarjuna of Sonnalige or Sholapur is confirmed by yet another inscription from Koṭabāgi.[254] This inscription contains the famous *vachaṇa* of Siddharāma. It also records a grant by Shashṭha to this deity. But the details are lost. The damaged portion of the record indicates that the grant village was situated in Halasige-dēśa.

Shashṭha III was the last known member of the Kadamba family. It is clear that his territory viz., Palasige-nāḍu and Goa regions became a part of the Sēuṇa kingdom.

The Goa plates of Shashṭhadēva[255] dated in Kaliyuga 4348 is worthy of mention here. It commences with the praise of lord Śiva under the name of Saptakōṭīśvara and Tryaksha, and mentions the genealogy of the family from Jayanta upto Shashṭha, son of Tribhuvanamalla and Māṇikadēvi. Shashṭha, mentioned here is Shashṭha III and not Shashṭha II as mentioned by Fleet.[256] The record is also interesting as it refers to a king named Kāma or Kāmadēva or Kāvanātha son of Lakshmīdēva and Lakshmī, and whose wife was the sister of the king Shashṭha and who is described as the establisher of Shashṭha. The record says -

> *Kāmadēva-nṛipah śrēshṭhō garishṭho-=guṇa-gumpitah |*
> *vārishṭha-Shashṭha-bhūpāla-pratishṭh-ādhishṭhō bhavat |*

This indicates the trouble Shashṭha had to face at the hands of the enemy king, obviously Sēuṇa Singhaṇa (1209-1247 A.D.) when Kāmadēva helped him in regaining his lost position and to come to the throne by 1247 A.D. The purpose of the record is to refer to the grant of a rice field to his *Guru, Rājaguru* and *Dikshita Jyēshṭha* Vishṇuśarman of the *Gārgya-gōtra.*

Interestingly, a hero-stone dated Śaka 1189, Prabhava, Paushya śu.5, which corresponds to 1267 A.D., December 5,[257] refers to a battle between *Mahāmandalēśvara* Gōveya Chaṭṭayyadēva and the Sāntara chief Sōyidēvarasa and Bommarasa.

According to the inscription Gōveya Chaṭṭayyadēva marched with his army and camped at Gutti (*chaturaṁgabala-sahita naḍadu baṁdu Guttoyolu biṭṭiralu*) and Sōyidēvarasa and Bommarasa were camping at Heddese. Sōyidēvarasa, the inscription says, ordered his *mahāpradhāna* Mākarasa to oppose the enemy. Mākarasa who fought against the enemy died in the battle.

Gutti i.e., Chandragutti in Shimoga district was a well known fort under the control of the rulers of Hanagal Kadamba family who were subdued by the Sēuṇas. Gutti was situated on the borders of the Hoysaḷa territory.

Gōveya Chaṭṭayyadēva mentioned in the record is identified with Shashṭhadēva III of Goa Kadamba family. Being the feudatory of the Sēuṇas he participated in the war against the Sāntara chiefs on behalf of the Sēuṇas. It is known from other records that there was rivalry between the Sēuṇas and the Hoysaḷas. The Sēuṇas intended to subdue the Sāntara chiefs whose territory was on the way to the Hoysaḷa kingdom.

A point worthy of mention here is the date of Chaṭṭayyadēva. 1264 A.D. was considered as the latest known date of this ruler when he was a feudatory of Sēuṇa Mahādēva.[258] But interestingly this hero-stone indicates that Chaṭṭayyadēva was in power till 1267 A.D. when he fought against the Sāntara chiefs.

It is interesting to note that the Kadamba family was first established by Mayūraśarma as early as fourth century A.D. at Banavāsi as the capital. The kingdom flourished as the first sovereign kingdom to be established on the Kannada soil. It received a severe set back when the Chālukyas of Bādāmi rose to power. It appears that his family split itself into several branches and the rulers of these branches were governing different regions. The Chālukya inscriptions claim, therefore, that the Chālukya king had to conquer different families of the Kadambas (*Kadamba-Kādambakaṁ*). Though beaten, the family was not wiped off. Though they were technically displaced from the original capital Banavāsi, they continued to bear the title *Banavāsi-puravarādhīśvara*. They were dormant during the days of the Rāshṭrakūtas. But, gradually, they raised their head during the time of the next rulers viz ., the Chālukyas of Kalyāṇa. Among the different branches of the family, to became more prominent, one was the Kadambas of Hāngal and another the Kadambas of Goa. Those of Hāngal had their capital at Hāngal, now, a small taluka place in Hāveri district of Karnataka state. They ruled over the Banavāsi region in which the Hāngal territory was situated. The other family as we know, ruled over the coastal region and are called *Konkaṇa Chakravarti* and ruled over the vast region of Halasige, adjacent to the coast. Both the families accepted the suzerainty of the Chālukyas of Kalyāṇa and both enthusiastically supported their over lords. This enhanced their prestige and they occupied a permanent position and enjoyed a prestigious status in the Chālukyan court. We have seen above that the Chālukyan masters honoured their trusted chiefs and even sought matrimonial alliance with them.

Being the absolute masters of their territory, they contributed most to the well being of the people of the territory by their good governance and brought peace and plenty to the region. By issuing large number of inscriptions, they contributed to the development of the Kannada language and literature. Their inscriptions, which are written in beautiful Kannada hand have also helped the development of Kannada script. They sponsored all the native religions like Buddhism and Jainism along with Śaivism and Vaishṇavism. They built several temples, which contributed simiultaneously to the growth of religion and the growth of architecture and sculpture. They built tanks, which promoted agriculture and the basic facilities of the people. Thus, they contributed to the cultural growth of the region, they governed, in a substantial way.

REFERENCES AND NOTES

1. GG., p. 94.
2. *KK.*, App.III, No.1.
3. *IIBS.*, Vol. I, pp.64 ff.
4. *KK.*, App. III, No.1.
5. B.R.Gopal, *Minor Dynasties of South India,* p. 49.
6. *GG.*, p. 94.
7. *KK.*, App. III, No.I.
8. *Maharāshtra State Gazetteer* - History (Part-I), p.263
9. *KK.*, App. III, No.1.
10. *Ibid.*
11. *JBBRAS.*, IX, p.266.
12. *JKU.*, XI, (1975), pp.146 ff.
13. *KK.*, App. III., No.1.
14. *JBBRAS.*, IX, p.287.
15. *IIBS.*, Vol. I, p.68.
16. *JBBRAS.*, IX, p.287.
17. *KK.*, p. 168.
18. *GG.*, p. 95.
19. *KK.*, p.168.
20. Gopal B.R. *Op.Cit.*, pp. 48 ff.
21. *KK.*, App., III, No.1.
22. *JBBRAS.*, IX, p. 286.
23. *SII.*, IX, (I), No.78.

24. *IIBS.,* Vol.I, p.68.
25. *Ibid.,* - - *nānā-Tarkka-niśānta-nirmala-matiḥ prauḍhaḥ kavīnāṁkaviḥ* |
26. *KK.,* App. III, No.1.
27. *EI.,* XIII, p.302.
28. *Ibid.*
29. Gopal B.R. *Op.Cit.,* p.51.
30. Unpublished.
31. From personal collection.
32. *SIM.,* p.110.
33. From personal collection.
34. *GG.,* pp.98 ff.
35. *EI.,* XXXVIII, p.286.
36. *IIBS.,* Vol. I, p.65.
37. *KK.,* App. III, No. 2.
38. *IIBS.,* Vol. I, pp. 65 ff.
39. *EI.,* XIII, p. 302.
40. B.R.Gopal, *Op.Cit.,* p. 141.
41. *JBBRAS.,* IX, p. 287.
42. *KK.,* p. 175.
43. Gopal B.R. *Op.Cit.,* p.52.
44. *GG.,* p. 96.
45. *EI.,* XIII, p. 302.
46. *KK.,* p.176.
47. *EI.,* XIII, p.302.
48. *Ibid.,* - *Śrī Mummuri-nṛipaṁ Śrī Chaṭṭa-bhūpaṁge neṭṭane-koṭṭam dhare mechche Chāga-jaga-jhampaṁ jhaṁpaḷāchāryyan*
49. *IIBS.,* p.65 ff.
50. *KK.,* App. III, No.2.
51. *IIBS.,* Vol. I, pp. 64 ff.
52. *Ibid.*
53. *KK.,* App. III, No.1.
54. *Ibid.*

55. *SIM.*, p.110.
56. *Ibid.*
57. *GG.*, p.98.
58. *EI.*, XXXVII, p.286.
59. *GG.*, p. 99.
60. *Ibid.*, p. 98.
61. *EI.*, XXXVII, p.286.
62. *GG.*, p. 99.
63. Unpublished.
64. *EI.*, XIII, p.303, - *Permāḍīdēvam baralk-idir-vvand-āgaḍe kūrppa tanna-magaḷaṁ Dhar-ānvitaṁ koṭṭu perchchid-alaṁpaṁ*
65. *IA.*, IV, pp.233 ff.
66. *KK.*, App. III, No.2.
67. *EI.*, XIII, p.303.
68. Gopal B.R. *Op. Cit.*, p.54.
69. *JBBRAS.*, IX, p.283.
70. Gopal B.R. *Op. Cit.*, p.54.
71. *EI.*, XXVI, p.306.
72. *Ibid.*, XIII, p. 303, - *tōḷ-valavumum padāti-balamuṁ pirid-unṭ-eneg-eṁdu garvvadiṁ-āḷvara-chakra*
73. *KK.*, App.III, No.2.
74. *GG.*, p.102.
75. *KK.*, p.186.
76. *GG.*, p.100.
77. *KK.*, p.186
78. *Ibid.*, p.187.
79. *EI.*, XIII, p.303; - *ā vasudhā-priyaṁge-Jasyakēśige kēsari puṭuvandadiṁ Gūvaladēvan- ūrjjita parākramaṁ puṭṭi*
80. *SII.*, XV, No.225.
81. *EI.*, XXX, pp.71 ff.
82. *SII.*, XI(II),No.177.(1025A.D.).*Śrīmat-Tribhuvanamallaṁ Gūvaladēvaru*
83. *EI.*, XXX, p. 74 (n).

84. *GG.,* p.103.
85. *Karnataka Bharati*, p.83.
86. *SII.*, XI, (II), No.177.
87. *Ibid.,* XV, No.225.
88. *Ibid.,* XI, (II), No.155.
89. *Ibid.,* XX, No.87.
90. From personal collection.
91. *SII.*, XI (II), No.160.
92. From personal collection.
93. *Ibid.*
94. *Ibid.*
95. *KK.*, App. III, No.1.
96. Unpublished.
97. *IA.*, IV, p..96 ff.
98. *SII.* XV, No.225.
99. From personal collection.
100. *Ibid.*
101. Ritti S.H. *"An Inscription from Kadarolli"*, JKU., (Soc. Sc.), IV, pp.178 ff.
102. *JBBRAS.,* IX, p. 278.
103. *KI.,* V, No..33.
104. *SII.,* XI (II), No.154.
105. *Ibid.,* No.177.
106. *EI.*, XIII, p.304
107. *SII.*, XI (II), No.154.
108. *JBBRAS.*, IX, p.273; KK., p.189.
109. *KK.,* p. 189.
110. *Ibid.,* p. 188.
111. *JKU.*, XI, (!975), pp. 146 ff.
112. *KK.,* p.188.
113. *Ibid.*
114. *SII.,* XI, (II), No.154.
115. *JBBRAS.*, IX, p.273.
116. *EI.*, XIII, p. 298 ff.

117. Gopal B.R. *Op.Cit.,* p.58.
118. *KK.,* p.191.
119. *GG.,* p.104.
120. *EI.,* XII, p.320.
121. *GG.,* p.104-105.
122. *Maharashtra State Gazetteer* – History (Part-I), p.270.
123. *GG.,* p.105.
124. From personal collection.
125. *EI.,* XIII, p.307.
126. *Ibid.*
127. From personal collection.
128. *Ibid.*
129. *EI.,* XIII, p.320.
130. *SII.,* XV, No.14.
131. *Ibid.,* No.16.
132. *JBBRAS.,* IX, pp. 304 ff.
133. *EI.,* XIII, p.304.
134. From personal collection.
135. *SII.,* XI (II), No.154.
136. *EI.,* XIII, p.304.
137. *Ibid.,* XXVI, pp.205 ff.
138. *SII.,* XV, No. 16.
139. From personal collection.
140. *Ibid.*
141. *Ibid.*
142. *Ibid.*
143. *EI.,* XIII, p.321.
144. From personal collection.
145. *Ibid.*
146. *KI.,* V, No.33 (1176 AD.)
147. From personal collection.
148. *EI.,* XIII, p.304.
149. From personal collection.
150. *EI.,* XIII, p. 305.

151. *Ibid.*, p. 320.
152. *Ibid.*, p. 306.
153. *SII.*, XV, No.14.
154. *KI.*, V, No.33.
155. From personal collection.
156. *Ibid.*
157. *EI.*, XIII, p.320.
158. *Ibid.*
159. From personal collection.
160. *Ibid.*
161. *Ibid.*
162. *SII.*, XX, No.252.
163. From personal collection.
164. *Ibid.*
165. *EI.*, XIII, pp. 316 ff.
166. *SII.*, XV, No.8.
167. *KI.*, V, No. 63, (1172 A.D.).
168. *JBBRAS.*, IX, p. 290.
169. *SII.*, XX, No. 252.
170. From personal collection; -
Rāma-Lakshmaṇa-teradiṁ Bhīm-ārjun-āndadind-esedarp-piriduo prēmadoḷe rājyalakshmi dhāmarp-Permāḍidēva vijayādityar
171. From personal collection.
172. *Ibid.*
173. *KI.*, V, No.64.
174. From personal collection.
175. *KI.*, V, No. 63 (1169 A.D.).
176. *JBBRAS.*, IX, p. 275.
177. *SII.*, XV, No.16.
178. From personal collection.
179. *JBBRAS.*, IX, p. 293.
180. *SII.*, XV, No. 229.
181. From personal collection.

182. *Ibid.*
183. *KI.*, V, No.64 (1173 A.D.)
184. *JBBRAS.*, IX, p. 293
185. *KI.*, V, No.30 (1192 A.D.)
186. *GG.*, p. 109.
187. From personal collection.
188. Gopal B.R. *Op. Cit.*, p. 59.
189. *GG.*, p. 109.
190. *JBBRAS.*, IX, p.294.
191. *Ibid.*
192. *Ibid.* p. 291.
193. *Ibid.*, p. 294.
194. *Ibid.*, p. 290.
195. *Ibid.*, p. 294.
196. *Ibid.*
197. *Ibid.*
198. *EI.*, XXIX, pp. 29 ff.
199. *Ibid.*
200. *JBBRAS.*, IX, p. 245.
201. *SII.*, XV,No. 16
202. From personal collection.
203. Unpublished.
204. *EI.*, XXIX, pp. 29 ff.
205. Gopal B.R. *Op.Cit*, p. 60.
206. *SII.*, XX, No.127; also see Gopal B,R .*Op.Cit.*, p. 81, Foot Note No. 144.
207. *Ibid.*
208. *Ibid.*
209. *KI.*, V, No. 63.
210. *EI.*, XXIX, pp. 29 ff.
211. JBBRAS., IX, p.242 .
212. *Ibid.*
213. *SII.*, XX, No. 252; *ā devargge keyyam biṭṭa kumāra Mallayya[na] pratāpa-ventendaḍe*

Turagaman-ēre khaḷgalate key-gaḷa vaṭṭire kumāra-Mallayyam-
Munidaḍe-māri mīṟidaḍe-mrittu kadimagidaḍ-ārdda Bhairavam
keḷarddaḍe siṁha-urrvidaḍehervvuli hāydaḍe kāla-rakkasam
maraḷdaḍe-moṟeya talare kurttuvan-ā-raṇarangadalli bhīkara-
madavāraṇa jitaraṇa Vijayārkkanagandhavāraṇ ||
Vijayādityana rājy-ābhyudayakkaṁ tandondu sāhasakkam tām
paḍedamnijagalitanamam dhareyoḷu raṇaranga-bhairavam Mallayaṁ ||

214. *JBBRAS.*, IX, p. 242.
215. From personal collection.
216. Unpublished - *piri-arasi Hampādēviyaru saṁpagāḍiya-nelevīdinoḷ-irdda samayadoḷ*
217. From personal collection.
218. *Ibid.*
219. *KK.*, p. 214.
220. *KI.*, V, No.31.
221. *SII.*, XX, No.217; Gopal B.R. *Op.Cit.*, p. 81.
222. *ARIE.*, 1927-28,B.K. No. 264; *SII.*, XV, No.155.
223. Gopal B.R. *Op.Cit.*, p. 62.
224. *KI.*, V, No. 70.
225. *IA*, XIV, p. 288.
226. *KI.*, V, No. 32 - *teṟadi puṇyātmakaṁ Puṭṭidamt-ā-naranātham Vajradēvaṁ Jitaripu Jayakēśi, kshitiśaṁge vīraṁ* ||
227. *Ibid.*, No. 69.
228. *SII.*, No. XV, No. 233.
229. *KI.*, V, No. 70.
230. *Ibid.*, No. 32.
231. *Ibid.*, No. 67.

232. *Ibid.*
233. *Ibid.*, No. 69.
234. *Ibid.*, No. 70.
235. *Ibid.*
236. From personal collection.
237. *KI.*, V, No. 67.
238. *SII.*, XV, No. 233.
239. *Ibid.*
240. Unpublished.
241. From personal collection.
242. *SII.*, XV, No. 231.
243. Ritti S.H., "*The Seuṇas*", p.133.
244. *Ibid.*, p. 134.
245. *Ibid.*, P.136.
246. *Ibid.*
247. *SII.*, XV, No. 231.
248. *IA.*, XIV, pp. 288 ff.
249. *Ibid.*
250. *Ibid.*
251. *SII.*, XV, No. 195.
252. *Ibid.*, XX, No. 328.
253. *EI.*, XXXVI, pp. 164 ff.
254. *SII.*, XV, N o. 195.
255. *IA.*, XIV, p. 288 ff.
256. *Ibid.*
257. Ritti S.H., *"Inscriptions from SaravatiValley"*, *JKU.*, (Soc. Sc.), Vol.III, pp.3 ff.
258. *ARSIE.*, No.447 of 1926.

CHAPTER - VI

ADMINISTRATION

The Kadambas of Goa, the feudatories of the Chālukyas of Kalyāṇa, were known for their good administration. Though they called themselves *Mahāmaṇḍalēśvaras* the titles like *Konkaṇa Chakravarti,*[1] *Paśchimāmbōdhinātha,*[2] *Konkaṇādhipati*[3] they assumed, indicate that they were complete masters of their own region. They enjoyed full freedom and ruled like independent monarchs, by following their overlords in the matters of political, social, religious, economic and cultural fields. The inscriptions speak of their attention towards almost all aspects of the human activities in the kingdom. The king was the head of the state. For easy and convenience of administration, the kingdom was divided into major divisions and these divisions were further divided and sub-divided into smaller units, the lowest unit of administration being the village. Officers and chiefs were appointed to look after the administration of these divisions which helped the rulers in safeguarding the interest and the safety of the whole territory.

THE KING

The king was the head of the state and the kingship was hereditary in character. Normally the succession went to the eldest son, as designated *yuvarāja* who was put in charge of administration. He assisted the king in all matters of administration. Sometimes, he was kept in charge of major administrative units before he assumed complete charge of the kingdom. Such princes jointly ruled with the king. A good example can be seen in the Savai-vare plaltes of Gūvaladēva II re-edited by Dr.M.G.Dikashit.[4] The editor of the record says that Gūvaladēva was a minor son of Shashṭha, who was entrusted with the administration of the kingdom, while he was on a pilgrimage to Sōmanātha in Kathiawad. An inscription from Mādanabhāvi mentions that Jayakēśi II was assisted by his son Permāḍi [5] who in turn was assisted by his younger brother Vijayāditya. The record from Kalkuṇḍi[6] says –

> *Rāma-Lakshmanara teradiṁ Bhīm-Ārjunar-andadim piriya prēmadoḷe rājya-lakshmīdhāma Permmāḍidēva Vijayādityru ||*
> *Ant-avara adhirāja – yuvarāja padaviyoḷ arasu-geyye*

i.e., Permāḍi and Kadamba Vijayāditya were governing together like Rāma and Lakshmaṇa or Bhīma and Arjuna of epic fame.

QUEEN

Some of the queens of the family played an important role in the administration. For example an inscription from Nūlvi says that Boppādēvi, the queen of Jayakēśi I was ruling along with the king, the administrative divisions such as Halasige-12000, Konkaṇa-900, Kundūru-500, and Sabbi-30.[7] Maiḷaladēvi, the senior queen of Jayakēśi-II was ruling from Bhōgāpura and Kundūru. An inscription from Siddāpur in Dharwad District, refers to her as ruling from Bhōgūru.[8] An inscription from Narēndra,[9] gives a list of divisions over which she was ruling from Kundūru. She commanded respect from her sons and others. For instance, when Kamalādēvi, the queen of Permāḍi desired to convert Dēgāve into an *agrahāra* and when she sought the permission of her husband, he gave the permission, after consultation with his mother Maiḷaladēvi.[10] Even her younger son Vijayāditya appears to have made grants to god Nṛsiṁha at Halsi along with his mother and the *purōhitas.*[11] Another queen who took part in administration was Hampādēvi, the queen of Vijayāditya II who was ruling from Sampagāḍi.[12]

MINISTERS AND OTHER OFFICERS

The king, as the head of the state, was assisted by his ministers. For instance Gūvaladēva-II had a group of ministers.[13] They were –

Adhyaksha	-	(president)
Pratihastaka	-	(Vice-president)
Mukhya svīkaraṇa	-	(finance minister)
Pradhānas	-	(ministers)
Mohalla	-	antaḥpurādhyaksha
Sandhi-vigrahika	-	(minister for foreign affairs)
Purōdhā	-	(royal priest)

Generally, the post of ministers was hereditary, obviously depending on the ability of the persons concerned. For instance there is a reference to one Kāḷapa, his son Nāgaṇa and grand son Kēlima who were working under Shashṭhadēva-II, Jayakēśi-I and Gūvaladēva-III, as ministers.[14] The Marcella plates refer to a family of *Purōdhā*. It is interesting to note that the post was passed on to his younger brother Nārāyaṇa by Gōvinda, on account of his old age, after obtaining the consent of Gūvaladēva. *Purōdhā* meant *Purōhita*, who was the chief advisor of the kingdom in conduct of administration, as well as religious practices. He also played the role of *Rājaguru* or a royal preceptor who guided the king in all affairs of the kingdom. An inscription from Dodwad dated 1209 A.D.[15] refers to Chandraśēkhaṛa Bhaṭṭōpādhyāya as the *Rājaguru* of Jayakēśi III. The Goa plates of Shashṭha III, mention Jyēshṭha Vishṇusharma as the *Rājaguru* of Shashṭha III.[16]

The minister was designated as the *mahāpradhāna, mahāmātya* or the chief minister. An inscription of Jayakēśi-I dated 1053 A.D.[17] refers to Sadano as the chief minister of Jayakēśi-I. He was highly powerful in carrying out the administration of the kingdom. Jayakēśi-III had Īśvarayya as his *mahāpradhāna* in 1201 A.D.[18]

It is generally seen that *mahāpradhāna* was also the senior military officer and was designated *sēnādhipati* and *danḍanāyaka*. He also held several other important offices like *sandhivigrahi, maneverggaḍe,* and *haḍapavaḷa.* An inscription from Tambur[19] refers to an officer, named Jayakēśi who has been mentioned as *Mahāpradhāna* and *Sandhivigrahi.* Lakshmarasa[20] and his grandson Singarasa[21] were holding the offices of *mahāpradhāna, antaḥpurādhyaksha, maneveṛggaḍe* and *pasāyita* of Maiḷaladēvi, the queen of Jayakēśi-II. An officer named Sōmēśvarabhaṭṭa has been mentioned as *mahāsāmantādhipati, pradhāna, hēri-sandhivigrahi, maneveṛggaḍe* and *daṇḍanāyaka*, in an inscription from Kadrolli dated 1075 A.D.[22] The same inscription mentions Kēśavāditya as *mahāsāmantādhipati* and *daṇḍanāyaka.* There were officers like *daṇḍanāyaka* who also shared the office of *Perggaḍe*. One such officer was Gangādharabhaṭṭayya mentioned in an inscription from Avarādi.[23] Another inscription[24] from Goḷihaḷḷi refers to an officer named Chāvaṇa-daṇḍanātha who has been described as *mahāpradhāna, sēnādhipati, haḍapavaḷa, maneverggaḍe* and *Gupta-Bhaṇḍāri*, obviously, was the chief treasury officer of the kingdom. There is a reference to the term *daṇḍanāyaki*[25] in an inscription from Narēndra. Perhaps this was the honorific description of the wives of the officers concerned rather than instances of women holding these positions in their own right.

The inscriptions speak of certain qualities and qualfications of the ministers. While describing the *daṇḍanāyaka* Sōma, the Narēndra inscription[26] says that they should have certain qualities like politeness, prowess, strength, courtesy, skill, resolution of counsel, noble conduct, majesty, literary art, famed ancestry, strength of arm, loyalty to the lord and safeguarding the interest of masters in every respect (*nijēśa hitadoḷ*). The Goḷihaḷḷi record speaks of the qualities of ministers as *sēvā-priya* (taking delight in rendering service), *vivēkadoḷ* i.e., sensible, and possessing three powers viz., *prabhu, mantra* and *utsāha* i.e., controlling, councselling and possessing zeal in work.[27] *Kulakramagataru* (born of noble families) *Nyāyadoḷ* (experts in state policy), trust worthy, brave and daring *(ārpinoḷ), chāturya, (*shrewed), *mantra-nischaya* (firm in taking decisions).

There were other officers to manage the affairs of the other sub-divisions. They were the *Nārggāvuṇḍas* to manage the *nāḍus.* For instance, an inscription from Mugad[28] refers to the family of *Nārgāvuṇḍa* of Mugunda-

30, who governed for over four generations, who served from Shashṭha-II (1010 A.D.) till Gūvala-III (1125 A.D.). Almost all the inscriptions refer to the *gāvuṇḍa* of the villages. For example, an inscription from Managundi refers to one gāvuṇḍa.[29] If Amminabhāvi[30] inscription refers to the twelve *gāvuṇḍas*, the Mummigaṭṭi record refers to sixteen (*padināruvaru*) *gāvuṇḍas* of Kundūru.[31] There are references to *Nāḍādhikāris, Mahattaras* and also *Ūroḍeya*, *Prabhu*, *Heggaḍe*, and *chakravarti* etc., in inscriptions. There is a reference to *Mahāprabhu* in an inscription from Māvaḷḷi.[32] The Kāmadhēnu inscription[33] refers to an *Ūroḍeya* of Sāsalu. An inscription from Miśrikōṭi[34] refers Dēsirāja of Pulivara as *Chakravarti*. Here obviously *chakravarti* is an honourific title of a lower officer.

ARMY

The Kadambas of Goa had maintained their own army like independent rulers. The inscriptioins state that they had maintained *Chaturangabala* , (viz., the four fold army consisting of infantry, cavalry, elephant force and the chariots). An inscription from Tambūru dated 1120 A.D.[35] of Gūvala-III describes him as *Chaturangabala-sūtradhāri* and *chaturanga-singa*.

Inscriptions refer to some terms *padāti*, and *kālāḷu* (foot soldiers), *Kudure* (horse) and *Turaga-bala* (cavalry) and *Billāḷu* (archers). There are sculptural representations of these different components of the army. A large number of hero stones referring to cattle raids and other fights graphically depict the participation of these components in battles. For example, the inscription from Dēvikioppa,[36] Bailandūr,[37] refer to the death of heroes after putting to death the horses and soldiers of the enemies. It is worth mentioning an inscription from Narēndra[38] which says that Jayakesi-I was proud of his infantry. The record says –

Tōḷ-valavmum-padāti-balamuṁ-pirid-unṭ-enag-endu
garvvadind- āḷvara chakravartti maleval Jayakēśi-nripālan .

There are references, as said earlier, to *Kālāḷu* and *Billāḷu* which indicate that the infantry consisted of both the soldiers and the archers. The sculptured representations on hero-stones of the period show, that the sword, Javalin and shield, were supplied to the cavalry.

The bow and arrow and shield (of different varities) were used by the foot soldiers as depicted on the hero-stones of the period.

The indication of the spirit for adventure and heroism is seen in inscriptions. For example a record from Kandli [39] says -

Jitēna- labhyatē- Lakshmī mritēnapi surānganā |
Kshaṇa- vidvamsini kāyekā chimtā maraṇēraṇē ||

As said earlier Cavalry was another important organ of the army. Some officers were experts in training horses which were un-controllable. For example *senapati* Singarasa was called *dushṭh-āśva-malla.*[40]

Depiction of elephants on hero-stones indicate that the princes or officers used elephants in wars. Elephants were sold at Kiru-Sampagadi [41] during the period under study.

There was a section of people in the society who were ready to sacrifice their lives for the sake of their masters. They were called *śastra-jīvīgaḷ* .[42] *Jōḷavāḷi* is another term appearing in inscriptions.[43] Similarly another term *ḍingariga* appearing in the inscriptions indicate a hero who sacrificed his life for the sake of his master. An inscription from

Dodwād refers to the death of one Lāhaḍa who was a servant (*ḍingariga*) of Jayakēśidēva.[44] Another inscription from the same place refers to the death of Vijayama-sāhaṇi, son of Rāya-sāhaṇi Sōḍapa, who was a servant i.e., *ḍingariga* of Vajradēva.[45]

NAVY

One speciality of the Kadambas of Goa was their maintaining a naval force. With their overlordship over the coastal region, they developed Goa as an important port, through which they conducted naval activities including naval expeditions against forces like Laṁka. There are copious references to their naval battles and there are visual representations of their naval activities in the form of hero-stones depicting pictures of their operating through water. In a poetic way an inscription from Dēgāve [46] states that the ruler conquered Laṁka with great ease, as a contrast with Śri Rāmachandra of the epic fame, who had to struggle hard for conquering Rāvaṇa through building a bridge over the sea. The inscription says that the Kadamba king did not undergo this ordeal since he also built a bridge of barks upto Laṁka, through which his army could reach Laṁka easily and over power it.

The rulers of the Kadamba family were called *paschima-samudrādhipati* i.e., the lord of western ocean. The *bahitra* or ships find their references in inscriptions. An inscription[47] refer to sea voyage undertaken by Gūvaladēva to worship Sōmanātha of Saurāshṭra. The inscription says that on this occasion he had to meet with a naval accident. His son Chaṭṭayya(II), according to an inscription from Narēndra,[48] also went on a pilgrimage to Saurāshṭra. He, the inscription says, selected the ships in proper condition (*neṭṭane-bhaitraṁgaḷa-mēle*), for this purpose. It further states that the ruler conquered Simhaḷa, Parāsika, and Kanaka-dvīpa obviously through naval battles. It also refers to the strength of the navy which was quite large. It also says that he went on an expedition to Lamka by building a bridge of ships. The record says –

Bahitra samtatigaḷ-indam Lamkēvaram sētuvam-kaṭṭi

The copper plate of Jayakesi-I[49] refers to his minister Sadano, who was permitted by the king to levy customs on local and other ships coming to Goa from other places.

The Dēgāve inscription[50] is interesting, as it refers to Vijayaditya(I) who led a naval expedition with a number of boats (*pōta-parampar-ābhih*) to various dvīpas. He is said to have attacked Lamka with *Nau-chakra* with *Kshēpakas,* which indicate that the ships were put for military use. Interestingly, the word kshēpaka probably represented some sort of a missile.

FORTS

Forts were very important and inevitable means of defence in the ancient period. Right from Kautilya all the writers on polity insist upon the construction of forts in stratigic places not easily accessible to the outside enemies. They were normally built, therefore, on rocky hills or high mountains or even amidst water. They normally mention four types of forts such as Giridurga. Jaladurga, Vanadurga and Neladurga. Our literature, also both Sanskrit and Kannada are replete with references to different types of forts, their seize and fights. A contemporary record from Katanur dated 1280 A.D.[51] speaks of four types of forts viz., Jaladurga, Neladurga, Giridurga and Vanadurga. Neladurga, is also refered to as Sthaḷadurga in a number of works. Jaladurga was the one surrounded by deep waters. Neladurga or Sthaḷadurga was built on plain grounds. In such cases the fort was normally surrounded by a deep and wide moat to be filled with water so as to make it inaccessible. Giridurga was the one built on high hills and Vanadurga was situated deep in the forest. The main idea behind this classification is to show that the fort was to be built in such a place which would be difficult to approach for the enemies for one can understand that in ancident days fort was the heart of the kingdom. It was the recluse of the king and his retinue and the state treasury was also housed there. Interestingly, near the village Baichawāḍa in Kalghatgi taluk of Dharwad district there is a dilapidated structure of a fort amidst the forest. Looking into the location, it can be guessed that it was a Vanadurga or a fort in the forest. An inscription from Kāvalavāḍa, Bailhongal taluk actually mentions a fight in the fort (kōṭe-kāḷaga).[52] The expression *Māvaḷḷi-thāṇe*[53] figuring in inscriptions indicates that it was a military centre. There are traces of fort wall at Mavalli area. It is a very lengthy foundation which is disturbed by the state high- way between Hubli-Karwar.

JUSTICE

Some inscriptions interestingly refer to offences and punishments also. For instance, an inscription of Jayakesi-I[54] mentioned above refers to one Sadano, the minister, who collected tax from the local ship owners and the ships coming from outside for maintaining a charity house built by him. Tax collection was made compulsory, and any one who tried to evade tax was peanalised.

An inscription dated 1107 A.D.[55] of Tribhuvanamalla is worth mentioning here. According to it a few Brāhmaṇa families were brought here and were given lands for their maintenance with a condition that they should enjoy the grant jointly and the lands allotted to them should not be alienated or sold to others. If the rule was violated both the parties would be fined and the land would be confiscated.

Another interesting information is supplied in an inscription from Halasi.[56] It refers to a theft of jewellary, worth 500 *nishkas*, belonging to the god Nṛsiṁha of the place by a person named Vaishṇava Padmanābha. When the theft was detected the king Jayakēśi-III appears to have ordered the recovery of land from the culprit. Further, the record states that the land was sold for 500 *nishkas* and the amount was returned to the temple of Nṛsiṁha.

A glimpse of judicial administration can be obtained from an inscription from Kittur[57] which deals with a disputes between two religious heads over a land which each claimed as belonging to his own institution. According to the inscription one Śivaśakti, the priest of the temple of Kallēśvaradēva of Attiyabhavi in Kittur objected to the claims of Kalyāṇaśakti the head of the temple of Mūlasthāna over the land belonging to the temple of Kallēśvaradēva. He complained that the piece of land was deceitfully acquired by the predecessor of Kalyāṇaśakti through Chanḍayyasāvanta. Further it is said that he got an inscription set to that effect.[58] The officer Īśvara daṇḍanāyaka referred the matter to the *Mahājanas* of Degave for settlement. The *Mahājanas* decided the case by following the method of *Phāla-divya*, according to which they were supposed to hold the red hot iron shaft of the plough. In this, it was Śivaśakti who came out successful and a decree (*jayapatra*) was issued in favour of Śivaśakti.

Such instances refer to the strong and just government under the Kadambas of Goa.

REFERENCES AND NOTES

1. *EI., XIII,* pp.303 ff.
2. *Ibid.*, pp. 302 ff.
3. *SII.*, XI (II), No. 154, (Line 76), 1104 A.D.
4. *SIM.*, p.110.
5. *SII.*, XV, No.16, (1138 A.D.) -
   Konkana-chakravartti Jayakēśi-dēvarasaruṁ Paṭṭamahādēvi Maiḷalamahādēviaṛun yuvarāja-Permāḍi-dēvianuṁ Vijayāditya kumāra sahita
6. Un-published - Another inscription from Siddapura also says –
   Śrī Kadamba Śivachitta Vīra Permāḍi dēvarasaru Śrīmad-yuvarājakumāra
   Śrī Vijayāditya dēvarasaru Saṁpagāḍiya-nelevīḍinoḷ-irddu (*SII.XV,* No.229)
7. Un-published.
8. *SII.*, XV, No.16 (1135 A.D.).
9. *EI.*, XIII, p.320 Another inscription from Mishrikoti (Personal collection) says -
   Kundūra nelevīḍinoḷ sukhadi rājyam – geyutt-ire
10. *JBBRAS.*, IX, p.390.
11. *KI., V,* No.63.
12. Personal collection -
    Hampādēviyaru Sampagāḍiya nelevīḍinoḷ-irddu
13. *KK.*, App.III, No.1.
14. *EI,* XXX, pp.75 ff.
15. *KK.*, App.III, No.2.
16. *JBBRAS.*, IX, pp.404 ff.
17. *JKU.*, XI, (1975), pp.146 ff.
18. *IA.*, XIV, 288 ff.
19. From Personal collection.
20. *EI.*, XIII, pp. 306 ff.
21. *Ibid.*
22. Un-published.

23. Un-published.
24. *KI.*, No.64, p. 24.
25. *EI.*, XIII, p.321.
26. *Ibid.*; p.306 -
    Nyāyadoḷ, śauryadoḷ-ārppinoḷ vinayadoḷ chāturyadoḷ mamtra-nischyadoḷ chāru-charitradoḷ Vaibhavadoḷ Sāhityadoḷ visrut-ānvayadoḷ dōrv-valadoḷ nij-eśa hitadoḷ Sāmarthyadoḷ sad-gun-āśrayan
27. *JBBRAS.*, IX, p.297.
28. *SII.*, XI, (II), No.211.
29. *Ibid.*, XV, No.233.
30. *Ibid.*, XI(II), No.191.
31. *EI.*, XVII, pp.117 ff.
32. From Personal collection.
33. *SII.*, XX, No.101.
34. From Personal collection.
35. *Ibid.*
36. *Ibid.*
37. *Ibid.*
38. *EI.*, XIII, p.303.
39. From Personal collection.
40. *EI.*, XIII, p.307.
41. *KI.*, V, No.33.
42. From Personal collection.
43. Ibid., - *Satēyanahaḷḷiya muttiḍalli bīdiṁ mun-nirdu kādi palaram konḍu-geldu tann-āḷdana jōḷiavāḷyaṁ nīgi sura-lōkamaṁ sūre-goṇḍu dēva-lōkakke-pōda*
44. Unpublished.
45. *Ibid.*
46. *JBBRAS.*, IX, p.287, -
    Na sētubandhō na cha-durgga-rōdhō na Vānarānīkapati prayāsaḥ nō vasumitr-ātmaja sambhramō-bhūl-Laṁkāpatis tasya tathāpi-vaśyaḥ
47. *KK.*, pp.171 ff.

48. *EI.*, XIII, p.302.
49. *KK.*, App. III, No.2.
50. *JBBRAS.* IX, p.287.
51. Un-published.
52. Ibid., -

    ... *mutti-kāduvalli kōṭe-kāḷagadoḷu hattikkalu kālāḷuvaṁ kureya (kudureya) n-ṟidu*
53. From Personal collection.
54. *GG.*, p.102.
55. *EI.*, XXX, pp.71 ff.
56. *KI.*, V, NO.63.
57. *JBBRAS.*, IX, pp.304 ff.
58. It is said that the fake inscription is also discovered in the locality recently.

CHAPTER - VII

SOCIAL CONDITIONS

Inscriptions of the Kadambas of Goa give considerable details regarding the social conditions prevailing in the period.

Inscriptions speak of the *chāturvarṇya* or the existence of the four *varṇas* as detailed in the *Dharmaśāstras*. These were the usual *Brāhmaṇa, Kshatriya, Vaiśya,* and *Śūdra*. Inscriptions speak of the same arrangements of the society, though sometimes using different terms. For instance – an inscription from Yelivaḷ in Dharwad district mentions these four classes as *Vipra, Mahīśa, Vaṇika* and *Chaturtha* (*vipra-mahīśa-vaṇik-chaturthar*).[1] An inscription from Mugad[2] speaks of *chāturvarṇya* ; and it says that arrangements were made in the *Saṁyaktva-ratnākara-chaityālaya* of that place for feeding of the *chaturvarṇas (nānā-dēśiya-chāturvarṇa-bhōjanakkaṁ)*.

The *brāhmaṇas* were held in high respect in the society because of their learning and religious practices. There are copious references in inscriptions to state their high moral values and expertise in different branches of learning. For instance an inscription from Halyal [3] speaks highly of such *mahājanas* who were proficient in all arts and sciences. They are described as an embodiment of *Dharma* and experts in the subjects like *Vyākaraṇa* and *Arthaśāstra.* An inscription from Doḍwād[4] speaks of several *brāhmaṇas* who were peroficient in *Ṛigvēda, Yajuṛvēda, Sāmavēda,* in the *Kāṇva śākhā,* reading *Purāṇas* etc. A record from Yelivaḷ, mentioned above, describes the *mahājanas* of the place as *sarvajñas*,[5] on account of their proficiency in *Vyākaraṇa, Kāvya, Nāṭaka, Purāṇa, Smṛiti, Tarka* etc. An inscription from Dēgāve[6] refers to the *brāhmaṇas* who were proficient in *Vēdas* and *Śāstras*. The inscription also refers to one Gōvindadēva, who composed the record on the orders of the Kadamba queen Kamaladēvi, was adept in *Tarkka, Tantra, and Kavitva.* Thus the *brāhmaṇas* enjoyed a high position in the society on account of their learning and religious pursuits.

Mahīśa, mentioned above, was one of the four *varṇas*, obviously represented the *Kshatriya* class. They held high offices in administration such as *daṇḍanāyakas*, *sēnādhipati* and the like. Many of them were placed as governors or administrators of different administrative divisions in the kingdom. They also participated in social and religious activities like making donations to the temples, free feeding houses, construction and maintenance of tanks and the like. For instance an inscription from Beṭdur dated 1122 A.D., of Jayakēśi II refers to one Baladēva as the *Sēnabōva.*[7] An inscription from Narēṇdra mentions an officer named Lakshmarāja as *mahāsāmanta* and *prachaṇḍa-danḍanāyaka.*[8] Siṁha-daṇḍādhīpa who has been described as *mahāsāmanta* and *prachaṇḍra-daṇḍanāyaka* in the same inscription, is said to have constructed a temple called Lakshmaṇēśvara in the name of his grand father Lakshmarasa.[9]

The *Vaiśyas*, the third of the *chāturvarṇas* were a trading class and they were generally known as *seṭṭis, seṭṭiguttas*, and *Nakras.* They also took active part in the social and religious activities. For example, a record from Kāmadhēnu dated 1129 A.D. refers to one Mallisetṭi, son of Chinnisetṭi and Kāḷiyakka, as a great devotee of Śiva.[10] There is a reference to the seṭṭis of Piriya-Gobbūru, Kuṇilagere, Sēḍiṁba, Poḷavase, Purigere, Lokkiguṇḍi, Hānuṁgalla-nāḍu, Māruḍige, and Gangāpura in an inscription from Goḷihaḷḷi, dated 1173 A.D.[11] The Seṭṭiguttas and other trading communities of four towns viz., Dāravāḍa, Narēndrapura, Taḍakōḍu, Ammeyanabhāvi and Vaiśya-Chandiseṭṭi, and others, who made grants to the temple of Lakshmīdēvi are mentioned in a record of Jayakēśi II from Dēvara-hubbaḷḷi dated 1206 A.D.[12]

There were other traders also like *Telligas* (oil merchants), *eleya-bojangas* (betel-leaf merchants), *Okkalu* (agriculturists), *Tōṁṭigas* (gardeners), *Ugura* (dealers in betel leaves) etc. in the society. They traded in different articles of merchandise and they formed their own group like a corporate body. For example, the oil merchants were known as the *Telligas* and they formed themselves into an association called *Telligar-aivattu-okkalu* indicated an association of fifty merchants dealing in oil trade. For example an inscription from Maṇigundage refers to *Telligar-aivattu-okkalu.*[13] Merchants dealing with betel-leaves were called *Eleya-bojaṁgaru.*[14] For example, an inscription from Maḍake-honnaḷḷi [15] mentions *sāsirvar-ainūr-nālvar-eleya bojaṁgaru.* They were also called *uguras.* They were known as *uguras* because they used a particular type of artificial metal nail to pluck betel leaves from the creepers. An association of such traders were called *ugura-mūnūrvvaru.* An inscription from Managuṇḍi refers to three hundred *uguras* of five places viz., Muguda, Huppavaḷḷi, Nuggiyahaḷḷi, Sattivura and Nīrusāgara who made grant to the temple of Tribhuvana-vīra-Jayakēśi also called Siddhēśvara temple at Maṇiguṇḍage.[16]

The people of the fourth *varṇa* generally called *chaturtha* were also an essential part of the society and they perhaps assisted the different professionals like the agriculturists and the merchants, in their professions. An inscription from Yelivāḷa[17] eulogises the *chāturvarṇa*. The inscriptions of the Kadambas do not contain any worth while references to this class.

Apart from these, there were other caste or classes in the society which were based on professions. They were the *Kammāra,* (black-smith), *Kuṁbāra* (potter), *Akkasāli* (gold-smith), *Maḍivāḷa* (washerman). A 12th century record from Bailur[18] speaks of Singōja the *Akkasali*, Kammāra-Dāsōja, Maḍivāḷa-Soppayya who made grants for the offerings and *chaitra-pavitra* celebrations of the god Hermēśvara of the place. The services of this class was also essential to the society. Obviously, such professionals were classed under *chaturtha-varṇa.*

Agriculturists were generally known as *okkalu* and they also formed their association like *arvattu-okkalu.* There is a reference to *aruvattu-okkalu* in an inscription from Siddāpura dated 1120 A.D.[19] which mentions *aravattu-okkalu* of the place. Another inscription from Goḷihaḷḷi dated 1173 A.D. refers to *aruvattu-okkalu.*[20] Similarly, *Tōṁṭigas* (gardeners) find their mention in records. For instance a record from Siddāpur dated 1158 A.D. refers to *Tōṁṭigar-ainūrvvaru.*[21]

Most of these traders and merchants formed their own guilds functioned as corporate bodies.

A word may be added here about the merchant community and others of the place who made grants for the social and religious activities of the place. The merchant community was generally economically well-off and there are copious references to its members, as said earlier, who made large donations to temples and the needy persons. They also built tanks for irrigation and drinking water purposes. They were also generous in providing food and shelter to the needy. Even others took interest in such activities. For example - an inscription from Mugad dated 1045 A.D.,[22] mentioned above, refers to the construction of a *Chaityālaya* and also grants made for feeding the people belonging to all the *varṇas* coming from different places. Another inscription from Hasaraṁbi[23] refers to Dēvagāvuṇda who was always (*santataṁ*) busy in supplying food to those who came to him (*āśrita-jana*). His daughter has been described as *Chintāmaṇi* in giving food to others. An inscription from Kāmadhēnu [24] mentioned above, speaks of one Mallisețți, who supplied rich and tasty (*rasōtkaṭa-vividh-ānna*) food to those who came to his door. The persons who came to him, are described as *naṭa* (actor), *bhaṭa* (soldier), *nagna* (mendicant), *bhagnapatha* (those who had lost their way), *Kaṁṭhaka-gāyaka* (musician), *dīna* (poor), *hīna* (the low), *Karppatika-jaṭādhara* (mendicants with matted hair), *dvija-digaṁbaras* (brāhmaṇa and jaina ascetics), *Tārkkiga* (logician). He supplied food untiringly (*āsarisade*) and without discriminating as high or low (*kiridu-hirid-id-ennade*). Even his wife was untiring in making *annadāna.* The twelve *gāvuṇḍas* of Ammeyanabāvi have been described as *āhāra dānigaḷu.*[25] An inscription from Kāmadhēnu mentioned above refers to Purōhita-Chāvaṇṇa as the one who could not withstand the sight of the hungry people (*pasidara mukha-nōḍa*).[26]

This generous attitude could be seen from the days of Jayakēśi I. His minister Sadano had started a house of charity for the poor and needy. He collected taxes from the native ships as well as those which arrived at Goa from outside and used it for the maintenance of this charity house.[27]

People had religious bent of mind which can be seen in their visiting religious centres like Gōkarṇa, Kollāpura and Sthānaka. The Gaṇadēvi [28] record of Shashṭhadēva II and Narēndra[29] record of Jayakēśi II refers to his visit to Prabhāsa, Gōkarṇa, Kollapura and Sthānaka and distribution of gold coins in hundreds to the learned (*anēka-vaidika-vidvān*) in a manner prescribed in scriptures and also sixteen *dānas* were made by him.

EDUCATION

Importance was given to learning and the learned. The kings being themselves learned, naturally gave due recognition to the scholarship of the brāhmaṇas who were learned in the *Vēdas, Vēdānga. Nyāya, Mīmāṁsa, Dharma-śastra, Jyōtiṣa, Vyākaraṇa* and the like and even used to invite them from different places and arrange for their settling in their kingdom by arranging for their stay. *Agrahāras* and *Brahmapuris* were created for this purpose. There were many such *agrahāras* in the region during the period under study. For example Ammayanabhāvi[30] was an *agrahāra* of the period. Ammayanabhāvi i.e., the modern Amminabhāvi in Dharwad taluk and district was a flourishing *agrahāra* in the times of the Kadambas of Goa. This *agrahāra* was reputed to have contained two hundred Mahājanas who were noted for their learning and character. Kanakāpur,[31] Kunduṁgoḷā,[32]

Dēvara-hubbaḷḷi,[33] Narēndra,[34] and Palliyal[35] were some of the *agrahāras* of the period. They were managed by the donees who were called the *mahājanas*. The number of the *mahājanas* in the *agrahāras* varied, probably, depending upon the size of the *agrahāra*. For example, if there were four hundred *mahājanas* in Ammayanabāvi *agrahāra*, there were five hundred and four at Managuṇḍi.[36] An inscription from Yalivaḷa refers to one thousand *mahājanas* of Kundaṁgoḷa.[37]

The *agrahāras* were granted as *sarvaṇamasya* or tax-free villages. Some times a certain amount of tax was fixed (*niyatakara*). The donees of the *agrahāras* were learned and their scholarship made the rulers invite such brāhmaṇas from different places to come and settle in their kingdom. One such *agrahāra* was Dēgāve.[38] It was a well known *agrahāra* in this period established by Kamalādēvi, the queen of Śivachitta Vīra Permāḍidēva of the Kadamba dynasty. The record says that she having heard of the excellence of the brāhmaṇas and also of gifts of land, praised in the *Purāṇas* and *Dharma-śāstras,* she desired to establish an *agrahāra* by bringing together these brāhmaṇas of great dignity, acquainted with all the *Vēdas, Vēdāngas*, in explaining the meaning of *Nyāya, Mīmāṁsa, Sānkhya, Yōga, Vēdānta, Smṛiti, Itihāsa* and *Purāṇas,* delighting in the performance of the six duties etc., and placed her desire before her husband. Permāḍidēva, "having with due consideration and with joy," gave his consent after having himself put to test the knowledge of the brāhmaṇas. The grant was made to the brāhmaṇas of various *gōtras* and *charaṇas* headed by Vindhyāvāsi-bhaṭṭōpādhyāya in the presence of the god Saptakōtīśvaradēva. The grants were given to the brāhmaṇas for their maintenance. The record also refers to the provision of grants made for study and teaching of *Śāstras* and *Vēdas.* Provision was also made for primary education (*Bālaśikshā*) in the *agrahāra.* Grants were also allotted for the subjects taught in the *agrahara*. For example, for teaching *Rigvēda* and *Yajurvēda* three-fourth share was given and for *bālaśikshā* half a share was given. Like the *Bhattōpādhyāyas* even *Ghaṭikōpādhyāyas* (teaching in *Ghaṭikasthānas)* received their shares depending upon their qualifications and expertise.

Doḍḍawāḍa[39] was another *agrahāra* of the period. Jayakēś III granted the village Doḍḍwāḍa, together with its six hamlets viz., Kummaḍige, Udukeṟe, Eḍavūru, Heggaḷde, Kūlavaḷḷi and Guṁḍavaḷḷi to several brāhmaṇas of different *gōtras* for teaching *Rigvēda*, two *Yajurvēdas* and the *Sāmavēda* in the *Kāṇva Śākhā,* for *satra* (for free feeding house), the reading of the *Purāṇas*, for arranging discourses etc. *Rājaguru* Chandraśekhara-bhattōpādhyāya and many other brāhmaṇas with their *gōtras* and shares are also mentioned in the record.

It is worth mentioning here once again an interesting inscription of Jayakēś II dated 1144 A.D. from Halyal [40] in North Kanara district. Its main interest lies in the unusual description of the Mahājanas of the place, who are stated to be experts in the subjects like *Vyākarṇa, Arthaśāstra*, arts and sciences, thorough in all languages like Sanskrit, *Apabhraṁśa* and *Paiśāchi* and experts in composing works in different styles of writing like *Gauḍa, Vaidarbha,* and *Pānchāla.* This inscription is a true reflection on the religious, social and educational conditions of the period.

BRAHMAPURIS

Like the *agrahāras,* the *brahmapuris* were also donated to the learned brāhmaṇas for their maintenance. Their main duty was *adhyayana* and *adhyāpana.* Mention may be made here in this context, the establishment of a *brahmapuri* i.e., the settlement of the learned brāhmaṇas, who were enjoined with the conducting of religious activities and pursuit of knowledge including imparting education to young aspirants. This *brahmapuri* was established at Gōpaka i.e., Goa by one Kēlima or Kēlivarma an official of Kadamba Tribhuvanamalla i.e., Gūvaladēva II.[41] He, according to the inscription, invited twelve families of brāhmaṇas from different regions *(nānā-dēśa-samāyāta)* and housed them in the locality which was named as *brahmapuri*. The names of the brāhmaṇas are given in the record. This was done in the presence of the king and other officers including *Purōhita*. They were given lands for their maintenance. And these brāhmaṇas engaged themselves in the six fold duties enjoined on them such as *adhyayana, adhyāpana, yajña, dāna* and *pratigraha* and they were engaged in learning and also imparting education and religious activities such as themselves performing sacrifices and also helping others to perform such sacrifices. Interestingly, it is laid down in the record that they would hold the grant lands jointly and share the income equally. They were not supposed to sell the property. If any one did it, he would be fined. The donee would enjoy the grant only so long as he lived in the *brahmapuri*. There was a provision to replace the deserting donee by a new competent one with the consent of others. It is a rare instance that so many details are given in relation to the establishment of a *brahmapuri*.

The *Ghatikāsthānas* were also centres of higher learning. But the information about them is scanty in the inscriptions of the period under study. An inscription from Dēgāve [42] refers to the grants made to the Ghaṭikōpādhyāyas of the place.

Ghatikāsthānas were essentially public halls where *ghatika yantra*, a device for measuring time was maintained for the use of public. Such halls were obviously used for educational purposes.

MAṬHAS

There are a few references in inscriptions for the *maṭhas* in the period under study. As it is well known, the *maṭhas* were religious centers which acted as educational centers also. *Maṭhas* were essentially residential places for the ascetics who engaged themselves in religious and educational activities. They were usually attached to the temples. Though there is copious information on the educationsal activities in the *maṭhas* in the inscriptions of other areas, the inscriptions of the Kadambas found so far do not speak much about the *maṭhas* of the period. *Maṭhas* acted as a meeting place also. Interestingly an inscription discovered by me during the course my survey in the Kalghatgi region, refers to a *maṭha* at Dāravāḍa.[43] The line of the teachers of the *maṭha* is given in the record is as follows - Agnimunīṁdra, Sōmēśvara Kalikāla, Śri Madvarēśa Śiva-Śakti jñāni, Śiva-siddhānta, and Yōga Vichhavi Śakti. The inscription describes the teacher Śivasakti jñani as "*lokōttama, akuṭiḷa-guṇa-nilaya śauchhika-tiḷaka, pravara-naishṭhik-ābharaṇa*" etc. Further the record describe Yōgavichhavi Śakti as a *tilaka* on the forehead of ascetics on account of his scholarship in all the śāstras etc., "*sakala śāstra-prauḍha nīraja-yama-niyama sucharitra sāma-dāna nishṭhita-tapaḥ-prabhāva.*" Unfortunately, the other details are not given. But it can be presumed that these ascetics and the *maṭha* mentioned in the record pertained to the *Kāḷāmukha* sect which was popular during the period under study.

There is a reference to Siddhēśvara *maṭha* in an inscription from Managundi.[44] It refers to the gift of an oil mill, income from taxes like *Bīravaṇa* and *Taḷasārige* by five hundred and four *mahājanas* in the presence of *eṁṭu-hiṭṭu*, *paṁcha-maṭha* and others headed by Tippa-gāvuṇḍa, who had assembled in the *Siddhēśvara-maṭha* of the place. *Maṭhas* also served as a meeting place of persons and officers for settling matters pertaining to social and religious activities. This *maṭha*,, perhaps belonged to the temple of Siddhēśvara which was also called *Tribhuvana-vīra-Jayakēśi* temple built by the *eleyabojangas* at the request of Chandrabhūshaṇadēva,[45] who was the *sthānāchārya* of the temple.

The temples had an important role in social life also of the people. Festivals, though essentially religious in character, had their social value also, when they brought people together which helped to lead a healthy community life. Festivals like *Dīpāvaḷi* and *Yugādi* and special occasions like *chaitra-pavitra* are mentioned in inscriptions.

An inscription from Managuṇḍi mentioned above speaks of a religious congregation on the occasion of *chaitra-pavitra* festival,[46] in the temple of Siddhēśvara of the place. *Chaitra-pavitra* festival is celebrated in the month of *Chaitra*.[47] It was obviously an auspicious occasion when people from different places like Mugunda, Huppavaḷḷi, Nuggihaḷḷi, Seṭṭihaḷḷi and Nīrusāgara came to this place to witness the festival. Even the merchants from far off places like Ayyāvoḷe (Aihole in Bijapur district), Kandamgallu, Sonnaligeyapura (Sholapur in Mahārāshṭra state), Kheḍa (in Gulburga district) and Nandagāve (in Belgaum district) came to this place and being pleased at the worship here, made profuse grants to the temple.

An inscription from Mādanabhāvi, dated 1138 A.D.[48] refers to Jayakēśi II as visiting Mandūra, every Monday to worship the god Kalidēvaswāmin. (*Sōmavārada-vāriy-āgirddu*) during *Chāturmāsa* period or four months of rainy season. The Budarsingi[49] inscription dated 1257 A.D. of Chaṭṭayyadēva refers to the gift of the village Vuchchaṁgi for the worship of the god Mallikarjuna and for the maintenance of tank, *abhisheka, nitya-hōma,* for students. (*ashṭa-sashṭi-tīrtha-siddha-taṭāk-khanana, chatushka-kaḷaś-ābhisēshēka, nitya-hōma* and *āvāsichhātra*). Further the inscription describes the place Sonnaligeyapura as *Abhinava-Śriśaila-yōga ramanīya-kshētra.* The Koṭabāgi inscription[50] of 1264 A.D. refers to the *vachaṇas* of Siddharama and it refers to a gift made to the deity by the chief Chaṭṭayya of the Goa Kadamba dynasty who is described as *Paśchimasamudrādhipati*. This indicates their devotion towards Siddharāma of Sonnaligeyapura, who was a great Vīraśaiva philosopher saint.

DRESS AND ORNAMENTS

Sculptures on the walls of the temples of the Kadamba period speak volumes on the dress and ornaments used by the people of those days. Interestingly, some of the inscriptions also refer to the ornaments worn by the people of the day. An inscription from Dēgāve[51] speaks of the golden ear-rings worn by the *puṇḍits* in the court of Jayakēśi I. The same inscription says that the wives of the enemy kings, who were brought as servants in the court of Shashṭhadēva II were wearing jingling anklets in their feet. The Doḍwāḍ inscription says that the ladies who prostrated before the queen of Jayakēśi III [52] were wearing jewels in their dressed hair. Reference is also made to the nail-paint which is said to have decorated the nails of the ladies. One of the inscriptions from Tambūr refers to the golden jewelry (*Kānchaṇ-ābharaṇaṁ*) given to Maiḷaladēvi by her father, the Chālukya emperor Vikramāditya VI.[53]

REFERENCES AND NOTES

1. *SII.*, XX, No. 293 (1181 A.D.).
   dorevetta-tāṇadoḷ vipra mahīśa vaṇika-chaturthar
2. *Ibid.*, XI (I), No.78.
3. From personal collectioin.
4. *JKU.*, XI,(1975), pp.146 ff.
5. *SII.*, XX, No.293 -
   Vyākarṇa kāvya nāṭaka purāṇa bharata. . . . smriti shaṭ-tarkk-ādi kalā sarvajñar-enisuvars-Sāsirvvar
6. *JBBRAS.*, IX, p.293.
7. *SII.*, XX, No.82.
8. *EI.*, XIII, pp.298 ff.
9. *Ibid.*
10. *SII.*, XX, No.101 -
    Śiva-pāda bhaktaṁ kēḷire |
    Śivaleṁkaṁ Śivana-tottu Śiva-gaṇa-mitraṁ ||
    Śiva-pāda-padma-bhriṁgaṁ |
    Śivan-āḷda Bammiseṭṭiyaṁ Pogaḷadar-āru ||
11. *KI.*, V, No.64.
12. *SII.*, XV, No.232.
    Halasige-hamneraḍu-sāsirada Dāravāḍa Narēndrapura Taḍakōḍu Ammeyanabāvi yiṁtu-na[la]kku-paṭṭaṇada Seṭṭiguttaru ā sthaḷada nakaraṁgaḷuvaiśya Chandiseṭṭi Kaṁni sāsaniseṭṭi Dēviseṭṭi
13. *KI.*, V, No.32.
14. *Ibid.*, No.66.
15. From Personal collection.
16. *SII.*, XV, No.233 (1216 A.D.).
17. *Ibid.*, XX, No. 293 (1191 A.D.).

Nālku-varṇṇa mogedattapar-alli chaturtha varṇṇaṁ-eṁbudu iḷā vinūtamati pūtavadaṁ Pogaḷalke ballavar-ār

18. Un-published.
19. *SII.* XI (II), No.194.
20. *KI.*, V, No.64.
21. *SII.*, XV, No.229.
22. *Ibid.*, XI (I) No.78.
23. From Personal collection.
24. *SII.*, XX, No.101.
25. *Ibid.*, XI, (II), No,191.
26. *Ibid.*, XX, No. 252 (1171 A.D.);

    pasidara-mukha-nōḍa |
    pusi-nudiyaṁ para-vanitey-oldu- bandaḍaṁ ||
    Muṭṭaṁ Śri Sōmanātha-dēvara |
    dāsa Pulivarada satvaraṁ Chāvaṇṇa ||

27. *KK.*, p.186.
28. *IIBS.*, pp. 64 ff.
29. *EI.*, XIII, P.306.
30. *SII.*, XI (II), No.121 (1071-72 A.D.)
31. *Ibid.*, No.154 (1104 A.D.).
32. *Ibid.*, XX, No.293.
33. *Ibid.*, XV, No.232 (1106 A.D.).
34. *EI.*, XIII, p.306 ff.
35. From personal collection.
36. *SII.*, XV, No.233.
37. *Ibid.*, XX , No.293 (1191 A.D.).
38. *JBBRAS.*, IX, pp. 283 ff.
39. Un-published.
40. From personal collectioin.
41. *EI.*, XXX, pp.71 ff (1107 A.D.).
42. *JBBRAS*, IX, pp.280 ff.
43. From personal collectioin.
44. *KI.*, V, No.31.
45. *Ibid.*

46. *Ibid.,*
47. *SII.*, XV, No.233.
48. *Kannada Nighantu*, Vol. III. p. 2798.
49. *EI.,* XXXVI, pp.164 ff.
50. *SII.*, XV, No.195 (1204 A.D.).
51. *JBBRAS.,* IX, p. 273.
52. Un-published.
53. From personal collection.

CHAPTER - VIII

ECONOMIC CONDITIONS

Glimpses of economic activities also can be gleaned from the inscriptions of the Kadambas of Goa under study. As elsewhere, agriculture was the backbone of the economy of those days. This is vouchsafed by a large number of agricultural lands donated to various persons. Lands of various types like wet land and dry land and different soils like *kari-keyi, ere-būmi* (black-soil), *hāḷu* (waste land), *haraḷu* (sand), etc., find their mention in the records. Barren-lands and forest lands were allowed to be reclaimed for agricultural purposes on stipulated conditions like the payment of tax or exemption there of. For example, the inscription of Jayakēśi I[1] mentions a grant of a village Laghumorambikā to an individual named Chhaddama on a condition that he should pay a stipulated amount of tax to the government. The land therein had remained uncultivated and the owners had deserted it. An inscription from Halyal dated 1144 A.D. speaks of a grant of land made by the *mahājanas* of the place to a tank for unhindered cultivation (*bevasāya-santataṁ*),[2] of land.

Huge plantations were raised and gardens developed. Varieties of trees like *honne, sura-honne, pannāga,* and *bāḷe* etc., were also grown,[3] An inscription from Muttage speaks of a plantation of three hundred trees.[4] A plantation of five hundred trees *(aynūru-marada-tōṁṭa)* is mentioned in a record from Tamburu.[5] An inscription from Narendra[6] speaks of a plantation consisting of a thousand trees and a groove consisting of one thousand creepers and also to one thoused eight hundred *(sāyirada-eṇṭunūru baḷḷiya)* creepers obviously of betel leaves and one thousand eight hundred (*sāyirada-eṇṭunūru-marada*) trees of the place. Flower gardens were also raised (*hū-dōṁta*). For example the village Tambur is described as a place of flower gardens.[7] An inscription from Malakinakoppa mentions a flower garden (*hūvina-tōṁṭa*).[8] Another inscription from Tambur refers to *Mālagāra-tōṁṭa.*[9] A record from Kamadhenu refers to a grant made to a servant who maintained a flower garden (*hūdōṁṭava-sākuv-āḷiṁge*).[10] An inscription from Jinnur refers to a lady named Basantikabbe, who is described as Mālakāra,[11] obviously a lady dealing with flower garlands. Interestinglhy, an inscription from Nulvi,[12] in Dharwad district, refers to a *Bāḍu-gāyi-tōṁṭa* (vegetable garden) consisting of vegetables like *hīre-kāyi* (ridged-goard), *saute-kāyi,* (cucumber), *badane-kāyi* (brinjal). According to the inscription five of each was to be given as *naivēdya* to the god every day by the gardeners of the place.

Most of the area covered by Goa Kadamba kingdom was known as *Malenāḍu* or hilly area with considerable rainfall. Naturally, the main crop appears to have been rice. Some inscriptions mention varities of rice like *Gandhasāḷi* or fragrant rice.[13] The grains like *urddu*[14] (black-gram), *hesaru*[15] (green-gram), *eḷḷu*[16] (jinjely) etc. find their mention in records.

Betel-nut grooves (*aḍake-tōṁṭa*) and betel-leaf plantations were also in plenty. All these go to indicate that the land was fertile and importance was given to agriculture.

Agriculture depended upon a good supply of water. Grants were made on a lavish scale for construction and maintenance of irrigational tanks. For example, an inscription from Guḍikaṭṭi [17] mentions a huge tank (*brihattaraṁ-enipa*) constructed by an individual named Niguṁbara-dāsa, in the name of the king Chaṭṭa (*Chaṭṭa-bhūnripatiya-pesaralu*), for the service of the world (*jaga-sēvyaṁ-āge*). Another record from Mugada[18] dated 1125 A.D. refers to a *sāmanta* of Mugunda-thirty named Bammadēva, who had it engraved on stone, the land and houses, granted to a tank constructed by his uncle Mārthaṇḍayya. The record while giving the genealogical account of the family it refers to the early members of the family viz., Chāvuṇḍayya, who had become famous on account of the construction of tanks, wells, *basadis,* temples, *aravaṭige, satra*, in the country.[19] Construction of tanks, temples, *basadis,* free-feeding houses etc. were an act of merit. But, they served also the public cause. Inscriptions of the Kadambas mention a large number of such tanks, constructed by different officers, merchants and other philanthropists. It is interesting to note that at least some of the tanks are in use even today.

TRADE

Trade activity was also considerably brisk. Mention is made above of the corporate bodies formed by different dealers as *Telligas* (traders in oil), *Nakaras*, *Ugura* etc. Inscriptions also mention the famous merchant guild known as *Ayyāvoḷe-aynūrvvaru,* which dominated the trade activities throughout south India and overseas also. An inscription from Goḷihaḷḷi dated 1173 A.D. refers to *Ayyāvoḷe-aynūrvvaru,*[20] who had contacts with the trade guilds existing in this region.

Oversea trade was also carried on through the port of Goa. As observed by Dr. G.M. Moraes[21] there was contact with other traders, many of whom had settled in Goa. They mainly dealt with horses. Inland trade was carried on through roads and by using animals and carts (*baṇḍi*). Roads are frequently mentioned in inscriptions. For example, an inscription from Narendra[22] speaks of *heddāri* or highway. An inscription from Managunḍi speaks of *baṇḍi-dāri* [23] or cart road, used for trading purposes. Oxen and donkeys were the usual beasts of burden.[24] Besides food grains, betel-leaves and nuts etc., there were other articles also, sold in some of the places in the kingdom. For example an inscription from Golihaḷḷi,[25] though mutilated, gives the list of articles for sale like jewels (mānika), *paḷi, pathāvaḷi,* betel-nut, pepper, etc. The list also includes elephants. This indicates that Kiru-sampagāḍi, mentioned in the record, was a trading centre during the period under study, from where even the elephants were sold along with gold and other mercantile goods which were sold or exported. It is worth mentioning here another trading centre of the period viz., Gōpaka-paṭṭaṇa, which was mentioned in the inscriptoin of Jayakēśi I, referred to by Dr. G.M. Moraes, in his *Kadamba Kula*,[26] which states that Gōpaka-paṭṭaṇa was one of the important emporiums in the westcoast. It is learnt from the record that many traders (*vaṇijas*) hailing from different countries such as Pantait, Kerala, Srytan (Sumatra), Bangla, Curgot, Latta, Pusta, Saurashtra, Sangamesvara. Chippalora, Shivapura, Pindiyanna, Valla-pattam, Simhala, Cudah and Zangawar (Zanzibar) visited the place.

The state economy, naturally, largely depended upon taxes collected from different sources. Agricultural commodities were taxed and so also there were taxes on commercial activities, transport and even professions. Taxes on agricultural land were generally known as *baṭṭe-suṁka, pannāya, tōṁṭada-āya, kuḷiya-suṁka. Siddhāya* and *Aruvaṇa* were taxes collected in cash. *Hejjuṁka* [27] and *vaḍḍarāvuḷa* [28] mentioned in records, appear to be taxes on income. *Baṭṭe-suṁka*[29] and *talasārige* [30] were taxes on transport. An inscription from Tambūr[31] mentions *Tōṁtada-Baṭṭe-suṁka*. An other inscription from Tambūr refers to *baṭṭe-sumka* and *kuḷiya-suṁka.*[32] *Baṭṭe-pannāya* is referred to in an inscription from Madanabhavi.[33]

There were various professions like *Sēṇiga, Agasa,* (washerman), *Baḍiga* (carpenter), *Kuṁbāra* (potter), *Kammāra* (black-smith), *Akkasāli* (gold-smith), and *Tellgias*, which came under taxation.

An inscription from Tambur mentions *Vāgila-vaṇa,*[34] which means door tax on house given by Mādirāja *daṇḍanāyaka* to the temple of the place. *Mane-dere* and *Koṭṭige-dere* also stand for a similar tax. Terms like *Handara-vaṇa,*[35] *Haseya-vaṇa,*[36] *Maduveya-beḷgoḍevaṇa*[37] indicate the taxes on marriages and similar occasions.

Suṁka and *Kara* indicate the tax in general though perhaps *suṁka* stood for tolls and *kara* for tax in general. There were also tax officers with different designations to collect taxes and manage the financial affairs. *Suṁkaverggaḍe* and *Sunkādhikāri* stood for officers collecting taxes in general. An inscription from Mavalli refers to *Suṁkaverggaḍe* named Nāraṇayya.[38] An inscription from Tambur dated 1140 A.D. refers to *Suṁkad-adhikāri* Vāvaṇayya who granted the *Taḷasārige* tax on a house of *Telligas* of the temple of the place.[39] *Sumkad-adhikāri* Dēvayya and Chandayya, who granted *taḷasārige* tax on oil mills of the temples of Siddhēśvara and Grāmēśvara are found mentioned in a record from Dārawāḍa.[40]

Interestingly, an inscription from Hasarambi refers to a lady tax-officer (*Sumkad-adhikāri*) named Lakshmidevi.[41] The term *Sumkad-adhishṭhāyaka,* obviously indicated an high officer in the finance department. An inscription from Kuradikeri,[42] refers to one Nāraṇa, brother of one Anantapālayya, as *pannāyada-sumkada-adhishṭhāyaka-perggaḍe* over the division of Palasige-12000, Noḷambavāḍi-3000 and Ālande-1000. It was expected from the officers that they should discharge their duties sincerely. A record from Madanabhavi[43] says – *dharmamsumkamampaḍed-adhikārigaḷ-sa-ddharmmadim-naḍeyisuvaru.*

MEASURES AND WEIGHTS

Inscriptions also mention the terms used for measuring different commodities. *Kamma* and *mattar* were the denominations for measuring the agricultural land. *Kai* or *hasta* indicated the term for measuring house-sites. Normally, a stick or a pole of specified length was used for measuring land. It is however, to be noted that there was no uniformity in the sizes in such measuring rods. For example we get references to measuring rods of different sizes such as *hattu-gēṇa-koḷu, ippattu-gēṇa-kōlu* and so on. *Gēṇu* stood for a span or the distance between the middle finger and the thumb of the stretched palm. Big and small poles were known as *piriya-gaḷe* and *kiriya-gaḷe* or *hiriya-kōlu.* An inscription from Mavalli[44] refers to *hiriya-kōlu.* Bammigatti inscription[45] makes reference to *kiriya-gōlu.* Some times such poles were named after individuals or rulers or places. For example *Śivchitta-kōlu*,[46] which was named after the ruler Śivachitta. *Kundūra-kōlu* [47] was a measuring rod prevalent in the administrative division of Kundūru-five hundred. Narendra had its own pole for measuring. It was known as *Narēndra-purada-piriya-kōlu.*[48]

Inscriptions also mention the terms indicating liquid measures and other commodities. *Soḷasige, sollage* and *soṁṭige* stood for liquid measures as well as measurement of grains. *Māna* was a unit of measuring oil. *Saṭṭuga* was used for measuring grains as well as oil. *Koḷaga* meant a vessel and a vessel of specified size which was used for measuring liquids as well as grains. A study of these details indicate that the agricultural and trading activities were conducted in an organized way throughout the kingdom and the finances were managed by various officers of different cadres under the control of the king.

Interestingly, an inscription from Golihaḷḷi [49] dated 1173 A.D. makes reference to selling of goods by *aḷate* (measuring) *tūka* (weighing), and *eṇike* (counting). The record says –

> *Chandr-ārkka-sthāyiy-āgi aḷate-tūka-eṇike-vilasapaḍi-int-āva-bhaṇḍamaṁ māridaḍaṁ māridavaru- hoṁge-arevīsa....*

COINS

Money has been a very important means of transactions and commercial activities in any period or kingdom and many matters were handled through coins. We have a very long history of coinage in our country. Right from the punch-marked coins of the very early days up to the minting of sophisticated gold coins, a history of coins presents a very fascinating study. In the days of the Kadambas of Banavasi, in Karnataka, coins of various denominations were put into use and right from those days inscriptions provide very interesting details about coins and their circulation. In the period under study also, the inscriptions provide information about a variety of coins in definite metals and denominations, used in administrative and commercial transactions.

Gadyāṇa was a very popular coin in this period. It was a standard unit of transactions. Indications are that both silver and gold *gadyāṇas* were very much in use. Many times gold *gadyāṇas* are specifically mentioned as *pon-gadyāṇas. Pon* means gold in Kannada. *Gadyāṇas* were named after the deities also, such as *Bhairava gadyāṇa* and *Brihat-Bharaiva-gadyāṇa.* They are mentioned in a copper plate grant of Tribhuvanamalla, dated 1107 A.D.[50] There is a reference to *Bhairava-gadyāṇa* and *Bhairava-nishka* in the same inscription. *Brihat Bhairava gadyāṇa* may be a gold coin of the *Bhairava* category, bigger in size than the normal ones.[51]

Ganga-gadyāṇa, Gangana-Pon-Gadyāṇa mentioned in records were possibly the coins issued by the Ganga chieftains holding sway over some regions in the Kadamba kingdom. For example an inscription from Kadaravaḷḷi, dated 1098 A.D.[52] mentions a grant of three *Ganga-gadyāṇas* made by one Taddavāḍi Indayya of Kadaravalli for offerings and perpetual lamp of god Rāmēśvaradēva, when Arikēsaridēva of the Ganga family was governing as the subordinate of Kadamba Gūvaladēva. Another inscription from the same place dated 1075 A.D.[53] refers to the grant of five *Ganga-gadyāṇa*s, given for *angabhōga* of the god Śankaradēva of Kādaravalli by *daṇḍnāyaka* Kēśavāditya and *daṇḍanāyaka* Sōmēśvarabhaṭṭa. The *gadyāṇas* were named after the place of the mint, where they were minted. For instance, *Lokkigadyāṇa,*[54] *Lokki-prīya-Śrāheya-gadyāṇa,*[55] *Hosa-Lokki-gadyāṇa*[56] and *Lokki-achchina-gadyāṇa* [57] referred to in inscriptions obviously were produced at Lokkiguṇḍi, i.e., modern Lokkundi in Gadag district, which had a famous mint during the days of Chālukyas of Kalyāṇa.

Nishka, was very popular coin from a very early days in our history especially in Northern India. But it had gained currency in the southern part also. As said earlier, some coins are called *Bhairava Nishka*.

Paṇa was a coin of smaller denomination. It figures frequently in inscriptions of this period. There are indications to show that ten *paṇas* made one *gadyāṇa*.[58]

Hāga or *pāga* or *hire-pāga* was another coin which was perhaps smaller in denomination than *paṇa*. It finds its mention in a record from Avarādi.[59] The record says that *Tōṁṭigas* and *Ugura-300* gave three *hāgas* and ten *hire-hāgas* to god Chaṭṭēśvara of the place. *Vīsa* and *bēḷe* mentioned in records were smaller coins. It is however, difficult to determine the exact ratio between these coins. There are also indications that these coins were normally of two denominations, big and small. For instance there are references to *Hiri-hāga*[60] or *hāga* of higher denomination, obviously anticipating the existence of *Kiriya* or small *Hāga*. Interestingly, many coins of this period also have been discovered from different places and scholars have tried to co-relate them in the terms like *Gadyāṇa, paṇa* and the like figuring in inscriptions.[61]

The Kire-halasige record mentions *Malavara-māri-nishka*. *Malavara-māri* was the title of Permāḍi.[62] *Paṇa* finds its mention in some inscriptions. It is said that a few *paṇas* were discovered at Chandrāpura.[63]

It is said that a few gold coins pertaining to the Period of Jayakēśi I, Jayakēśi II and Jayakēśi III have been noticed. The coins containing the legend *Saptakōṭēśvara-*

labdha-vara-Vīra-Jayakēśidēva Malavara-mari[64] and *Śivachitta-vīradēvarasara-Malavara-māri*[65] are refered to in *Kadamba Kula* by Dr.G.M.Moraes. They are pure gold coins. Dr.Moraes also refers to the coins collected by some Institutions in India[66] viz., The Bombay Branch of Royal Asiatic Society, The Indian Historical Research Institute and Indian Museum, Calcutta.

REFERENCES AND NOTES

1. *KK.*, , App..III, No.2.
2. From personal collection.
3. *Ibid.*
4. *Ibid.*
5. *Ibid.*
6. *EI.*, XIII, p.321.
7. From personal collection. -
   Sogayipa-pūga-saṁkuḷad-aśōka-mahijada peṁpuvetta
   Saṁpageya podaḷdu Pūṭa-nava-pātaḷad-orppava
   Nāḷikēradim bagegoḷisirppa. . . .ele-vaḷḷi-baḷḷi Mallige-
   gaḷa līle kaṇg esedu tōṟugaṁ-ā puraṁ-eṁṭu-nōrpaḍa ||
8. *EI.*, XXVIII, p.311, -
   Hosa-gaddeya keḷagina-hūvina-tōṁṭakke
9. From personal collectioin; - *Mālalgara tōṁṭada*
10. *SII.*, XX, No.101.
11. From personal collection.
12. *Ibid.*
13. *Ibid.*
14. *SII.*, XX, No.101.
15. *Ibid.*
16. From personal collection.
17. Un-published.

18. *SII.*, XI (II), No.177.

19. *Ibid.*

    Keṟe-bhāvi-dēgulaṁ-aravaṇṭige-satraṁ-eṁba dharmmamavā-inituṁ neṟedavu Mugunda-mūvattara vibhu Chāvuṇḍarāyanindaṁ-jagadoḷ

20. *KI., V., No.64.*

    It is well known that this guild carried trade with not only the inland regions like Chōḷa, Chēra, Pāṇḍya, Magadha, Saurāshṭra and other kingdoms but also outside countries like Kamboja, Persia, Nepala and others. The inscription says that they travelled by both water routes and land routes. The merchandise included not only commodities of day today use needed but also prescious stones and even animals like elephants and horses. It is learnt that they sold these by whole sale or hauked them. They paid *suṁka* (tax) regularly. Filled the treasury with gold and jewels. *EC.*, VII, Sk.118.

21. *KK.*, p. 283.

22. *EI., XIII,* pp.316.

23. *SII.*, XV, No.233. –

    Baḍaga-desey-iṁdaṁ Haḷḷigēriyiṁ-banda-bhaṇḍi-dāri.

    Another Inscription says –

    Navilūr-iṁda Haḷḷiṁgerege banda bhaṇḍi-dāriy-iṁ ettu-katte-kōṇaṁ-eṁb-ivarall-āva bhanḍam hēṟidad-irppattakkaṁ....

24. *KI.*, V, No.64.

25. *Ibid.*, No.33 -

    Ayinūrvvarubiṭṭadharmmaṁ-ent-eṁaḍe āne-māṇika-paḷi- paṭṭhāvaḷi-aḍake- Meḷasu. . . . . ā- sthānadalu vikrayav-ādaḍe hoṁge – kāni....

26. *KK.*, page 283.

27. From personal collection.

28. Un-published.
29. From Personal collection.
30. *KI.*, V, No.66, (1206 A.D.).
31. From Personal collection.
32. *Ibid.*, -
    dēvara-tōṁṭada keyya-baṭṭe-suṁkamaṁ kuḷiya-suṁkamaṁ
33. *SII.*, XV, No.16.
34. From personal collection
35. *Ibid.*
36. *SII.*, XV, No. 233.
37. From personal collectioin. (Siddarahalli)
38. From personal cpollectioin.
39. *Ibid.*
40. *KI.*, V, No.67.
41. From Ink impression.
42. From personal collection.
43. *SII.*, XV, No.16.
44. From personal collection.
45. *Ibid.*
46. *Ibid.*
47. *EI.*, XIII, pp.316 ff.
48. *SII.*, XV, No.230.
49. *KI.*, V, No.64.
50. *EI.*, XXX, pp.73 ff.
51. *Ibid.*
52. Ritti S.H. *An Inscription from Kadaravalli*, *JKU.*, (Soc.Sc.), IV, 1968, p. 168 ff.
53. *Ibid.*, No.15.
54 *KI.*, V, No.67.
55. *Ibid.*, No.68.

56. *SII.*, XV, No.22 .
57. *Ibid.*
58. Ritti S.H., *The Seunas,* p.240.
59. Un-published.
60. *Ibid.*
61. For details see Dr. A.V.Narasimha Murthy's *Coins of Karnataka* (New series).
62. *JBBRAS.*, IX, p.293.
63. *KK.*, p.383.
64. *Ibid.*
65. *Ibid.*
66. *Ibid.*

CHAPTER – IX

RELIGIOUS CONDITIONS

The Kadambas of Goa contributed considerably to the growth of different religious sects in their region. They encouraged and patronized saints and ascetics of all the prevailing religious sects in their period by constructing temples and by strengthening them with liberal donations for their maintenance.

The heydays of Buddhism were over long back. But this religion lingered on through centuries as can be seen from a few remains at Goa, however scanty.

JAINISM

Jainism however, which was born along with Buddhism in our country survived and flourished throughout the historical period and has continued to influence a large section of the population in our country even today. Copious references to Jaina *Basadis* and the Jaina teachers found in the inscriptions of the period testify to the fact that this religion flourished in the region during the period under study. It was patronized by the rulers and their subordinates and supported by the populace, particularly the merchant community, through centuries. Consequently, it grew from strength to strength in Karnataka, so much so that it came to be considered as the home of the Jainas *(idu Jina dharm-āvāsam-ādattu. . . .chāru-Karnāṭa-dēśaṁ).*[1] It is well known that the Chālukyas of Kalyāṇa and the Hoysaḷas were enthusiastic patrons of this religion. During their regime, Jainism flourished throughout the kingdom through different sects like *Anvayas, Gaṇas, Gachhas* and the like. These rulers were responsible for the creation of many architecturally attractive structures like *Basadis* and *Chaityālayas* and numerous sculptures of the *Tīrthankaras* big and small and the marvelous pillars known as *Mānasthaṁbhas.* Their subordinates, the Kadambas of Goa were no exception. They also patronized and supported Jaina ascetics and they helped them to pursue their religion without any hindrance. They built many *Basadis* which became at once the centres of religion, education and culture. Following are a few details about their activities in the promotion of this religion.

Mugunda i.e., the modern Mugad in Dharwad district was an important Jaina centre during the rule of the Kadambas of Goa. An inscription from this place, dated 1045 A.D., mentions a Jaina temple called *Samyaktva Ratnākara-Chaityalaya.*[2] It was constructed by *Nāḷgāvuṇḍa* Chāvuṇḍa-gāvuṇḍa, in this place. Chāvuṇḍa-gāvuṇḍa also made grants of land and money for the maintenance of this temple and for feeding the people of all the communities. That it was a famous institution is indicated by the fact that it gives a lengthy line of teachers, belonging to this place. The earliest member to be mentioned is Kīrtigorava, who is described as a Grammarian and an expert in Tarkka and

Siddhānta. The following generations of ascetics were also highly learned persons. Traividya Gōvardhanadēva, in this line is also described as an expert in all arts and sciences. His disciple Muni Gaṇḍavimukta, seems to have been incharge of this *Chaityālaya*, Interestingly, the inscription states that Mahāsāmanta Mārthaṇḍayya, the grandson of Chāvunḍa-gāvuṇḍa, the builder of the *Chaityālaya* renovated it and added a *Nāṭakaśāla* to it.[3] Another inscription from Mugad dated 1125 A.D.[4] refers to an interesting event that Bammayya, the grandson of the above mentioned Mārthaṇḍa, had that grant of land previously made by his uncle Mārthaṇḍayya for the upkeep of the tank mentioned in the inscription. The grant land was exempted from all kinds of taxes. This inscription pertains to the period of Gūvaladēva III. Interestingly, the inscription calls Gojjiyakka, the wife of Mārthaṇḍa as Ghaṭāntaki i.e., Attimabbe, a Jaina devotee at Lakkuṇḍi.

Anilāpura, i.e., modern Alnavar also in Dharwad district, was another prominent Jaina centre under the Goa Kadambas. The inscription from this place dated 1081 A.D.[5] and belonging to the rule of Guvaladēva III also refers to the grant of land made by Narasimhaseṭṭi in favour of the Biḷiya *Basadi* constructed by an officer (*pradhāna*) named Māchaṇṇa at *rājadhāni* Anilāpura for feeding the ascetics in the *Basadi* . The inscription mentions the lineage of these Jaina ascetics. But, the details are lost because of the damaged condition of the inscription. The names of the ascetics like Rāmachandra and Bālachandra are noticed in the record. These names also appear in the Mugad inscription mentioned above. An inscription from Kulavaḷḷi dated 1040 A.D. refers to a grant of a land and a house for the renovation of the *Basadi* built by *Aravatt-okkalu* of the place, by the king Vīra-Permāḍideva.[6]

The Malakinakoppa inscription also of Gūvaladēva III dated 1103 A.D.[7] refers to the construction of a *Basadi* by one Puligōḍa Bammiseṭṭi, obviously, a prominent merchant of the town. The *Basadi* was headed by an ascetic named Śāntivīramuni of *Yāpanīya-sangha Maiḷapānvaya Kārēyagaṇa* whose predecessors are mentioned as Vijayakīrtidēva, Nāgachandradēva, Kāmahara-Saiddhānta-Śirōmaṇi, Kanakaśāntimuni, Abhayēndu-mōnidēva and Mahēndrakīrti. Śantivīradēva is described in the inscription as a great scholar with mastery over *Tarkka*, *Vyākaraṇa*, *Kāvya,* and *Nāṭaka* and was an embodiment of compassion and was the one who was striving hard for the growth of *Kāreyagaṇa*.

Māvaḷḷi was another important Jaina centre in this period. The inscriptions indicate that there were a number of *Basadis* in the place. An inscription from Māvaḷḷi belonging to Jayakēśi II [8] speaks of Śāntinātha Basadi constructed by Heggaḍe Bammachayya, an officer under Hākiballadēva who appears to have been the brother-in -law of Jayakēśi II. Heggaḍe Bammachayya was a devoted Jaina, always enjoyed the worship of Jina. The inscription also mentions the Jaina teachers belonging to *Sēna-gaṇa and Mūla-saṁgha.* The inscription records a grant of land to this Jaina *Basadi.* The grant was entrusted to Vārisēṇa-paṇḍitadēva of *Sēna-gaṇa* and *Pogari-gachha*. Māvaḷḷi has been described as a religious centre with many Saiva and Jaina temples. The inscriptions also record other grants in the reign period of Bhūlōkamalla. Interestingly, Bhāviyakka, the wife of Bammachayya was also a Jaina devotee. She is described as having surpassed Attimabbe, an ardent Jaina devotee of Lakkundi in the earlier period.

Tammiyūr i.e., the modern Tambur, in Kalghatgi taluk, was yet another famous Jaina centre of the period. An inscription of Jayakēśi II[9] gives interesting details. It states that the officer Barmachayya and Rāchamallayya constructed a *Basadi* or Jaina *mandira* at Tambur. It was headed by Mēghachandra-paṇḍitadēva of *Mūla-saṁgha* and *Sūrastha-gaṇa*. Rāchamalla mentioned here appears to have been an officer under Jayakēśi. It is worth noting that Tambūr is here called Tāṁbrapura and described as a city of great repute with tall buildings and flower gardens. Another inscription from Mavaḷḷi, dated 1169 A.D.[10] narrates an interesting event that when Hākiballa desired to construct a *Basadi* for the *parōksha-vinaya* of his father Māvulidēva, he was advised by his ministers Barmachayya and Rāchamalla, to construct a *Basadi* at Tammiyūru, situated in Māvaḷḷi-500. The work was executed by these ministers themselves. The chief of this *Basadi* was Mēghachandra-paṇḍitadēva, belonging to *Mūla-sangha* and *Sūrastha-gaṇa*.

Another broken inscription in this place dated 1158 A.D.[11] introduces a Jaina teacher Guṇanandi who belonged to *Sūrastha-gaṇa* and *Chaitrakūṭ-ānvaya*. The record states that *Mahāsāmanta* Rudrayya constructed a *Basadi* in the village Bīranahaḷḷi and made a grant of land for the maintenance of the *Basadi*. The grant was entrusted to the ascetic Nēmichandra, the disciple of Guṇanandi. The name of the ruling king is lost. But on the basis of the date it can be ascribed to Śivachitta-Vīra-Permādidēva. Another inscription of Permādidēva[12] from the same place speaks of the same *mahāsāmanta* Rudrayya, as having constructed a *Basadi* at the instance of the members of *Kuruṁba-Sēṇiga* community. The description in the inscription indicates that this *Basadi* was an expansive structure (*vistāraṁ-āgi*).[13] The priest of this temple also was Guṇanandi-brati, described as *Siddhanta-chakravarti*. The date of the inscription is lost.

Another *Basadi* in this place was called Nakara-Jinalaya,[14] obviously because it was constructed by the *Nakara* or the merchant community. The record states that a lady named Padmāvati, made a grant of land for feeding the ascetics in this *Basadi*. Several other officers like *Sandhivigrahi* Basavaṇṇa, *Sunkad-adhikāri* Vāmayya are also stated to have made grants to this *Basadi*.

Bammigaṭṭi, another place in Kalghatgi taluk was also a Jaina centre. An inscription of Permāḍi in this place[15] states that his officer named Singhaṇa constructed a beautiful *Jina Bhavana* at Honnehaḷḷi. Grants were made for the worship of *Jina* and for conducting other austerities in the temple. The ascetic in-charge of the temple appears to have been Chandrakīrti-Munīndra of *Yāpanīya-Saṁgha* and *Kundūr-gaṇa*.

Gōlihaḷḷi in Khanapur taluk was also a famous Jaina centre. Three merchants of Kiru-sampagāḍi (identified with Gōḷihaḷḷi, the find spot of the record), constructed a *Basadi* here. Mallisetṭi, Dēvisetṭi and Madurasetṭi, the sons of Gangisetṭi made grant of land, house site and oil-mill for the maintenance of these temples. The grant was entrusted to Vāsupūjya Bhaṭṭāraka, the disciple of Nēmichandra Bhaṭṭāraka. These ascetics belonged to *Mūla-saṁgha* and *Baḷagāra-gaṇa*. The spiritual genealogy of these ascetics is also given in the inscription. The record belongs to Permāḍidēva and is dated 1176 A.D.[16]

An inscription from Dharwad[17] refers to a Nagara *Jinālaya* and gives a list of Jaina teachers as Ēkavīra-āchārya, his disciple Rāmachandra-brati and his disciple Bāhubalimuni. The last one was incharge of the *Basadi*.

Different grants were made to this *Jinālaya* by different donees on different dates.

An image of Pārśvanātha is found in a Jina temple at Havage near Aḷnāvar. An inscription found in tne pedestal of the image[18] refers to a Kotara-Kollagāvuṇḍa who got the idol of Pārśvanātha prepared for the Nakarājinalaya at Anilapura. The record says that he was a *guḍḍa* or disciple of a lady named Guṇavatiyavva, who was *śshithi* or a disciple of the preceptor Māghanandi of the *Kāreya-gaṇa* and *Maiḷpānvaya* in the illustrious *Yāpaniya-saṁgha*. A record worthy of mention here is that there were lady disciples of religious preceptors who had in turn their own followers.

A *Nishidi* stone found at Garag[19] in Dharwad taluk and district refers to the death of a preceptor named Śantivīradēva of *Kummadi-gaṇa* of *Yāpaniya-saṁgha*. Another *Nishidi* stone found at Chhabbi[20] dated 1060 A.D. refers to the death of a Jaina teacher named Kanaka-nandi, a disciple of Bāhubali of Sēnagaṇa. It was erected by Kanti Bāgiyabbe.

A sculpture of twenty-four *Tirthankaras* in a Jaina *Basadi* at Amminabhavi indicates the existence of *Digambara* sect during the period under study.

The above details make it amply clear that the Jaina religion received benevolent patronage from the Goa Kadamba chiefs and their officers and also the common public like the merchants. Many of the monuments have come down to us to this day to vouchsafe this fact.

ŚAIVISM

It is a known fact that Śaivism was a very dominant religion in the period under study. It was sponsored zealously and with devotion by the Chālukyas of Kalyāṇa. This is vouchsafed by a large number of Śiva temples, which have come down to us, as well as numerous inscriptions mentioning the construction of temples, the installation of deities and similar other activities. The Kadambas of Goa also followed their overlords and contributed considerably to the development of this religion, through construction of temples, making munificent grants and providing shelter to the ascetics and learned men by creating *agrahāras*. A few such important examples are reviewed below.

We have seen above that Tambur, former Tammiyūr, the headquarters of a small division viz., Tammiyūr-12 in Māvaḷḷi-500 housed Jaina temples. Tammiyūr was a Śaiva centre also. An inscription[21] in the present day Uttarakumāra temple near this place speaks of the temple Uttarēśvaradēva, which is obviously known as Uttarakumāra in the modern times. The inscription speaks of Piriyakka, wife of *daṇḍanāyaka* Jayakēśi who made a grant of land and an oil mill for the worship in the temple and for the maintaining the lamps. A large number of gifts made by different individuals recorded in the inscription show that the temple was fairly big and wielded considerable influence on the people. The inscription further states that Chaṭṭimayya, the chief of Tammiyūr (*Ūroḍeya*) and Kētapayya, the *Perggaḍe* of Māvaḷe-nāḍu made grants for maintenance and also for the worship in the temple. The inscription is dated 1087 A.D.

Yet another inscription from Tambūr[22] found in a field belonging to Sri Nandikatti Saheb, gives detailed description of the temple of Permēśvara or Hermēśvara, constructed by Kaggaṇa or Khaḍga, a prominent officer under Permāḍi. The inscription states that this temple was built by this officer in the name of the ruler Permāḍidēva, as a mark of his loyalty to his master. This Kaggaṇa is said to have been born of Śāntivarma and Tippavve. He is highly eulogized in the inscription. From this we come to know that he was valorous and generous. Interestingly, the ascetics incharge of this temple appear to have been related to the *Maṭha* of Dārawāḍa (*Dārawāḍada maṭha*). Dārawaḍa is obviously the same as the present Dhūrwaḍ. This ascetic was called Vichchavi śakti. His spiritual genealogy is also given in the record and it is as follows:

Agnimunīndra
|
Sōmēśvara Kalikāla
|
Śrī Madhvarēśa
|
Śivaśakti Jñāni
|
Śiva Siddhānta
|
Yōgivichchavi Śakti

The inscription speaks of Śivaśakti Jñāni as *Lōkōttama, akuṭilaguṇālaya, Śauchchika-tilaka, pravara-naishthikābharaṇa* and also describes Vichchavi-śakti as *Sakala-śāstra-prauḍha-nīraja* and follower of *yama, niyama suchcharitra sāma-dāna-isthika-tapaḥ-prabhāva* etc. Kaggaṇa also made a grant of several lands to this temple for the worship of and offerings to god and for feeding the temple priests and the guests. Several other officers like *Gāvunḍas, Prabhus* and *Ainūrvvaru, Nakara samūha, Telligas* of Tammiyūr-12 and Huligōḍu-12 made grant of money for the continued worship of the god Permēśvara.

This Kagga was the subordinate of Mādirāja *danḍanāyaka.* The inscription is broken at both the ends.

The village Kāmadhēnu in kalghatgi taluk which was known as Sāsalu in ancient times was a noted holy place with the temple of Kalidēva in the days of the Kadambas, now called Kalmēśvara. One of the inscriptions dated 1129 A.D., of this place extols this as a place where god Śankara came and stayed.[23] Another inscription of Permāḍi dated 1171 A.D. says that this place was sanctified by the river Urvā,[24] flowing in the southern part of the village, to the west. Presently, this river is called Śālmalā, which, as said by the local people, has its origin at the place called Sōmēśvara near Dharwad. The inscription describes the secredness of the river thus -

> *ā Sāsala dakshiṇa bhāgadalli paridaḷ-paśchima-mukhadim dhareyoḷ-ure-chōdyav-ensid-Urvvā-nadiya vaṛad-ormme snāna māḍida phaladi Śivalokadalli sukhadin-irvvaru*

The temple was visited by several devotees in those days and the inscription speak of the grants made to this temple by the devotees Bhaṇḍa-saleya Mallisеṭṭi, and Kumara Mallayya and other officers. An inscription dated 1129 A.D.[25] mentioned above describes Mallisеṭṭi as *Śivapāda-bhakta, Śivana-tottu, Śivagaṇa-mitra, Śivana-pāda-bhringha, Śivanāḷda* as he was a great devotee of Śiva. He was very liberal in treating the people without any discrimination. He used to feed *Naṭa, Bhaṭa, Nagna* (nacked), *Bhagna,* (disappointed), *Kanthaka, Gāyaka, Hīna* (poor), *Dīna, Kapartika, Jaṭādhara* (ascetic), *Dvija* (brāhmaṇa), *Digambara* (Jaina), *Tarkkiga* (logician). Even his wife was untiring in feeding such people.

An ascetic (*purōhita*) of this temple was Chāvaṇṇa[26] who has been described for his chaste character thus –

Pasidara mukha-nōḍa pusīnuḍiya para-vanitey-oldu bandaḍam muṭṭa Śrī-Sōmanātha-dēvara-dāsa Pulikarada sutvaram-Chāvaṇṇa

In tune with their masters, the Chālukyas of Kalyāṇa, the Goa Kadambas also sponsored and patronized the Śaiva religion, which was very prominent in the period and the region concerned. A number of inscriptions of these chiefs refer to several grants made to the Śaiva temples, some of which were constructed by themselves or their officers. They claim that they were favoured by Saptakōtīśvaradēva. Kings like Shashṭa II were ardent followers of the God Sōmanātha of Saurashṭra. Gūhaladēva of this family is reported to have gone on a pilgrimage to Saurāshṭra for the worship of the deity.[27] Jayakēśi II is said to have donated the village Kanakūr to the temple of this deity in Saurāshṭra on the occasion of his marriage.[28] Their devotion to god Śiva is well illustrated by Permāḍi, who bore the title Śivachitta. There are examples of several officers and subordinates who made sumptuous grants to the Śiva temples. Several inscriptions mention the existence of Śaiva temples in many places. The Kāmadhēnu inscription of Permāḍi[29] mentioned above, refers to the temple of Sōmanātha in that place. Similarly, there were Śiva temples in places like Tambūru,[30] Dārawaḍa,[31] Mandūra,[32] Siddāpura,[33] Amminabhavi,[34] Avaṛādi,[35] Narendra,[36] Managundi,[37] etc., under different names like Permēśvara, Kalidēvaswami, Panchalingēśvara, Mallikārjuna, Chaṭṭeśvara, Śankaradēva, Tribhuvana Vīra Jayakēśidēva also called Siddēśvara and so on.

Most of these temples were headed by śaiva saints of the Kāḷamukha Lākulīśa sect. These ascetics are highly eulogized as learned scholars and followers of serene life.

An interesting feature about the Goa Kadamba rulers is their devotion to the god Kapilasiddha Mallikārjuna of Sonnalige which was situated far beyond the territorial limits of the Goa Kadambas. Two inscriptions of Chaṭṭayadēva of the family, one dated 1257 A.D.[38] and another from Koṭṭagi in Dharwad district dated 1264 A.D.[39] which refer to the above are worth mentioning here. The former comes from Budarasingi in Hubli taluk, Dharwad district. It contains the *vachanas* of Siddharāma figuring in other inscriptions also. It records that Chaṭṭayadēva made a gift of village Uchchangi for the worship of the god Mallikārjuna of Sonnalige and for other purposes like *nithya hōma* (i.e., offering oblations to god every day), *āvāsa-chhātra* (i.e., meant for the maintenance of the students in the temple) and for the maintenance of *Ashṭa-shashṭhi-tīrtha-siddha-taṭāka.* It is well known that the temple of Mallikārjuna was constructed by the famous *Vīraśaiva* saint Siddharāma at Sonnalige (Sholapur). It is also well known that he excavated a tank in that place, which is referred to in the present inscription as *Ashṭa-shashṭhi-tīrtha-siddha-taṭāka,* that means the holy tank with sixty-eight *tīrthas.* The inscription dated 1264 A.D. from Koṭṭagi, which is damaged, records a grant to this very temple. The details, however, are lost. The fact to be noted here is that the Kadamba rulers were attracted by this holy place and even went there on pilgrimage.

VAIṢNAVISM

Comparatively speking, references to Vaiṣṇava temples in the Kadamba inscriptions are not many. But there are evidences to show that Vaiṣṇavism also did flourish in this regime. Just as Permādidēva called himself Śivachitta i.e., his mind intent on Śiva, his brother Vijayaditya called himself Vishṇuchitta.

Inscriptions show that there was a Visṇu temple in Tambur and the deity was known as Nārāyaṇadēva.[40] Halasi was a famous Vaiṣṇava centre with the temple of Naṛasiṁha. This deity is said to have been installed by a saint called Matayōgi or Matēsa,[41] obviously during the time of Śivachitta-vīra-Permāḍi. The inscription in this place, in the famous temple of Naṛasiṁha, is a composite record containing the records of both Śivachitta-vīra-Permāḍi and his brother Vishṇuchitta Vijayāditya. The first record says that Śivachitta-vīra-Permāḍi made a grant of the village Sindavaḷḷi in Kāḷagiri Kaṁpaṇa of Panasi-deśa. The grant was made over to Maṭayōgi, who constructed the temple. The second inscription records the grant of the village Bhalikā in the same *Kaṁpaṇa* in Panasi-dēśa. The first record is dated 1169 A.D. and the other is dated 1172 A.D.

The most prominent Vaiṣṇava centre in this period was Dēgāve, which housed the temples of Vishṇu called Kamala-Nārāyaṇa and also Śri Mahalakshmi.[42] It was constructed by Kamalādēvi, the chief queen of Śivachitta-vīra-Permāḍidēva. This indicates that encouragement was given to Vaishnavism during the rule of the Kadambas of Goa.

ISLAM

The Panjim plates of Jayakēśi-I[43] mention a family which hailed from Tājiya Vishaya or Arab lineage who appears to have come from Vaimūlyapura, the identity of which has not been established. The name of the first known person of this family was Aliyama, son of Madhumada i.e., Mohammad. His son was Sadano, who appears to have been in service of Jayakēśi-I. The inscription states that a village called Laghu-Morambika[44] was granted to this Sadano or Chhadama, by Jayakēśi-I. Obviously, these were Arab traders, some of whom settled in the Goa region. It is interesting to note that the grants of certain taxes made to the mosque at Gōpaka established by his minister Chhadama, for its maintenance, is mentioned in the grant of Jayakēśi-I dated 1073 A.D.[45] This indicates that patronage was given to Islamic religion also.

REFERENCES AND NOTES

1. *EC.*,VII, Sb.
2. *SII.*, XI, (I), No.78.
3. *Ibid.*
4. *Ibid.*, No.177.
5. *Ibid.*, XV, No.225.
6. Un-published.
7. *EI.*, XXXVII, pp.307 ff.
8. From personal collection.
9. *EI.*, XXXIX, pp.62 ff.
10. Un-published.
11. From personal collection.
12. *Ibid.*,

    dhareyoḷe saṁda Kuṟumba-sēṇiga-samūhaṁ bhaktiyiṁ
    Jaina-Mandiramaṁ Māḍisal-akkuṁ-eṁdu pirid-
    ōtsāhadiṁ pūṇdu nirbharadiṁ vistaraṁ-āgi-chelv-eseye
    puṇya-puṁjam-ādante Bhāsura-vijhyāti-pogaḷd-urrvere
    Jinēndr-āvāsamaṁ māḍidar
13. *Ibid.*
14. From personal collection.
15. Un-published.
16. *KI.*, V, No.33.
17. *Ibid.*, No.68.
18. Un-published.
19. *SII.*, XV, No.610.
20. Un-published.

21. From personal collection.
22. *Ibid.*
23. *SII.*, XX, No.101 (1129 A.D.).
    Sāsalim-tenkaṇa-deseyali bandu nelesiye nindaṁ Śankara Svayambhuv-enisida kuṁkuma-lōlam Kāpāli Kalidēvēśa ||
24. *Ibid.*, No.252 (1171 A.D.).
25. *Ibid.*, No.101.
26. *Ibid.*, No.252.
27. *KK.*, p.171.
28. *SII.*, XI (II), No.154.
29. *Ibid.*, XX, No.252.
30. From personal collection.
31. *KI.*, V, No.16.
32. *SII.*, XV, No.16.
33. *Ibid.*, No. 229 (1158 A.D.).
34. *Ibid.*, XI (II), No.191.
35. Un-published.
36. *EI.*, XIII, pp.316 ff.
37. *SII.*, XV, No.233.
38. *EI.*,XXXVI, pp.164 ff.
39. *SII.*, XV, No.195.
40. From personal collection.
41. *KI.*,V, No.63.
42. *JBBRAS.*, IX, p.294.
43. *KK.*, App.III, No.2.
44. *Ibid.*
45. *GG.*, P.102.

CHAPTER - X

CONCLUSION

It is interesting to note that the Kadamba family was first established by Mayūraśrma as early as in the fourth century A.D. with Banavāsi as the capital. The kingdom flourished as the first sovereign kingdom to be established on the Kannada soil. It received a severe set back when the Chalukyas of Bādāmi rose to power. It appears that his family split itself into several branches and the rulers of these branches were governing different regions. The Chālukya inscriptions claim, therefore, that the Chalukya king had to conquer different families of the Kadambas (*Kadamba-Kādaṁbakaṁ*). Though beaten, the family was not wiped off. Though they were technically displaced from the original capital Banavāsi, they continued to bear the title *Banavāsi-puravarādhīśvara.* They were dormant during the days of the Rāshṭrakūṭas. But, gradually, they raised their head during the time of the next rulers viz., the Chālukyas of Kalyāṇa. Among the different branches of the family, which became more prominent, one was the Kadambas of Hāngal and another the Kadambas of

Goa. Those of Hāngal had their capital at Hāngal, now, a small taluka place in Hāveri district of Karnataka State. They ruled over the Banavāsi region in which the Hāngal territory was situated. The other family as we know, ruled over the coastal region and were called *Konkaṇa Chakravarti* and ruled over the vast region of Halasagi, adjascent to the coast. Both the families accepted the suzerainty of the Chālukyas of Kalyāṇa and both enthusiastically supported their overlords. This enhanced their prestige and they occupied a permanent position and enjoyed a prestigious status in the Chālukyan court. We have seen above that the Chālukyan masters honoured their trusted chiefs and even sought matrimonial alliance with them.

Being absolute masters of their territory, they contributed most to the well being of the people of the territory by their good governance and brought peace and plenty to the region. By issuing large number of inscriptions, they contributed to the development of the Kannada language and literature. Their inscriptions, which are written in beautiful Kannada hand have also helped the development of Kannada script. They sponsored all the native religions like Buddhism and Jainism along with Śaivism and Vaishṇavism. They built several temples, which contributed simultaneously to the growth of religion and the growth of architecture and sculpture. They built tanks, which promoted agriculture and the basic facilities of the people. Thus, they contributed to the overall growth of the region which they governed.

Appendix

Select Inscriptions of The Kadambas of Goa

APPENDIX

I

Mavalli, Kalghatgi Taluk, Dharwad District
Ist pillar erected in the field of Hanumantappa Irappa Walikar

Rāshtrakūṭa Gōvinda-IV – 931 A.D.

The record is dated Śaka 853, Nandana, which is equated to 931 A.D. The record is fragmentary. It refers to the rule of Goṇḍarāja Vallabha, who on the basis of the date to be identified with Rāshtrakūṭa Govinda-IV. It also mentions Kanaha Maharāja as the governor of Palasige-12000. The village Kerewada in Tammiyūr is also mentioned in the record.

Text

1. Svasti Śrī prithvī-vallabha mahārājādirā [ja] paramēśvara Gondara vallabha pri...
2. vi rājya geye | Śrī mat-Palasige pannir-chchāsira ma Kaṇṇaha mahārāja rājyaṁ-ge..
3. Śaka-nripa-kālātīta sataṅgaḷ eṁṭunūṟa-ayvatta-mūraneya-Nandanam-eṁba Saṁvatsara
4. pravarttise Tammavurada paḷḷi Keṟavadaṁ.. ma na [o] ṇiga niṟindo

II

Sedambi, Kaḷaghatagi Taluk, Dharwad district
Slab lying outside the temple of Kalmēśvara

Jayakēśi I : 1062-63 A.D.

The record is dated Śaka 984, *subhakṛit, Pushya, Su.5, Guruvāra, Uttarāyaṇa Sankrānti,* equated to A.D.1062. *Subhakrit,* December 9, Monday. The cyclic year was *Shobhana.*

It refers to the rule of Jayakēśi of the Kadamba family, as ruling from his capital Anilāpura. It records a grant of land made by the ūroḍeya of Tammiyūr named Jayadēvayya for the worship and offerings to God Mūlasthānadēva, built by Indeya Holleya who belonged to the *Okkalu* of Sēḍimba in Tammiyur region. It also refers to the grant of *mudrāpaṇa* to the deity by *Mummuridaṇḍa* and *Aravattokkalu* of the place.

Text

1. *Svasti samadhigata paṁcha-mahā-śabda mahāmaṇḍḷēśvaraṁ Banavāsi pu-
2. ravarādhīśvara Trilōchana Kadamba-kuḷa-kamaḷinī-vikāsi bhāskaran || anēka
3. samara vijayō-pārjitaṁ Vīra-Śrīnivāsaṁ dakshiṇadōrddaṇḍa malege mārttaṇḍa
4. n-ubhayabaḷa-gaṇḍa mukha-darppaṇ-āyud-āchāryyan-aparimita śauryyaṁ
5. Kādaṁba kūrmma Kūrmmāvatāra śaraṇāgatā vajra-panjara kīrtti-mārttaṇḍa mū-
6. rtti-Nārāyaṇa maṇḍḷika lalāṭa-paṭṭa vairi-gharaṭṭa subhaṭa rāja-lakshmī-

7. ty-akhiḷa-rājāvaḷi-samāḷaṁkritar-appa śrī maj-Jayakēśidēvar-nnija rājadhā-
8. niy-Anilāpuradoḷ sukha saṁkathā vinōdadind-uttarōttar-ābhivriddhi
9. pravarddhamānam-ā-chandrārkka-tāraṁbaraṁ vijaya-rājya[o] saluttaṁ-ire ||svasti||
10. samasta bhuvana jana-vandya Kamaḷajāśva vaṁśōdbhava chatur-vvōpādhi-ka
11. ḷā-pariṇata dharāmara nivaha pari-rakshaṇa dakshiṇa-dōrddaṇḍa kadana pracha-
12. ṇḍa vibudha-jana vanaja vana-haṁsa Sarasvatī-karṇāvataṁśa niśita diggaja-gha
13. ṭā parivartita dhavaḷa yaśō viḷāsinī kucha-yuga-hāra | vairi-saṁhāra
14. sukavi-jana-kalpavriksha | sujana-Jana-kārya-daksha | sakaḷa-kaḷā-pravī
15. ṇa saraṇāgatā-jana-trāṇa vairi-subhaṭa paṇṇāga Vainatēya | satya
16. rādhēya chatura-chārāyaṇa Tāṭaka-Nārāyaṇa Kaliyuga-Vi
17. kramāditya tandeya-gandha-vāraṇa nāmādi samasta praśasti sahitaṁ
18. śrīmat Tammiy-Ūrōdeya Jayadēvayyaṁgaḷ Śaka-nirpa-kālā
19. tīta saṁvatsara śataṁgaḷ 984 neya Subhakritya saṁvatsa
20. rada Pauśya śudha 5 Guruvāradand-uttarāyaṇa Saṁkrāntiy-andu
21. Tammiyūra-Kālpaḷḷi Sēḍimbige okkala-magan-Indeya-Holleyamaṁ
22. māḍisida dēgulakke Kongiya-kuṇṭeya Guṇigana eraḍu-ma
23. ttar-gaddeya dēvara nivēdyake biṭṭar-idan-āvan-ōrvan-aḷida Bāna

24. rāsi Kurukshētra Prayāgeyoḷ sāsira-kavileyaṁ sāsira-brāhma
25. ṇaraṇ-aḷida dōsa | Svarang-ati bhakta Sōmēśvara dāsi Hollimayya-Chandrā
26. si-jīyarige sthānavaṁ koṭa (ṭṭa) || Sāmānyōyaṁ dharmm, a-sētu nripāṇāṁ
27. kāle kāle- pālaniyō bhavadbhiḥ sarvva-nētān-bhāvinaḥ pārthivēndrān
28. bhūyo bhūyō yāchatē Rāmachandraḥ || Śrī Mūla-stāna
29. dēvargge Mummuri-daṇḍa Aṟuvattokkala-makkaḷu sahitav-āgi vichāra...
30. .....mudrā-paṇavaṁ sarvva-namasyav-āgi koṭṭaru || dēvara.....
31. .... keya mane ||

III

Sangamēśvara, Kalghatgi taluk, Dharwad district
Engraved on central bay of *Sabhā-maṇṭapa* of Sangamēśvara temple

Jayakēśi I - 1069 A.D.

The inscription refers itself to the rule of Jayakēśi-I, who was ruling over Konkaṇa-900 and Hanasige-12000. It mentions Baḷḷagāvuṇḍa, a Lenka or a servant of the king, who made a grant of two *mattar* of land for the worship and offerings to god on the date specified.

The given date in the record is *Śaka* 991, *Kīlaka, Samkrānti*, equated to 1069 A.D. The other details are insufficient for equation.

Text

1. @ Svasti-samadhigata paṁcha-mahā-sabda-mahā-maṇḍalēśvaraṁ Banavāsi Puravarēśvara-ajjādēvi labda-vara prasāda Kādaṁba kuḷa-tiḷakaṁ-tyāga-jaga-jhaṁpa Jhaṁpaḷārya male-
2. ge mārttaṇḍaṁ śrīmat **Jayakēsidēvar Hanasige-pannichchāsiramuṁ Konkanad-oṁbhai-nūṟumaṁ** suka-sankhatā-vinōdadiṁ-dushṭha-nigraha sishṭha prati-pāḷana
3. māḍiy-āḷuttamire @ Svasti samasta-guṇa-saṃpannar vinaya saṁpannar-Kaliyuga-Karṇa para-vadhū putraṁ gōtra-pavitraṁ Achaṭana-putraṁ . de giṟe-mallaṁ pusi-ilad-ātaṁ prajege-nallātaṁ śrimatu... Ha
4. ḷḷa-gāmaṇḍa ātana-tammam Sānta-gāmaṇḍaṁ para-nārī-dūraṁ gōtra-pavitram Sōmēsvara-dāsi Hoḷḷāgāmaṇḍana putraṁ Sānta-gāmaṇḍana aṇugaṁ śrī-matu Jayakēśi-dēvara leṁka Chaṭṭa-gāma-
5. ṇḍaṁ **Saka-varsha 991 neya Kīlaka-saṃvatsarada Sankrānti-andu** Baḷḷigaṭṭina keṟeya-keḷage Guṇigana eraḍu matta keyaṁ dēvararchana-nivēdyake-biṭṭam

IV

Sangamēśvara, Kalghatgi taluk, Dharwad district
On the central beam of the *Sabhā-maṇṭapa* of Sangamēśvara temple

Jayakēśi I - 1069 A.D.

The record is dated *Śaka* 991, *Kīlaka, Bhādrapada, Shashṭhi, Tuesday*, equated to 1069 A.D. August 25. *Tuesday*.

It refers to the grant of paddy land jointly made by Chaṭṭa-gāvuṇḍa and Haḷḷa-gāvuṇḍa to Śiva temple, constructed by Śānta-gāvuṇḍa, for the worship and offerings to the same deity.

Text

1. **Saka-varusha 991 neya Kīlaka-saṁvatsarada Shashṭhi-Mangalavārad-aṇdu** Māvaḷi-nāḍoḷagaṇa Kūḍala Achatta-gāmaṇḍana putraṁ Dēvageṟe Mallaṁ pusiyiladāta nuḍidu- matt-e. kiṟiya…
2. nna kīḷegeyde kūrppaṁ sujanaika-mitraṁ tandeya-gandha-vāraṇa aṇṇana-siṁga-baṁtara bova prajege-nallāta-śrimat Kūḍala Haḷḷagā-maudana tamma Mārasinga-gāṁaṇḍan-ātaniṁ kiṟiya Śiva-dharmmanemma
3. gōtra-pavitra siva-pāda paṁkaja-bhrāmaran-āhāra-dāni ekkōtiya-torttu….devara sishya Śāntagāmaṇḍanu māḍisida Sivālayake śrimat-Jayakēśi dēvara leṁka Chaṭṭi-gā-
4. maṇḍanu Haḷḷagāmaṇḍanuṁ-iḷdu dēvar-archana-nivēdyake biṭṭa bhūmi Baḷḷi-gaṭṭina-keṟeya-keḷage Guṇigana matta-gaḷde 1 khaṇḍuga bījada haḷalaṁ biṭṭa @ Idan-aḷidaṁ Baṇarāsiyalu-sāsira-kavi

5. leya sāsira Tapōdhanaran-aḷida pātaka || mattaṁ temkaṇa Mūlasthāna-dēvara nitya nivēdyake Baḷli-goḷada kẹlage biṭṭa gaḻdeya matta 2 ḍarkke sarva-bādā-parihāra @@

V

Nūlvi, Hubli taluk, Dharwad District
Engraved on a slab set up near the village in survey No.217

Shashṭha II and Jayakēśi I - 1073 A.D.

The record refers itself to the rule of Shashṭha-dēva over Konkaṇa-900. There is reference to the rule of Jayakēśi and Boppādēvi over Konkaṇa-900, Halasige-12000, Kundūru-500, Sabbi-30 from the capital Gōve. It mentions to the twelve-*gāvuṇḍas* and *aravattokkalu* of Nūle who appears to have made grant of wet-land, betel-nut, betel-leaves, income from taxes to an *āchārya* (name lost) of the temple (name lost) .

There are four dates given in the record [1] *Śaka* 994, *Paridhāvi, Pushya, śu.* 8, Monday. *Uttarāyana Sankranti,* corresponding to 1073 A.D. January 4, which was Friday. *Sankrānti* did not occur on that day. [2] *Visvāvasu, Āshadha, ba. Amavase,* Sunday, Solar eclipse, equated to Solar year was probably *Saka* 987, in that year the tithi can be equated with 1065 A.D., July 6, which was Wednesday. There was no eclipse on that day. [3] 14th regnal year year of Śivachitta Vīra Jayakēśi, *Raudra, Phalguṇa, śu. Punnami, Sōmavāra* corresponding to 1064 A.D. *Krodin,* February 23, Wednesday, Puṇṇami. [4] 12th regnal year of Śrī Kādamba Śivachitta

1. 'Ka' is written in small script between 'da' and 'do' on the top

Vīra Tribhuvanamalla, *Hēmalambi, Aśvayuja, Amavāse, Sōmavāra* equivalent to 1238 A.D.

Grant of land by Appana daṇḍanāyaka at the instance of a ruler for the worship of god Sakalēśvaradēva, and grant of vegetables (specified) to be made by the *Tōṇtigas* of the place, for the daily offerings to the deity is mentioned. The record also refers to twelve *gavuṇḍas* and *aravattokkalu* of the place who made grants (not specified) to one Dēvarāśi Pandita. The other details are not available.

Text

1. * Namas-tunga śiras-chuṁbi chandra-chāmara chāravē Trailōkya-nagar-āramcha [bha] mūla stambhāya
2. Śaṁbhavē || Svasti samasta praśasti-sahitaṁ śrī-prithvī-vallabhaṁ rājādhirāja paramēśvara parama-bhaṭṭārakaṁ Satyāsra-
3. ya kuḷa-tiḷakaṁ Chāḷuky-ābharaṇaṁ śri mad-Bhuvanaikamalla dēva-vijaya rājyaṁ-uttar-ōttar-ābhivriddhi-pravarddha
4. mānam-ā-chandrārka-tāraṁ [baraṁ] salutaṁire || Samadhigata paṁcha-mahā-śabda mahāmaṇḍaḷēśvaraṁ Banavā-
5. sī puravar-ādhiśvaraṁ samasta bhuvana saṁsthūya-māna Hara-Dharaṇī-prasūta Trilōchana-Kadaṁba-vaṁśa
6. mahōdaya-mahī-dharēndra-śikhar-ābhyudaya mānaṁ mahā-prachaṇḍa-mārttaṇḍa karāti tībra nija pra-

7. tāpa vaśīkrita sakaḷa-mahī-maṇḍaḷanuttuṁga simha-lānchchanaṁ Vānara-mahā-dhvajaṁ Permạ=ḍi (ṭṭi) tūrya nirghō-
8. shaṇaṁ Tyāga-jaga jhaṁpaṇ-āchāryya śaraṇāgata vajra-prākāraṁ saṁkrānti-dhavaḷaṁ mūrtti-Nā-
9. rāyaṇaṁ kīrtti-mārttaṁḍa maṇḍalika-lalāṭa-paṭṭā śrīmad-**Chaṭaya dēvarasaru Koṁkaṇa-900** man-āḷdu su
10. khadiṁ rājyaṁ geyuttaṁ-ire ||@ tat= putra samadhigata-paṁcha-mahāśabda mahāmaṇḍaḷēśvaraṁ Banavāsi
11. puravar-ādhīśvaraṁ Triḷōchana Kadamba-kuḷa-kamaḷinī vikāsī-bhāskaran-anēka samara-Vijayōpārjjita-vīrā-Śrī
12. nivāsa dakshiṇa dōrddaṇḍa pagevaran-erbbaṭṭi-gaṇḍa mūrtti-Nārāyaṇaṁ kīrtti-mārttaṇḍa maṇḍalika lalā-
13. ṭa-paṭṭa śrīmaj-**Jayakēśi dēvarasaruṁ Boppādeviyaruṁ Koṁkaṇa-900 Halasige-12000 Kundūra-500**
14. **Sabbi-mūvattuman**-āḷdu nija **rājadhāni Gōveyoḷu** sukha-sankathā-vinōdadiṁ rājyaṁ-geyyu-
15. ttaṁ-ire || Kuntaḷa vishayada raṁjita kāntā-niṭaḷakke tiḷakaṁ-enisida nādatyunnata Halasigeya-
16. yadaṛada... ti... noḷa-koṇḍu Nūle-sogayisi tōrkkuṁ || ant...... nū-Beḷavalada sale-sī-maḍal-enisi
17. baḷasidupa-vanadiṁđaṁ .... vati-viḷasita me........ chelvan-āvarisikkuṁ || ant-enisida Nū-
18. leya Hannirbbar-gāvuṇḍugaḷuṁ sukhadind-ire maṛeguvarige vajradoḷ-paṁjaravārtti janakke beḷpudaṁ

19. salisuv-udārām-uddatahitolige kāḷa-kritāntan-endoḍe........ Paschima... ḷeya

20. hanneraḍaṁ prabhu........ gaḷ-peraraḷave......... raṁ || @ Kiṟikataṁ.....

21. modal-alli tāṁ-bagedu mūṟuṁ lōkamaṁ ....gi madhya ....

22. .... utpr̄ekshisi māḍidan ...... janarkkaḷā.... ṟuvatt-okkalan-ene

23. doḍe vogaḷpudu peṁpaṁ dharā-chakradoḷ || Svasti-yama-niyama-svādhyāya dhyāna-dhāraṇa

24. mō (mau)nānushṭhāṇa-japa-samādhi sīḷaguṇa saṁpannar-appa śrī-ma .... dēvar-āchāryya

25. Sōma .... varige hannirbbaruṁ aṟuvattokka......... **Śaka varshaṁ 994 ne**

26. **ya Paridhāvi saṁvatsarda [Pu]shya Śuddha 8 [Sō] mavār-Uttarāyaṇa saṁkramaṇadoḷu** neredu kā

27. laṁ-toḷedū dhārā-pūrvvakaṁ māḍi-koṭṭa dānav-ent-endeḍe || mūḍa ....

28. .. aḍake-dōṁtamgaḷoḷu aḍakeya[1] kone-vondu ho/ deya.... kuṁḍu Chaitradal-ele-nūṟu-paivi-

29. tradal-ele nūṟu yint-ini... koṭṭa-dānavaṁ ā-Chandrārkka Tāraṁ-baraṁ saluttam-irppa.... ravadoḷ-āḷgaṁ ||

30. @ Svasti śrī **Kādaṁba Śivachitta Vīra-Prmmaḍidēvarasara Vijayāditya-dēvara** [sa] .... **Viśvāvasu**

31. **saṁvatsarada Āśāḍha Bahuḷa Amavāse Ādivāra Sūryya-grahaṇad**-andu śrīma-

32. d-arasara besadiṁ Appaṇa daṇḍa-nāyakaruṁ hannirvvr-mukhyar-āgi [Śa]kaḷēśvar-āryyargge dhāra-

33. pūrvvakaṁ māḍi koṭṭa keyya-sthaḷam-ent-endaḍe || Hindavaḷan-oḷage gāḍi [ya] keṟeyiṁ baḍa

34. gaṇa kōḍiyiṁ paḍuvalu gadde-hakkalu-kamma 250 || adarinda mūḍala koṁkaṇa hakkaliṁ puḍuva

35. lu-gadde-hakkalu kamma 250 akkasāliya-maneyiṁ-mūḍalu rājahasta 15 agala-hastā -1 mane ||

36. @ Svasti śrī **Kādamba Śivachitta-Vīra-Jayakēsi-dēva-varshada 14 Raudri-Saṁvatsarada Phālguṇa-Śuddha-puṇṇami**

37. **Sōmavāra**.................

38. ...... dhārā-pūrvvakaṁ māḍi-koṭṭa || bāḍukāya-tōṇṭdoḷu saute-kāyi 5 badane-kāyi-5 hīrekāi 5 maṁ

39 -dinaṁprati nivēdyakke Tōṇitigaru koṭṭaru || yint-initu vrittiyuṁ sarva-namasya || yinti-ī dharmmamanāvaṁ prati-pāli

40. sidan-ātaṁ vāraṇāsiyoḷu gō-sahasrama-brāhmaṇage koṭṭa-phaḷa 1 yī-dharma-maṁ kiḍisidavaṇ-ananta-kōṭi varshaṁ Kuṁ-

41. bhī-pākadoḷ birddu ghōra dukhaman-unaga ||* **Svasti śrī Kādamba śri Śivachittā Vīra-Tribhuvanamalla-dēva**

42. **varieśada 12 neya Hēmalaṁbi saṃvatsarad-Āśvayujad amāvase Sōmavārad**-aṁdu haṁnnirvvar-ggā

43. vuṇḍugaḷu aṟuvatt-okkala-makkaḷuṁ **Dēvarāsi-dēvargge** dhārā-pūrvvakaṁ-māḍi-koṭṭaru ||

The imprecatory verses are found written 5-6 lines after this line

VI

Tambur, Kalghatgi taluk, Dharwad district
Found in the forest area called *Doddakeremaḍḍi*

Gūvaladēva - 1077 A.D.

It is a damaged record. It refers to a *mahāmaṇḍaḷēśvara* (name lost), who was ruling over Palasige-12000. A *daṇḍanayaka* named Jayadēvayya finds a reference in this record as administering Tammiyūru and twelve villages.

Dandanāyaka Mādirājayya is also mentioned in the record. There is a reference to 18th Chālukya Vikrama *Kāla* and also certain grants. But the details are not obtainable as the record is damaged.

It is dated Śaka 999, *Ānanda, śu. Uttarāyaṇa Sankranti, Vyatīpa*ta corresponding to 1077 A.D. The details are insufficient for equation.

Text

I – Panel

1. Namastunga śiraschuṁbi-chandra-chāmara-chāravē Trailōkya- nagarārambha mūḷa sthaṁbhāya-
2. śambhavē ||

II – Panel

3. @Svasti-samasta-bhuvan-āśraya śrī prithvī-vallabha mahārājādhirāja paramēśvara paramabhaṭṭāraka ssa
4. tyāśraya kuḷa-kiḷakaṁ Chālukya-ābharaṇaṁ **śrī ma-Tribhuvana-malla-dēvara** vijaya-rājyam-uttar-ōttar-ābhi-vriddhi pravardha

5. ṁānam-āchandrārkka-taraṁbaraṁ saluttaṁ-ire tat-pāda padmōpajīvi samadhigata paṁcha-mahāśabda
6. mahā-maṇḍaḷēshaṁ nahitamaṇḍaḷika madana-māhēśvara nija kuḷa-tiḷaka kuvaḷaya sudhārita-vinaya....
7. ratnākara.... su-maṇḍaḷika teṟeya kara-pattala ninava chārudattan-udbha guṇa nutaṁ......
8. ṇḍaḷika... yana dēva maṟivurge kāva vishama-turag-ārūḍha prauḍha-dēva-tamna-hita śrī
9. Śrī Mallikārjuna-dēva labdha vara-prāsādan-ubhaya..... baraṇ-āchāryan-achaḷa tadādhairya
10. na Mala-dēva pesaṇa-garuḍa nāmādi samasta prasasti sahitaṁ śrīman-mahāmaṇḍaḷēśvara dē....
11. varasanu **Palasige-pannichhāsiramaṁ dushṭha**-nigraha śishṭha prati-pāḷaneyiṁ sukhadind-āluttam-ire ||.....
12. ta pañcha-mahā-śabda mahā-prachṇda daṇḍa-nāyaka vidvajjanō phaḷadāyaka sarusa.....
13. hā-samasta... nyasa nija-nisita kau. ya kavigaḷo-muktā phaḷālaṁkrita vijaya śrī ka.....
14. paratu Jīmutavāhana atyanta bhuja-baḷāvaḷe prodipta vidvishṣtha mahā... khivisiko....
15. mayā-rudraṁ paḷāhādaridra kaḷi maḷakaḷaṁka pakaṁtita durābharṇa [birabata.....]
16. ḷa guṇā-gaṇa ..... gha akaḷankānēka mēgha Kādaṁba Kuḷa-Kamaḷa-mārthaṇḍa śrī.....
17. Charaṇāravinda śadvatanādi tīrthajana muddharaṇa nityakhiḷa-nāmābhi.....
18. prachaṇḍa-daṇḍanāyakaṁ Jayadēvayya Tammiyūru-ma Panneraḍu......
19. prabhu sāmyadoḷu sukhadind-āḷuttam-ire || Samadhigata pañcha.....
20. śrīmatu **Gūhaladēvana** Vijaya-rājyadoḷu śrimatu.....

21. ka Jayadēvayya **Saka varsha 999 neya Ānanda-saṁvatsara....**
22. **rāyaṇa Śankrānti vyatī-pātam**-āge tatu puṇyādhi ni......
23. ā dēvarggeṟeya keḷage śatra-śāleya tōṇṭada pū.....
24. .....Shattugaṇa kōlalu mattalu eraḍu Svasti-ya.....
25. shaṇa japa-samādhi sīḷa sampannar-appa śrī-ma.......
26. sarvva-namasya sarvābādha pariahāramāgi cha....
27. pañcha-mahāśabda mahā-prachaṇḍa daṇḍa-nā.....
28. ..... Mādirājayya ta..... ya.....
29. **Chālukya Vikrama-kālada 18 neya ga......**
30. .... ṇa māgi ma..........
31. .... navada. holaga. bhōga
32. .... bigaralte paṇa po ......
33. .... laṇaya a..........

Broken

VII

Mukkal, Kalghatgi taluk,Dharwad district
Slab set up at the entrance of the Rāmalingēśvara temple

Gūvaladēva III – 1078-79 A.D.

It refers to the rule of the *mahāmaṇḍalēśvara* Gūvaladēva over Konkaṇa-900 and Palasige-12000, and also to the rule of Śāntivarmadēva who was in charge of Hānumgal-500, Kontakuḷi-30. The record refers to grant of land for the worship, offerings and renovation of Barmēśvaradēva temple constructed by Barmadēvayya of Pannasōge after laving the feet of Nirvāṇaśaktijīya, on 1st year of *Chālukya Vikrama Kāla, Śiddharthi, Pushya su....* Corresponding to 1076 A.D. In the absence of *tithi* the exact equation cannot be given.

It also refers to Bīrayyadēva son of S`āntivarma who made grants for supply of food and clothing of ascetics in the temple of Barmēśvaradēva after laving the feet of Nirvāṇaśaktijīya of Pannasōge. This instance appears in the 7th year of *Chalukya-Vikrama-kāla,dundubhi, Uttarāyana Sankranti,* corresponding to 1083 A.D. In the absence of *tithi* the exact equation cannot be given.

Text

1. Namaśtuṅga-śiraschuṁbi chandra-chāmara-chāravē-Traiḷōkya nagar-āraṁba [mūla-stam]
2. bhāya śaṁbhave || Svasti samasta bhuvan-āśraya srī prithvī-vallabha ma [hā-rājādhirāja-paramēśvaraṁ parama bhaṭṭārakaṁ]

3. Satyāśraya kuḷa-tiḷakaṁ Chāḷuky-ābhaṇaṁ Śrīmat-**Tribhuvanamalla-dēvara** vijaya-rājyam-uttar-ōttar-ābhivriddhi pravarddha
4. [māna]ṁ-āchandr-ārkka-tāraṁbaraṁ-saluttam-ire-samadhigata paṁcha-mahā-śabda-mahāmaṇḍaḷeśvaram [**Banavāsīpura**-varā-
5. dhīśvaraṁ samasta bhuvana-saṁsthūyamāna hara-dharaṇī prasūtaṁ Triḷōchana-Kadamba-vaṁsa mahōdayaṁ saka-
6. [ḷa-mahi-] maṇḍaḷan-uttuṅga Siṁha-lānchhana Vānara mahā-dhvajaṁ chaturā-sīti nagar-ādhishṭhitān-ashṭhādaś-āśvamēdha dīkshā
7. [dīkshita] kuḷa-prasūta himavad-girīndra rundra śikhara saṁsthāpita mahā śakti prabhāvaṁ tyāga-jaga jhampa-ḷāryaṁ ni
8. [śśaṁka] rāma subhaṭa-kanaka nikaśōpaḷaṁ saraṇāgata-vajra-prākārā lōkaika kaḷpadrumaṁ saṅkrānti-dhavaḷa-mū
9. rtti-Nārāyaṇa kīrtti mārttaṇḍa maṇḍlika lalāṭa-paṭṭa subhaṭa-rāja śikhāmaṇi-ty akhila-rājāvḷi-samāḷaṁ-kritar-appa
10. śrī-man-mahā maṇḍalēśvaraṁ **Gūvaladēvarasaru Koṁkaṇa-voṁbhainūrumaṁ Palasige-pannirchchhāsira mumaṁ**-sukha- saṁkathā-vinōdadiṁ
11. rājyaṁ geyyuttam-ire || Samadhigata paṁcha-mahā-śabda-mahā-maṇḍaḷēśvaraṁ Banavasī-puravar-ādhiśvaraṁ Triyaksha-kshmā-saṁ
12. bhavaṁ Chaturāsīti nagar-ādhishṭhitā lalāṭa lōchana chaturbhujaṁ Jagad-vidhit-ashṭhādaś-āśvamēdha dīkshitaṁ Himavad-girīndra-rundra

13. [śi]khara-śakti-saṃsthāpita sphaṭika śiḷā-stambha baddha mada-gaja mahā-mahimāmbharāmaṁ Ḳādaṁba-chakrēśvara nāmādi-samasta pra
14. śasti sahitaṁ śrīman-mahā-maṇḍaḷēśvaraṁ **Santivarmadēvarasar Hānuṁgal-aynūṟumaṁ Kontakuḷi-mūvattumaṁ sukha saṁ**
15. kathā vinōdadiṁ rājyaṁ geyuttaṁ-ire || @ śrī Sakaḷēśanuṁ Kamala-saṁbhavanuṁ sa........ ri vāsava kinnarar-ōragaruṁaṁ kiṁnara
16. kiṁpurusharkaḷu-sura Vyāsa-munīndraruṁ Sasiyu-tāra... ulvi Vindhya-vāsiyuṁ sāsa......... neredu Barmma-gāvuṇḍana putraṁ
17. mitra .... dind-esedu māḍuge mangalam-utsava......|| .... poḍavige sale negaḷda-Hannasōgeya Barmmaṁ- Mri-
18. ḍan-ālayamaṁ-māḍisi paḍedaṁ yaśa-kīrtti-khyāti-mukti [śrīyaṁ] anti-enisi negaḷda prabhugatyantaṁ strī-ratnar-enisi-patibratā-guṇa
19. doḷ .... doreyant-appaḷ Jātikabbe-ipparb-ī-jagadoḷ || Barmmaga Jātikabbege permmaga-Chāvuṇḍa-Chāva-maḷiga-
20. n eṁba .... nūrmmaḍi migil-enisi negaḷdar-intu su-putrar || Śaraṇāgataraṁ kāvudu meradavargg-īvudu mu-
21. dāra-chāru.... niruta......... parahita chittarvvudhā .... ra..... yarbbu-pūjyar || Ishṭha jana-kaḷpa-vrikshaṁ sishṭha jan-ādhāra
22. n-ugra-vīran-udāraṁ kashṭha-jana dūra negaḷd-utkrishṭhaṁ para-nārī-sōdaraṁ Chāvuṇḍaṁ || Anavarata dāni chāvaṁ-navanī-taḷadoḷ vipra-janaka
23. vandi-janakaṁ-mamnidanta-vairi...... Manu-muni-chāritra negaḷda gōtra...... || Bhalada-chalada-kalitanada-chāgada-kulada-mahātmikeya guṇada...

24. peṁpina-Tējō-balada parākram-ārppina sale negaḻda Chāva-gāvuṇḍa [be]rppara namṭaṁ || Tōṟeyaṁ-balade-sura-nadiyaṁ keṟeyaṁbu-

25. de Harana-koraḷa hāḷa-hala-maṁ peṟeyaṁbudu-mrita kiraṇanirppa puruśannōrvvan-eṁbaram Māḷiganaṁ || Ārppa-gunaṁ nija śau-

26. ryyaṁ-dōrppa-guṇaṁ ṭannan-āsi vaṭṭavargellaṁ kūrppa-guṇaṁ upakāraṁ mārpa-gunaṁ Māḷigaṁage sahaja-guṇamgaḷ ||mattaṁ|| Surar-asu

27. [ra]rpaḷgaḍalaṁ bharavasadi kaḍedu paḍedasura-vimānada-volu dharega[va]tarisidud-eṁbaṁt-ire māḍida Bammi-seṭṭi **Barmmeśvaranaṁ** ||

28. Svasti-samasta bahujana stutva satya-vākyan-upāya Chāṇakya palarig-ādhāra paranārī-dūra gōtra Divāka-

29. raṁ Śiva-pāda-śēkara lōka-vikhyātaṁ prajege nallātaṁ nuḍidu-matt-ennaṁ vinaya-saṁpannar-appa śrīmat Pannasōge

30. ya Barmma-gāvuṇḍaṁ śrī Barmmēśvara devargge **śri Chālukya Vikrama-kāḷa 1 neya Siddhārthi saṁvatsarada Pauśya suddha...**

31. **Ādityavāram-Uttarāyaṇa Saṁkrānti vyatīpātad-andu** || **Niruvāṇa-śakti Jīyara** kāḷaṁ kārchchi dhārāpūrvva-kaṁ māḍi-dēvara-

32. nivēdyakkaṁ khaṇḍa-sphuṭita jīrṇṇōddhārakaṁ ūriṁ-mūḍaṇa keṟeya-keḷage biṭṭa gaḻde mattar-ondu || int-i-dharmmaman-āva-

33. n-ōrvva pratipālisidavargge Vāraṇāsi Kurukshēṭradoḷ sāsira-kavileya kōḍum-kaḷagumaṁ Paṁcharatnagaḷṝṁ

34. kaṭṭisi sāsirvvar-Vedāpāragar-appa brāhmaṇarg-ubhaya-mukhiya-dānaṁ-goṭṭa phaḷam-akkuṁ || Int-i-dharmaman-aḷidavanig-ā-

35. puṇya-tīrthaṁgaḷoḷ sāsira-kavileyuman-aḷida paṁcha-mahā-pātakan-akku ||
36. śrīman-mahāmaṇḍalēśvaraṁ Śāntivarmmarasara-magaṁ Bīravadēvaṁ Pannasōgeyaṁ manneya-sāmyadoḷ rājyaṁ-geyyu
37. ṭṭire || **Vikrama-kāla 7 neya Dundubhi-saṁvatsarada-uttarāȳaṇa Saṁkrāntiy-aṁdu** Bīrajadēvaṁ Pa
38. nna-sōgeya **Nirvvaṇāśakti-Jīyara** kālaṁ-karchhi dhārāpūrvvakaṁ-mādiy-alliya Siddhāyadoḷage Brahmēsvara
39. dēvargge bitta-gadyāṇa ondu | mattaṁ tapōdhanargge kappaḍak-achchuḍakke biṭṭa-gadyāna ondu || @ Sāmānyōyaṁ-dharma
40. sētuṁ nripāṇāṁ kāle kāle pālaniyōbhavadbḥi sarvva-nētān bhagi (vi)naḥ pārthivēndrān bhūyōr-bhūyō
41. ryyāchate Rāmabhadraḥ || Svadattaṁ (tām) paradattāṁ vāyō harēti Vasuṁdharām shashṭhir-vvarsha sahasrāṇi vishṭhāyāṁ
42. jāyate-krimiḥ ||

VIII

Tersikoppa, Kalghatgi taluk, Dharad district
Stone lying near the temple of Basavanna in the village

1080 A.D.

It refers to the rule of Chālukya Tribhuvanamalla and also mentions a Kadamba chief (name not mentioned) who was ruling over Konkaṇa-900 and Palasige-12000 from his capital Chandrāpu (ra).

It mentions one Mūkagāvuṇḍa and his wife Nanniyabbe and their son Māla-gāvuṇḍa who made grants of land and oil for the worship and offerings to god Kalidēva of Māḷavēśvar.

It is dated Śaka 1002, *Raudra, Jyēshṭha, Amavāse, Brihavara, Uttarāyana Sankramaṇa* equated to 1080 A.D. *Raudra* June 20th, Saturday.

Text

1. Śrī-prithvī-Vallabha mahārāja-paramēśvara parama.......
2. kyābharaṇa Śrī ma-Chālukya Vikrama Śrī Tribhuvanamalla dē....
3. pravarddhamānam-āchandrārkatārambaram saluttam-ire tat pāda............
4. ..ṇḍaḷēsvara Banavāsi-puravar-ādhīsvara samasta bhuvana saṁ............
5. Treḷōchana Kaḍamba-vaṁśa mahōdaya-mahīdhara (ruṅ)dra śikhara............
6. .. Simha-lāñchana Vānara mahā-dhvaja Permmaṭṭi-tūrya nirghō............

7. tyāga jaga-jhaṁpi-Jhaṁpaḷāchārya subhaṭa kanaka nikashōpaḷa
8. mūrtti-nārāyaṇa kīrtti-mārttaṇḍa-maṇḍaḷika lalāṭa-paṭṭa vairi............
9. **Konkaṇa-vombhainūṟuṁ Palasige-panni-chhāṣiramuva............**
10. **karṇāvataṁśa ottumanāḷutaṁ-nija rājaḍhāni Chandrāpu............**
11. ....sukha saṁkathā vinōdadiṁ rājyaṁ geyyuttaṁ-ire ||Vritta|| viyad embudu ....
12. .. madud-āchārateyiṁ kiṟid-allade voḷa. . . . . .
13. .... māge avana sati Panchikabbeyu............ nijeyo dhātri.........
14. .... Bhuvana Bhavāniya varadiṁ tavada-guṇaṁgaḷane paḍedaḷinene pesarvvaḍedaḷā
15. Śivana-padāṁbuja-yugaḷa satvada (Śaṭpada)n-enipa kavi-gamaki-vādi-vāgmigaḷ-avarge-nellaṁ
16. ...ṇḍa-negaḻdu || Ant-enipa Mūkagāvuṇḍana-kānte āchāramante vinayada kaṇi
17. ..... panavenalu Nanniyabbe Māḷana janani || Ā Māḷa-gāuundaṁ ... chi.
18. ....ḷ || Jaḷadi parivrita tiḷakaṁ-enalu.....
19. ....nile suputra kuḷa-dīpakan-enisi Māḷagāvuṇḍane....
20. .... na-dān Mūka-gāvuṇḍana Singhapa.........
21. gāmaṇḍa anugataṁ-anna dānadol-anna.....
22. .... vinoḷ anavaṛaṭaṁ... Māḷan-īgalu.... nira........
23. .... vinoḷ rugṃiyoḷ Bhuavana-bhavāniya...tava.... ḍada

24. Svasti **Śaka-varsha 1002 neya Raudra-Saṁvatsaraṁ prȧvarttise tatu-Jēshṭhad-Amāvāsse Briha..**
25. **Vuttarāyaṇa Saṁkramaṇamum-āge Māḷavēsvarada Kalidēva**
26. gaṁ khaṇḍa-sphutita jīrṇṇōdhāraṇakaṁ ūriṁ-tenkaṇa.... keḷage-āya
27. ...... na-kōlalu mūṟru-matta gaḻdeyumaṁ.... paḷḷadiṁ mūḍaṇade..
28. du terppa. galumaṁ sarva-namanyam-āgi dēvargge bi....... mōkshame baḷa...daḷdareke dānad ga..
29. rthamaṁ māḍi.......................
30. .... pud-enal-i-prākaṭamā.. kīrtti. ta.... Kaliyugada....
31. kya ko... negaṟda karppur........... vesaṟi naḍa-kalvesagadalu khaṇḍiya-Kētaṇa
32. .... gadyā ant-ā Kalukaṇḍiya baḷiya bāḍa-kōṇana-paḷḷiya
33. Kalidēva-svāmiya aṁga-bhōgakkaṁ sarva namasyam-āgi biṭṭa gaḻdeya.......
34. .. sana.. maryyādeyan-āvan-ōrvva-prati-pāḷisidan-ātange. Kurukshētradoḷaṁ
35. ....mikkuṁ-ātana vaṁśaṁ-utar-ottar-abhivriddhi....... pravarddha-manȧm-āgi-salu
36. .... yādan-āvan-ōrvvan-ākramisi manyana vaṁśa nirvaṁśaṁ-akku
37. kuḍitapō dhanaruva lōkade kavilegaḷaṁ brāhmaṇruman-aḷisutiya... ni su-strīyaru
38. .... bagaḷumaṁ brahma pa.. Mahēsvara-Navagrahō.... rābśōḍa Rudrāshṭhalōka-voḷa saptava....

IX

Sangamesvara, Kalghatgi Taluk, Dharwad District
Engraved in the middle bay of sabhā manṭapa of the temple

Gūvaladēva III – 1082 A.D.

This inscription refers to a grant of money and oil for the worship and offerings to the temple of Śiva constructed by one Sānta-gāvuṇḍa son of Mārasinga-gāvuṇḍa, and it was stipulated that the grant was to be managed by Kēta-gāmuṇḍa and the *aruvattokkalu* of the place. It was Gūvaladēva of the Kadamba family who was ruling over Palasige-12000, Konkaṇa-900 from his capital Analāpura.

It is dated *Śaka* 1004, *Dundubhi, Pushya śu.*5, Sunday, *Uttarāyaṇa Sankrāṇti* equated to 1082 A.D. *Dundubhi,* December 27, Tuesday.

Text

1. .... mahāmaṇḍalēśvara **Banavāsīpura-** varēśvaram Ajjādēvi labdha vara-prasādaṁ Kadamba kuḷa tilakaṁ tyāga Jaga-Jhaṁpaḍāchārya malege mārthaṇḍaṁ
2. .... Śrī mad-**Gūvaladēvaru Palasige-pannichhāsira-Konkaṇa-voṁbhainuṟumaṁ Aṇalāpurada-rājadhāniyoḷu** suka-saṁkathā vinōdadiṁ dushṭha-nigraha sishṭha pratipāḷane-mādi āḷuttam ire ||@ **Saka-varsha 1004 neya**
3. **Dumdubi-saṃvatsarada Pushya śu 5 Ādivārd-Uttarāyaṇa Saṅkrāntiy-andu** Svasti-samasta praśasti sahitaṁ Śrīmad-Mārasinga-gāmaṇḍana magaṁ svasti samasta guṇa-saṁpannaṁ vineya-saṁpūrnaṁ

4. ……para vadhu-putra gōtra-pavitra sujanaika-mitra tandeya-gandharāraṇa Sōmēśvara dāsa Śivapād-paṁkaja bhramaran-āhāra-dāni Siva-dharmma nirmmaḷa erkkōtiya tottu-…. Sānta-gāmaṇḍana māḍisida de
5. va layad nandā-dīvigeya naḍasal biṭṭa ga 5 tiṁgalige poṁg-ondu pāgavridhivya (vriddhiya) mūṟu-daraṇa ponge… loḷu manenneya ā-chandr-ārkkaṁbara nandā-dīvigege bitta || intī-dharmava Kētagāmuṇḍan-um-**aṟuvatt-okkal** prati-pāḷisu
6. u du int-ī dharmama

X

Mukkal, Kalghatgi taluk, Dharwad district
Slab set up at the entrance of the Rāmalingēśvar temple

Gūvaladēva - 1103 A.D.

The record mentions the rule of Gūvaladēva over Konkaṇa-900 and Palasige-12000. Reference is also made to the rule of a *mahāmaṇḍalēśvara* named Tailapa over Pānumgal-500 and Kontakuḷi-30.

It makes reference to the construction of a Śiva temple by Barma-gāvuṇḍa of Pannasōge, which has been described as *Naḍu-nāḍa-tirtha.* Further, the record mentions Māla-gāvuṇḍa, son of Barma-gāvuṇḍa. It is said that he made grant of land to god Mūlasthānadēva, after laving the feet of Vaidīśvara pandita, the deciple of Vikalēśvara-paṇḍita of Bankēśvara of Hangal.

The given date is Chālukya-Vikrama era…. *Subhānu, Pushya, śu. Panchami.* Sunday. *Uttarāyana*

Sankranti corresponding to 1103 A.D. In the absence of solar year the exact date cannot be given.

Texts

1. Namas-chandra śiraschumbi chaṁdra-chāmara chāravē Traiḷōkya-nagar-āraṁbha mūla-stam-
2. bhāya śaṁbhave|| Svasti samasta bhuvanāśraya śrī prithvī-vallabha mahā
3. rājādhirāja paramēśvarṁ bhaṭṭarakaṁ Satyāśraya kuḷa-tiḷakaṁ Chālukyā-
4. bharaṇaṁ śrī mat-**Tribhuvanamalla** dēvara vijaya-rājyam-uttar-ōttar-ābhivriddhi pravarddhamāna
5. m-āchandrārkka-tāraṁbaraṁ saluttam-ire|| Samadhigata paṁcha mahāśabda mahā-maṇḍalēśvarṁ Bana
6. vāsi-puravarēśvarṁ samasta-bhuvana saṁsthū-yamānaṁ Hara-dharaṇī prasūtaṁ Triḷōchana-Kadaṁba vaṁśa-
7. maho-dayaṁ sakaḷa mahī-maṇḍaḷan-uttunga Simha-lānchhanaṁ Vānara-mahā-dhvajaṁ-chatura-
8. siti nagar-ādhishṭhitan-ashsṭhā daśāśvamēdha dīksha-dīkshita kuḷa prasūtaṁ himavad-girīndra
9. rundra śikhara saṁ-sthāpita mahāśakti-prabhāvaṁ tyāga jaga-Jhaṁpalāryya nisaṁka-rāma su
10. bhatā kanaka nikshōpaḷaṁ saraṇāgata vajra-prākāraṁ subhaṭa rāja śikhāmanī-tyakhiḷa rajāvaḷi
11. samāḷaṁkritar-appa śrīman-mahā-maṇḍalēśvaraṁ **Gūvaladēvaru Konkaṇa voṁbhai-nūrumaṁ Palasige-panni**

12. rchhasira mumaṁ suka-saṁkathā vinōdadiṁ rājyam-geyuttaṁ-ire|| Samadhigata paṁchamahā śabda
13. mahāmaṇḍalēśvaraṁ **Banavāsi** puravarādhisvaraṁ Triyaksh... saṁbhavaṁ chaturāsīti nagar-ādhishṭhi
14. ta lalāṭa-lōchana chaturbhujaṁ jagadvidit-ā-shṭhādaśāsva-mēdha dīkshitaṁ Himavad-girīndra rundra
15. ...... saṁsthāpita sphaṭika śilā-sthambhaṁ baddha madagaja mahā-mahim-ābhi-rāmaṁ Kādaṁba Cha-
16. krēśvara nāmādi-prasasti sahitaṁ śrīmanu mahā-maṇḍaḷēśvaram **Tailapa-dēvara Pānuṁgal-ainū**
17. **ṟumaṁ Kontakuḷi mūvattumaṁ su**[ba]kha saṁkathā-vinōdadiṁ rājyam-geyyuttam-ire|| **Naḍu-nāḍa**
18. **tīrthaṁ**-enisida poḍavige sale negardda Hannasōgeya... Barmaṁ **Mriḍanālayamaṁ** māḍisi paḍada[ṁ]
19. yaśa-kīrtti khyāti-mukti-śriyaṁ|| Ātana-tanaya|| Vīran-udāraṁ guṇa-gaṇādhāraṁ Manu-nīti
20. mārgga gōtra-pavitraṁ sārataraṁda nannige paranārī-sōdara-mideni danalte Māḷa-gavuṇḍa|| Ātana
21. sati|| Vinaya-nidhi sahaja-chalvina vanitāratna pratibratā guṇadoḷaruṁ vadhatiy-enisida daye dha
22. rmma bhakti Gauripāda-paṁkaja-bhramara mad enisidene rāṇi... g-uḷida satiyar-doreye||
23. Svasti samasta-guna-saṁpannaṁ śrīmatu Hanna-śōgeya Barmma-gāuṇḍana magma Māḷa-gāvuṇḍaṁ Mūla
24. sthāna-dēvargge śrī-**ma Chchāḷukya Vikrama-kālada Subhānu-saṁvatsarada Paushya Śuddha paṁchami Āditya-**

25. **vāra Uttarāyaṇa Sankrantiy-andu** Hānuṁgallā Bankēśvarada Vikaḷēśvara paṇḍitara sisyaru Vidhiśvara
26. Paṇḍitara kālaṁ karchchi dhārā pūrvvakadiṁ sarbba-namasyavagi ūriṁ tenka Haḷa..... Barmmayyana keṟe
27. ya tenkaṇada koḷa ā koladiṁ mūḍaṇa hakkala arevattaramaṁ bittar|| Idan-aḷidaṁ Bāṇarāsi
28. Gurukshētra prayāge kurukshētradoḷ sāsira kavile brāhmaṇaram tapōdhanaraṁ konda paṁcha mahā
29. pātakan-akkuṁ|| Svadattaṁ paradattaṁ vāyō-harēti vasundharām shashthir-varisha sahasrā-
30. ṇi mi(vi) shṭhāyāṁ jāyatē krimi || Purvvara-haḷḷiya Kāḷōjaṁ besa-geyda|| @@

XI

Kandli, Kalghatgi taluk, Dharwad district
Stone lying infront of ruined Īśvara temple outside the village

Jayakēśi -II - 1132 A.D.

This hero-stone is dated *Śaka* 1054, *Paridhāvi, Chaitra, śu. Ashṭhami*, Sunday, equivalent to 1132 A.D. *Paridhavi* March 26th Saturday. It refers to the death of a hero named Mallayya, son of Bammaja-gāvuṇḍa in a boundary dispute.

Text

I panel

1. * Svasti **Śaka-varsha sāsirad-aivatta-nāl-kaneya-Paridhāvi-saṃvatsarada chaitra-śu..**
2. **Ashṭhami Ādivārad-andu** śrīman-mahā-pradhānaṁ sandhi-vigrahi

3. daṇḍanāyakaṁ Jayakēsi-dēvana Tammiyūra gaḍi(yi)

II panel

1. ndaṁ Kōṭekiṟuvattiyaṁ-Ajjagāveyaṁ Taileya-Sōvanaṁ-iṟidu seṟe ..... mavāya..
2. ... ka vaḷḷiyali... Bammaja-gāvuṇḍana-magaṁ āhu-Mallayya-nāyakaṁ Hūvayya leṁka.
3. labhyate Lakshmī mritēṇa-vāpi surānganā kshaṇa-vidhvaṁsini-kāye-kā-chintā maraṇē-raṇē
4. .. daṁ bagedu Sangana-bayalalli parid-aḍḍaṁ-bandu tāgi mēreveri.......
5. ... kontadaṇigaṁ Ballāḷaṁ moggarakaṁ seraguṁ baraguṁ... bage ....
6. danamaṁ magurhchi-bīramaṁ meṟedu sura-lōka prāptan-āda kāḷaga..........
7. ... ha bala ba.... kahaligeyindaṁ ... ki kālaṁ toḍa ....

III Panel

1. ant-ā-Kannaleya Bamma-gāvuṇḍanu Bācha-gāvuṇḍanu.... traruṁ Jaga.....
2. negarddu parōksha vinayārtham-āge ... ta.... ge..... Bīra-kallaṁ-māḍi ....

XII

Jinnur, Kalghatgi taluk, Dharwad district
Engraved on stone set up infront of Kalmēśvara temple

Jayakēśi II - 1138 A.D.

While making a reference to the rule of Jagadēkamalla of the Chālukyas of Kalyaṇa dynasty, the record says that a grant of land was made by one Bīchaṇa, for the worship and offerings to god Grāmēśvaradēva, after paying respects to the feet of Santi-gāvuṇḍa of Huligōḍu. The latter, in his turn made grant to the deity after laving the feet of Sankarāsi-Panditadēva. Another person named Nēma-gāvuṇḍa and the community of *Telligas, Jeḍas* and *Senigas* also appears to have made grants for the *Chaitra* and *Pavitra* festival of the temple. A lady named Basantikabbe made grant of land for the worship in the temple. The record refers to *Telligas (Telligar-aivattokkalu)* who made grant of oil for the lamp in the temple.

The date of the record is *Śaka* 1060, *Kālayukti, Akshaya-tritiya Amavāse*, Solar eclipse, Sunday. It is equivalent to 1138 A.D. The details are incorrect.

Text

1. Namas-tunga...... chāmara-chāravē
2. Trailōkya-nagar-ārambha mūla... śambhave
3. ....
4. ....
5. ḍi biṭṭa-dharmma | Svasti-samadhigata paṁcha-mahā-śabda mahāmaṇḍaḷē-śvara Banavāsi puravarādhīsvara manneya Bhaira-

6 va Kāḍaṁba kūrmma-Kūrmmāvatāra mūrtti-
Nārāyanaṃ kīrti-latā-kandaṁ Saṁkrāntīni-dhavaḷa. sura-Rāmana-

7. bhuvana Pārtha subhaṭara tīrtha nind-irivātaṁ pāradhi-
Parasurāman-ubhaya dēsi vallabha Tribhuvanama-

8. lla-maṇḍaḷika-śikhāmaṇi Kādaṁba-chūḍāmanī-tyē[ka]
rājyāvaḷi samāḷaṁkritar-appa śrī maj Ja-

9. yakēśi-dēvara-vijaya-rājyam-uttar-ōttarābhivriddhi
pravardha-manam -āchandr-ārkka tāraṁbaraṁ salu

10. ttaṁ-ire anjidara guṇa-tējadim-anjisidaṁ pesara jisama
nelamaṁ deseyoḷu punjisidaṁ nripa-sabheyaṁ

11. . ranjisidaṁ Sānti-gāvuṇḍan-eṁba mahātma svasti
Saka-varsha 1060 neya Kāḷayukti saṁvatsarada

12. **Akshaya-tritīyāmavāse Āditya-vāra Sūrya-
grahaṇad-andu** Hulagō

13. ḍa Sānti-gāvuṇḍana pāda-pūjege Heggaḍe-Bīchaṇaṁ
koṭṭa Grāmēśvara-dēvara

14. nivēdyakke Hosageṟeya-hariya gadde kammayinnūru-
hakkalu

15. kamma-nānūrumaṃ Bīchaṇaṁ haḍedu-biṭṭa mattaṁ
sānta-gāvundana-pā-

16. da-pūjege [a]rvaḷara Bīcha-gāvunḍaṁ koṭṭa
Gramēsvara-dēvara naivedya

17. kke-yarakereya mūḍal-ēriya gadde kamma [yi]
nūṟippatt-aidu

18. maṁ Bīcha-gāvuṇḍaṁ paḍedu biṭṭav-intidaṁ
dharmmamaṁ Sāntagāvu-

19. ṇḍaṁ Sankarāsi-paṇḍita-dēvara kālaṁ karchchi
dhārāpūrvakaṁ māḍi

20. biṭṭa dharma matte goṇḍa.. sabala kaṇa Muddagāvuṇḍana pā-
21. da pūjege kuṭṭu Grāmēsvara-devara nivēdyakke Hosageṟeya
22. hariya-gadde-kamma Nūṟ-ayvatumaṁ biṭṭan-int-ī-dharmmamaṁ pratipāḷisidaṁ
23. Vāranāsi Gurukshetra prayāgey-arghya tīrthaṁgaloḷ sāsira kavileyaṁ
24. kōduṁ koḷaguṁ paṁcharatnadoḷ kaṭṭisi brāhmaṇargge mahādānam geyda phaḷa-
25. makkuṁ yi-dharmmaman-aḷidange yint-appa tīrthaṁgaḷoḷ sāsira-kavileyuṁ
26. sāsirvva brāhmaṇaruman-eḷkōṭi tapōdhanaru-man-aḷida paṁcha-ma-
27. hā..... mattaṁ Nēma-gāvuṇḍanuṁ Samastav-aṟuvattokkalu Telliga-
28. .... Jēḍaruṁ Sēṇigaruṁ initu-varsha
29. .... rmmav-ent-endaḍe Sarga-gāvuṇḍiya maneya hattira paḍuvaṇa |
30. .... taḷa-sārigey Bīravaṇa-mānya-sahita sarvva-bādhā-parihārv-āgi
31. Chaitra-Pavitrakke... ge vakkalu hēṟiāṁge anāmikaru... Saga varisaṁ
32. ... hāgamaṁ biṭṭaru || Mattaṁ Sānta-g-āvuṇḍana pāda-pūjege koṭṭu mālagāṟa Basan
33. tibbe Grāmēśvara dēvara nivēdyakk-eṁdu Hiṟiyakeṟeya bachchala mēgeyuṁ keḷageyuṁ biṭṭa-gadde ka-

34. mmav-ayadumaṁ sarvva-namasya || Int-ī-
dharmmamaṁ nā-rērvvaruṁ prati pālisuvudu..

35. @ mattaṁ **telligar-ayvatt-okkalu** dēvara soḍar-eṇneg-
endu okkalali koṭṭa soṭige-vondu ||

XIII

Hunasikatti, Kalghatgi taluk, Dharwad district
Engraved on stone set up out-side Mallayya temple

Permāḍiēva - 1142 A.D.

The record is dated *Śaka* 1065 *Dundubhi, Pushya, śu.*12, Thursday, *Uttarāyaṇa Sankrānti* corresponding to 1142 A.D. December 20, Monday, *Sankramaṇa* occurred on December 25, Saturday.

It mentions to a grant of land for food and offerings to the god Hellēśvara of Kaḍaleganahaḷḷi, by Mudda-gāvuṇḍa, belonging to *Sagalara Vaṁśa,* and who was a subordinate of *mahāmaṇḍaḷēśvara* Permāḍidēva of Kadamba family after laving the feet of Chandrabhūshaṇa Paṇḍita, son of Śivaśakti Paṇḍita.

The record also refers to another grant of land made by Nēma-gāvuṇḍa, the brother of Mudda-gāvuṇḍa, for the perpetual lamp in the temple after laving the feet of Chandrabhūshaṇa Paṇḍita.

Text

1. Namas-tunga-śiraschuṁbi chandra-chāmara-chārave
Trailōkya-nagar-ārambha mūla-staṁ [bhā]

2. ya Śambhave || Svasti samasta-bhuvån-āśraya śrī-
prithvi-vallabha......

3. …….. [kaṁ satya] …………..
4. ḷakaṁ Chāḷuky-ābharaṇam śrīmaj-**Jagadekamalla-dēvara** vijaya-rājam-uttar-ōtta
5. ābhivriddhi pravardhamānam-āchandr-ārka-tāraṁ-baraṁ saluttam-ire || Svasti samadhigata
6. paṁcha mahā-śabda mahāmaṇḍḷēśvaraṁ **Śrīmad-Vira-Permmādi-dēvara** sthiram jīyatu || Śrīma-
7. t-Kadaṁba va[ṁ]śa lalāma sangrāma-Rāma sāhasa-Bhīma sāmade ripu-nīḍe-śauryō-
8. dhāmam- Permmādi dēvananari ghaṭe-malla || kaḍupiṁpe Permādi dēvaṁ nija-vijaya-gajā-
9. rūḍhan-āgalke Lāḷaṁ guḍigitt-ā-gaṇḍa-garvva Draviḷan-aḍagidaṁ Māḷavaṁ-bhītan-āda || śede
10. da[ṁ] Nēpāḷanaṇmaṁ toreda-ka[ḷe]van-ā-Gūrjjaraṁ Pāriyātra-tān-anji-ninda Malepan-aḷḷi-
11. paṁ Māḷavaṁ bhītan-āda || Tat-pāda padmōpajīvi-daya-dāna-nirataṁ na
12. ..viddant-anēka-vākyan-amaḷa charitraṁ niyataṁ shāḍguṇya-yutaṁ priya
13. ..chanaṁ Chāyi-gauṇḍan-enisutirdda || Tat-putran-ent-appan-ent-endaḍe ||
14. ..va-balaḍāya dāyad-ā rvina kalitanada baṇaṁja dharmmadaynūrbba-
15. tula taṁnna-kulav-enippaṁ sale jagadoḷ-Mudda-gauṇḍan-ūrjjita tēja || Sāga
16. [la]-kulake-tiḷakaṁ Sāgala-kuḷābhavaṇa-virājita mitraṁ Sāgalara-vaṁśado-

17. .... lāgirdda Mudda-gaundanaṅ-avanī-taḷadoḷ || āyan-oḍauṭida || Paladigu-
18. ḷanaddēsi palaraṁ kaykonḍu poredu bhūmaṇḍaḷadoḷ kula-dīpakan-enisi
19. sale sāhasa-bhīman-enisi Nēmagoṇḍa || avara putra[ṁ] Prabhu-Nēma-gāvuṇḍa-
20. param-āyuṁ śrīyuman-ādaradiṁ Nēmange kuḍuge Hellēśvaran-ī-dhare
21. yuṁ vāridhiyuṁ suragiriyuṁ chandr-ārkkav-endu uḷḷ-annevara || ayana pra
22. tyada-haḷḷi || Kaḍalegana-haḷḷi satataṁ poḍavige migil-enipudu bhaya [dvā-]
23. sigaḷ-ār-irppaḍeyendare baṇṇipar-āru baḍavara vaneyanon
24. .. lageyanara || alliya Hellēśvarad-āchāryaru || Paramēśa Sadāśiva-
25. riyisi hrit-kamalad-oḷage praṇamādi ShaḍākshMaramaṁ paṭhiyisut-ī
26. Śivayōgi Chandrabhūshaṇadēva || **Svasti Śaka-varsha 1065 neya Dundhubi-saṁ-**
27. **... tsa[ra]da Puśya sudda 12 Guruvāradandu Uttarāyaṇa Sankrānti vya-**
28. **[tī] pātadandu** śrīmatu Huligōḍa-Mudagāunḍaṇanu . Hollagā-
29. [uṇḍa] [He]llēśvara-dēvara nivēdyakke Śivaśakti-pandittura-putra Chandra-bhū[shaṇa]
30. paṇḍitara-kālaṁ-karchihi dhārā-pūrvvakaṁ mādi sarbba ma-

31. [ḍa] la geṟeya-pariya paśchima.. rada-gardde kamaṁ
32. ḷr-int-ī-dharmamaṁ prati-pāḷisida[ṁ]ge Vāra[ṇā]si Kurukshētrā-
33. . rghya tīrthaṁgaḷoḷ sāyira kavileya[ṁ] kō[ḍu] koḷa[ga]-.....
34. .... ṭṭisi sāsirbba-brāhmaṇarige mahā-dānaṁ-ge[yda]
35. .... dharmmaman-aḷidange-yī-puṇya tīrtha[doḷ]
36. brāhmaṇaruman-eḷkōṭi ta[pō]-
37. .... pātakar-apparu || Svasti śrīmatu sa .
38. ... [va]ra nandā-dīvigegondu ta ....
39. . pūrvvakaṁ-māḍi-koṭṭaru

XIV

Tambur, Kalghatgi taluk, Dharwad district
A slab lying near the Barkol Basavanna temple outside the village

Tribhuvanamalla (Vikramāditya VI) – 1144 A.D.

The record is damaged. It refers to the construction of a Śivālaya at Tāmbrapura and also to a *dandanayaka* named Mādirajayya who was administering Tammiyūr-12 and Huligōḍu-12, Kōte-kiruvatti and Nelkunda. Grant of land, garden, oil for the worship and offerings to the deities Narasingadēva, Bōdēśvaradēva, Vāgīśvara, by the *Nakaras, Honnavanigas, Telligara-aivattokkalu*, on the date specified, find a mention in the record. The given date is *Śaka* 1066, *Raktakshi, Pushya, Amavāse, Monday, Uttarāyaṇa Sankramaṇa* equated to 1144 A.D. December 25, f.t.d.25.

Text

1. .... nimāra
2. .... yēdiniyoḷ Pē........
3. ṇdiga Boppan-ene Kritakritya dainya......... girīndra....... chelviniṁ māḍisi.....
4. daṁ dēvālayavānāyatiya........ ntu ......nindesevaṁ Tāṁbrapurakke śōbheyā-
5. giral nōḍidirgge-lā...... kolinudinadipandu vettu....... mudadiṁdeḍeyy pulugava dāna-dharmma parahita........
6. ḍe-yoḷ... biḍad-ittum aṟu-bhavakkaṁ maḍagittavan-intu... nappaṁ Boppaṁṁ || @ Antavara gurukulaṁ Mūvara-kōṇeya-samtati...śa

7. permmeyaṁ Parvvatāvaliyu-enisida Kundaṁgoḷada śrī Svayambhụ devatā-sthānad-āchāryar-ent-appar-endaḍe || Surabhūjaṁjeḍe pottundaṁ bā-
8. ri tapōveśakkeḍarppāytu Mandara śaiḷam yati rūpamaṁ taḷedu deṁbant-atyudāratva-diṁ vara gaṁbhīrate-yiṁ vaniśchaḷateyiṁ Vāgīśvara sanmu-
9. nīśvara chūḍāmaṇi tāne-rajisidapaṁviśvaṁbherā chakradolu @ śri_man mahā-prachaṇḍa daṇḍanāyakaṁ Mādirājayyaṁgaḷ Māva
10. ḷe-nāḍa baḷiya-bāḍaṁ Tammiyūruṁ Pannirppaḷḷi yumaṁ Huḷigōḍu-pannirppaḷḷiyu-maṁ Māvaḷe-pannirppaḷḷiyumam Kōṭekiṟuvatti Ne
11. lkuṇdav-intinitumanēka prabhusāmyadiṁd-āld-arasu geyuttaṁire|| Svasti **Śaka-Varshaṁ 1066 neya Raktākshi saṁvatsarada Pushyad-amāvāsye**
12. **Sōmavārada Vuttarāyaṇa Saṁkramaṇa vyatīpātamaṁ** samanisi-banda puṇya tithiyoḷavagaṁ śrī Nārasingadēvarige parōksha-vinamā[yā]rtha vā-
13. gi Śrī Chouḍēśvara-dēvara aṅga-bhōga raṅga-bhōgakkaṁ | chaitrakkaṁ | pavitrakkaṁ | āhāra-dānakkaṁ khaṇḍa-sphuṭita- jīrṇṇōddārakkaṁ | paḍisalisuvant-āgi bitta
14. dharma-bhūmiy-entendaḍe | ā Dēvaḷageṟeya-baḍagaṇa tuṁbina modala mạdav=ayal-ainūru-marada tōṇṭamumaṁ Dāvina gaṭḥina
15. hariyalu Haḍavaḷageyya hattuge-iṁ Mūḍalu hiriya-gaḷẹyalondu matter-gaddeyumaṁ adaṟa baḷiya ṃelvannu ..
16. tana keṟeyim mēge haḍuvaṇa bhāgadalu hiriya-gaḷeyal-eraḍu mattal hakkalumaṁ | sarvabādhā pariah=raṁ sarvnamasyav-āgi

17. Śrī Vāgīśvara dēvarige | dhārā-pūrvaka māḍi-koṭṭar | **Nakara-samūhamaṁ Hanna-vaṇigara-samūhamaṁ** | chaitrakkaṁ | pavitrakkaṁ śrī Nakarēśvara dēvari-
18. ge koṭṭu harikeyaṁ śrī Chauḍēśvara dēvarige koṭṭar | Nakara-samūha saṭṭuga-bhattamaṁ koṭṭar | Hannavaṇigaru hēṟige nūṟ-eleyuma tale
19. .... voṟeg-aivatt-eleyumaṁ koṭṭar || Telligar-aivattokkaluṁ | chaitrakkaṁ Nirpāgamaṁ | pavitrakke pāgama | nandā-dīvigege soṇṭige yeṇṇeyuma ko
20. ṭṭar | Sēṇigarokkalellaṁ Chaitrakke pāgamaṁ Pavitrakkaṁ pāgamma(ma) koṭṭar | śrī Mādirāja-daṇḍa-nāyaka mānya-mannaṇey-ennade... bāgilvā-
21. gamaṁ koṭṭar @ Janakaṁ Jātōjanantātana kulavadhu Jīkavegaṁ puṭṭidar-sadvinayāmbhō-rāsi Kētaṁ sakala-guṇa gaṇālaṁkritaṁ Mudan-eṁba (ba)
22. rttanayarttā Mādarantāyavarggaḷe kaḷaśārōpaṇaṁ māḍi-viḍvajjanakke śrī Mādirājaṁg-ati mudade manōtsāha-vantāduduāgal | Ant-avargge
23. Kāruṇyaṁ-geydu śrī Mādirāja-daṇḍa-nāyakara Dāveyagathina Hiriya śrī Chauḍēśvaradēvara gaḷdeya hattugeyiṁ-mūḍalu-hiriya
24. gaḷeyalondu mattalu gaḷdeyumaṁ | ā dēvarige biṭṭa hakkalaṁ Tenkalu kōtaḷiya hattugeyiṁ hiriya gaḷeyal-eraḍu mattal hakka-
25. lumaṁ dēvara-puravarggadoḷage hadinaydu kayya-maneyaṁ Vāgīśvara-dēvaru koṭṭar | Nakara-Jinālayada haṟage-ḥaṇṇerdu kayyal-eraḍu maneyumaṁ Daṇḍnāyakar-āḷva-naḍoḷage geyida bannaṇiya-kayyalu dasavandamaṁ yintinitumaṁ Sarvabādhā-parihārav-āgi koṭṭar ||

26. ī-dharmaṁ prati pāḷisidavarggalu Gangā-sāgara Vāraṇāsi Prayāgē Kurukshētram-embarghya-tirthaṁgaḷoḷ koṇḍuṁ-koḷagumaṁ Suvarṇṇadiṁ Kaṭṭisi
27. dubhaya mukhiy-appa sāsira kavileyumaṁ Sāsirvvar-Vēda pāragar=appa brāhmaṇarige koṭṭa puṇyada phaḷaman-yaiduvar || Ī-dharmmamaṁ
28. pratipāḷisidavarggaḷ || Gangā-Yamunagaḷal-eraḍara sangamadoḷ-agaṇya-puṇya-vara-tīrtha-sthānaṁgaḷoḷ iṟppa-tapōdhanaraṁ gō-brāhmaṇaranaḷida
29. nint-idan-aḷida || Svadttaṁ paradattaṁ vāyō-harēti vasundharā shashsṭhirvvarsha shasrāṇi vishsṭhāyāṁ jāyatē-krimiḥ bahubhir-vvasudhā bhuktā
30. [rājabhiḥssagarād]hibhiḥ yasya yasya tadā bhūmi tasya tasya tadā-phaḷaṁ @@

XV

Haliyal, Haliyal Taluk, North Kanara district
Engraved on stone set up near Mallikarjuna temple

Jayakēśi II - 1144 A.D.

The inscription is dated *Śaka* 1066 *Raktākshi, Pushya, Amavāsya*, Tuesday, Solar eclipse equated to 1144 A.D. *Raktākshi,* December 26, Tuesday, Solar eclipse.

It mentions the rule of Jayakēśidēva and refers to Palliyala i.e., modern, as *Mahāgrahāra* and eulogises the scholarship of the *Mahājanas* of the place, as experts in the subjects like *vyākarna arthaśāstra*, art and sciences and thorough in languages like *Sanskrit*, *Apabramśa* and *Paiśachi* and also experts in composing works in different styles of writing like *Gauḍa, Vaidarbha* and *Pānchāla*.

It also registers a grant made for the continuous cultivation in the place.

Text

1. Ōm-Svasti [||] Samadhigata paṁcha-mahā-śabda mahā-maṇḍalēśvaraṁ
2. Banavāsī puravarādhīśvaraṁ Kadaṁba kula-tila
3. kaṁ śrī maj-Jayakēśidēvaṁ vijaya-rājyam-uttar-ōttar-ābhi
4. vriddhi pravardhamānam-āchandr ārka-tāraṁ-baraṁ saluttam-ire || Svasti yama-niya
5. ma svādhyāya dhyāna-dhāraṇa maun-ānushthāna pārāyaṇa japa-samādhi śīḷa saṁpaṁ-
6. nnaruṁ nuḍidu matt-ennaruṁ Agnishṭhōm-ādyānēka yajñav-ābhritāvagā hana pavitrīkrita śarī -
7. raruṁ vidvajjan-ābjini mitraruṁ yajana-yājana adhyayanādhyāpanadāna pratigraha [hā]
8. dy-anushṭhāna vidhāna-nidhāna-dīpa-varttigaḷuṁ dharma-mūrttigaḷuṁ sakaḷa Vyākraṇ-Ārthaśastr ākhila
9. kaḷā-kaḷāpa parijñāna shaṇmukharuṁ ḍambha-krōdha lōbh-āsūy-ādyāvaguṇa bahir-mmukharuṁ kavi-gama
10. ka (ki) vādi vāgmi-sujana-manaḥ padminī-rāja-haṁsaruṁ Sarasvatī karṇṇāvatāraruṁ Gauḍa-Vaidarbbha-Pānchā-
11. ḷādi nānā-rīti saṁyukta mridu-madhura vachana-rachana smita spandini Samskrit-Āpabhraṁśaruṁ Paiśāchi
12. ka pada-nichaya nichita sukara-duśkara śrabya-kābya-gōshṭhi-vinōdaruṁ anavarata-vinuta
13. divija danuja yaksha-rākshasa-kinnara-nara-tiriṭa-kōṭi sandarbhita taruṇa taraṇi-bhāruṇa
14. mayūkhā vikāsita taruṇgita charan-āravindvaṁ dvaṁ dvaṁdy-ēnipa śrīmat-Kānchi-dēvi labdha vara prāsāda–

15. ruṁ Chaturddhaśa bhuvana-bhavana vistārita daśa-śata gabhasthi-māḷaṁkrita Bhāskara-dēva charaṇa-pū
16. jā-karaṇa pariṇatashkaruṇaruṁ Hiraṇya-Kaśipōra-sthaḷa nirddārita sakaḷa daityāri Śrīman-Nā-
17. rasimhadēva pādārādhana tatparāyaṇaruṁ yāchaka-jaṇa-paritōshaṇa vitaraṇaruṁ-appa
18. Svasti **Śaka-varsha 1066 Raktākshi Saṁvatsarada-Pauśyad-Aṁavāse Mangaḷavāra Sūryya-graha-**
19. ṇad-andu śriman Mahāgrahāraṁ Palleyāḷa aśesha mahā-janaṁgaḷu Dēvingeṟege byavasāyaṁ santataṁ naḍevant-āgire sarbba- bādhā [parihāra] vāgi pebboḷadoḷage bhāga
20. vatyā-sthānadiṁ baḍagalu Sathikaṁbadōḷage biṭṭa mattal-aidu || Intī dharmamaṁ pratyēkaṁ
21. prati-pālisuvaru | pratipālisade kiḍisidantavaru Vāraṇāsi Pra –
22. yāge Kurukshētradalli sahasra brāhmaṇaruvaṁ sahasra kavileyan-aḷida-dōsha |
23. sva-ddātuṁ samahachchakyaṁ-dānamaṁ yasya-pāḷanaṁ | dānaṁ pālanaṁ rē
24. ti-dāna chchrēyōnu pālanaṁ || [1] Bahubhir vasudhā dattā rājabhih sa
25. garādhibhiḥ || Yasya yasya yadā-bhūmi tasya-tasya-tadā phalaṁ || [2] || @
26. Svadattaṁ (ttāṁ) paradattam(āṁ) vāyō harēti (ta) vasuṇ-dharāṁ [I] shasṭhirvvarsha sahaśrāni vishṭhā
27. yāṁ jāyate-krimiḥ || [3] na vishaṁ vishamikyā huḍe brahmasvaṁ visha
28. muchyatē [1] Vishamēkākinaṁ haṁti brahmasvaṁ putra-pautrika (o) || [4]

XVI

Bammigatti, Kalghatgi taluk, Dharwad district
Slab kept in the village Panchayat Office

Permāḍi - 1147 A.D.

The record gives the eulogy of a chief named Sāmanta Suriganripa also called Surigamayya and describes him as Bharaṇīpurādhipa. He was administering Bharaṇi-12, another 12 divisions (name lost) and Kampila, when Permāḍidēva of the Kadamba family was ruling over the divisions viz., Palasige-12000,and Konkaṇa-900.

The purport of this inscription is to record the construction of a *Jina bhavana*, at Hoṇṇeyahaḷḷi by a *sāmanta* named Surigamayya and also grant of land, house sites, for the perpetual lamp in the temple. The grant was received by Anantavīra Siddhānta munīśvara of *yāpanīya sangha* and *kandūra-gaṇa.* The date mentioned in the record is *Śaka* 1069 *Prabhava*, equivalent to 1147 A.D. Regarding date other details are not mentioned.

Text

1. .... nātha Jayekēśi dēvane...
2. ma doḷe rājya-lakshmī-dhāma Permmāḍi..
3. daṁbōdaya Śaiḷa-tuṁga śi[kha.]
4. rtyanānyavanitāpatyam.... ya dontaja
5. ..... mahā maṇḍalēśvaṟa ..... marttaṇḍaṁ |
6. ..chanaṁ-vānara mahā-dhvajaṁ Permmaṭṭi-tūrya
7. nirghōshaṇaṁ | chaturāsīti nagarā....
8. giriṁdra ruṁdra-sikhara-sthāpita saṁ.... siḷā-sṭhambha śaraṇāgata vajra-prākāraṁ
9. .... mārttaṇḍaṁ saṁkrānti-dhavaḷaṁ maṇḍaḷika.

10. lalāṭa paṭṭaṁ | nōpura subhaṭa-rāja śikhāmaṇi-ma-
11. hā-maṇḍaḷēśvaraṁ **Permmāḍidēvaṁ Palasige-pannichchāsiramumaṁ Konkaṇa-vombhaiy-nūṟrumaṁ du-**
12. shṭha-nigraha visishṭha pratipāḷaneydikhadin-āḷuttaṁire @ tatpāda-payōja Shaṭpada ||vri|| ...sedaṁgā..
13. ..ṇḍa....saniprōd-griha-mukti śaurya... ḷadiṁd-āntaṇminindaṁ gagana... śālōpaman-anganā janakangaṁgaṁ
14. ..... Suregaṁ peṁpiṁde dhātri..antu sāmanta kauntēyaṁ sukhadin-ire || ra... su..meni....
15. ḷdini pposatāgalvariṁ ramjikuṁ... dēśaṁ samentati śobhisuguṁ Māvaḷḷe-nāḍu pancha-śata-saṁkhyā.....
16. sogayikuṁ nānāvi.... rājini.... ḷayadoḷaṁ.... niḷayadoḷaṁ ... na ....
17. [dva] Jana niḷayadoḷadhika chelvu.. bhū . ḷeseguṁ Bharaṇīpura-varādhipanī-bhuvana vyapta kīrti-ramaṇa.
18. Charaṇaṁ suṟiganneḍaṟa todaḷdā.. tat-priy-ātmajaṁ subhaṭa... jana stut-anudyad-vibhavaṁ-vairībha daḷana kēsari
19. .. khiḷa prabhu tiḷakaṁ kamman-ugra... dune... tad-anujaṁ|| muni-dvijaruṁ.... dhanamaṇapēksha....
20. kara-virōdhi sura-kunjam-enipa manavārya-śauryōdāryaṁ || Svasti samadhigata panchamahā....
21. ... llita digantaṁ Kavi-iamaki-Vādi chyūdaṁ jaṁ .... | Kōdaṇḍa pārtha-subhaṭara-tīrtha śaraṇā.....
22 sūtradhāra Kādaṁba-rāja.... māvana-gandha-vāraṇaṁ || subhaṭa jana-stutyaṁ vasuvara........
23. kadanaika Bhairava subhaṭa... ṇi bandhuchintāmaṇi... suṟi munīśvara-dēva-labdha vara prasā.....
24. .... madi samsta-praśasti... sāmanta Suṟigamayya Bharaṇi-hanneraḍu .... ha

25. nneraḍu kaṁpila.... prabhratī-nāmanēka vīra-bhōga prabhu sāmyadinā-
26. Suṟiganagra.... viṇana[bhā] jananivaha.... saṁhārana mari
27. .. singa ā [ma] ... yāvatāram-entene ||vri|| Krita-puṇyan-amaḷachari....
28. Kādaṁbēśa .... nanupama Barmmaṇaṁ vistrata-bhāgyaṁ Ba..... maṇi-ramaṇi
29. ..lōkaṁ gōtra-maṇi balakaṇanaudārya kalvā vani baṁ negardda Baṁka
30. Barmmaya... vinutanuḷiyisidanamaḷina Jinapada sarasija... bhringaṁ......
31. tmaku.... natyanta vistara puṇyodayanishṭhasishṭha janatā [dhāraṁ] nijādhīśa Bhāsu....
32. pu.... Mantri-raṇad-bhūshaṇan-eṁdu.. dhātri-pogaḷguṁ sauryanganaṁ Singanaṁ || Jina
33. [ni] mmiyakkaṁ ...... ta .. na-sārdhaṁ dāna-chintāmaṇi Suṟiga nripaṁ-Śōbhaṇaṁ Dēvaṇaṁ tannanu...
34. re... neṭṭanaī-dhanya Singanātyantika vidaḷa-yaśōttuṁga . sad-bhrājitānga..
35. pati kārya-dakshanupadhā-śuddha-niratiśaya vibhavan-end urvvare pogaḷguṁ
36. nanabhyadaya śrī Sangamanati vishada-kīrtti-dhavaḷita [bhā] vanōttungadanana [nany] āvanī
37. vasuḍhā-taḷadol || Bhū-bhuvanaṁ pogaḷalu [suta] vicha raṇa .... tiśaya Singaniḷāvyā..
38. shajya Śāstra-dānōtkaramaṁ||vri||Vidita suvase Singanahaḷḷi dhānya saṁ......
39. .... haḷḷi samasta bhōga saṁpadaṁene [baṇṇipa] ∴... sāmya vrittiyaṁ bēḍada

1 'ru' is not written.

40. bandu sangane || hennaṁ Bettabbege.. mahōnnata.... navikīrṇateyindaṁ be...
41. manameṟagisuguṁ || Honne, Sura-honne .... ge pannāgavili-Bāḷegaḷiṁ saṁ
42. pinnummunnūra puragaḷēṁ paṁpude || Dharaṇige taḷa.... denisuva Bharaṇi... baḷiya bā ..
43. tavarmmane Manumathanaramaneyene-Honnehalli pariranjisuguṁ ||....bha sama...
44. .... nyaraksha || karatyana viśuddha-dharmma nirata [Trai]varṇya bhāphaḷar ssukritō-pārji phala
45. chāra sātvika sārarssale....Honnehaḷḷiy-aṟuvattokkalgaḷaṁ dhanyaro ||.. ase.........
46. pannanāgi sukhadin-irddu ||vri|| polvige vāradintida [ra] śobhe mandara tunga-śriṁga..
47. thāvaḷi-kūrttu baṇṇisalveseyal-Jinēndra-grihamaṁ [sachivāgraṇi] Honnehaḷḷiya..
48. .... ttariyāgi Singanā || Aṁtu Bhuvana-vidhitaṁ enipa Jina-bhavanamaṁ nirmisi-svakīya-
49. .... nāthasya Gaṇēśvarō-bhut-saddharmma nāmā pravidhūta karmmā tadanvayē Śrimat-Yāpanīyē......
50. vikhyāta-Gaṇēśa-babhū-vuṟvvīrā-munīndrā-bahāvō-mahāntāḥ || Tatōnya . vādībha pha...
51. Jayatu Śubhachaṁdra-dēvaḥ Kandūrggaṇa Puṇḍarīka vana-mārttaṇḍah khaṇḍaḥ Tridaṇḍa dū .....
52. Yāpanīya Sanghāynāmāna-tiḷakam-enipa Kaṇḍūrggaṇadoḷ... nyāya
53. negardda || Chandrakīrtṭi-munīṁdrō sau... Siddhānta-i gamāgraṇi bhāti kaṇḍūr-gaṇe-khyā-
54. .... ||vri|| mahīdharendra ku.... Jina śāsana-dīpakaṁ
55. ..... hī-taḷā Śanta-vivartti-kīrtti ramaṇaṁ maru.... puran-Nanta-vīryya Siddhānta-munīśvaraṁ

56. Śriman-mahāsāmantaṁ Suṟiyamayyaṁge pāda-
pūjeyaṁ koṭṭu kā..ge..... ṟa....
57. me mēṟey-āge piriyagaḷeloḷ-erạdu mattar-gaddeyman-
adara baḍa...
58. yiṁ baḍagalu mūṟu-maneya nivēshaṇamumaṁ dēvara
nandā-dīvige....
59. bādhā parihāram-āge paḍedu svasti Śaka-varsha-1069
neya Pra[bhava]....
60. .... vyatī pātamuṁ samanisi baṁda puṇya-tithiyoḷ
61. vri|| viḷasan-manṁgaḷa tūryan-ā...khiḷā śā...
62. ḷina śrī Jina-pūjegutsavakke koṭṭa.. Singaṇaṁ....
63. ..... vanacharitar-mmahātmar-aruvattokkalu....
64. . pūjege sarāgadiṁ nereda śēsha-gāvuṇḍa....
65. .... yana savasadiṁ pāpiye.....
66. ..... vēti dānachchrēyō.....
67. Kālē kāle....
68. dtatāṁ paradattāṁ

XVII

Tambur, Kalghatgi taluk, Dharwad district Slab lying in the compound of Basavaṇṇa temple

Permāḍidēva - 1155 A.D.

It records the rule of Vīra Permāḍidēva over Konkaṇa-900, Palasige-12000, from his capital Gove it refers to a sāmanta named Kagga as administering Tammiyūru-12, Huligōḍu-12 and Māvaḷḷi-12. It also refers to Biravaṇa for the worship and offerings to the deity Nārāyaṇadēva by the sumkadadhikāri Mādhavarāja daṇḍanātha the ūrodeya of Tammiyur. It further mentions the grant of taxes like *handaruvaṇa, baṭṭe-sumka, kuḷiya-sumka* it refers to Chāvundayya and also the construction of temple. The date of the record is Śaka 1077, Dhatu, Pushya śu.11, Sōmavāra, Uttarāyaṇa samkrānti equated to 1155 A.D. December 6, Tuesday, Sankrānti occurred December 25th. The cyclic year was Yuva.

Text

I – Panel

1. @ Namstunga śiraschumbi chandra-chāmara chāravē
Traiḷōkya-nagar-ārambha mūla-stambhāya śambhavē
2. …….. Jayatya-vishkritaṁ vishnōrvārāha chit-ārṇava
da…. ṇinnata daṁshṭrāgra vikrānta bhuvanaṁ vapuḥ ||

II – Panel

3. Svasti samasta bhuvan-āśraya śrī-prithvī-vallabha
mahārājādhirāja paramēśvara parama-bhaṭṭā

4. rakaṁ Satyāśraya kuḷa-tiḷakaṁ Chāḷuky-ābharanaṁ Śri mat-Traiḷōkya malla dēvara vijaya-rājyam-utta
5. rōttar-ābhivriddhi pravardhamānaṁ-āchandr-ārkka-tāraṁ saluttire || ta-chchhakravarti Vikrama-sahā[yan-enipa]
6. Śrīmat-Kādaṁba vaṁs-ōdaya śikhari-samūdbhūta-tigmāya vīra Śrī mādyannarttana prāṁ.....
7. bhuja śikhara kīrtti kāntā-vihāra vyemaṁdārē śrīnivāsa pramuda vadana nīrēja.....
8. dudhātri-bhāmākarṇṇavataṁśaṁ ripu-viṇata pāda-**Vīra Permmāḍi-dēvaṁ** || Āmahī.......
9. **Konkaṇa-vombhaynūrumaṁ Palasige pannichhāsiramumaṁ sukhadin-āḷu....**
10. Tat-pāda padm-ōpajīvi Tammiyūra-prabhu ||Ka|| sal-lalita guṇa gaṇāspada.
11. llasita viḷāsa vibhava nībhuvana lasatpa || amita kirti-ramaṇaṁ Mallarasaṁ daṇḍanātha......
12. dha-ratnaṁ || ā Mallarasanaṁ nija sant.. doḷ-nilisida mahātmaṁ ||ka|| sāmaṇōraga.....
13. Ruḍam- sāmanta kujatya-khaṇḍanaika-kuthāraṁ sāmanta-kadīra vajraṁ sāmanta-dine.......
14. śa Sembīkeyaṁ Kaggaṁ || Ā sāmanta chūḍāmaṇi Tammiyura[1] Hūligōḍu Māvaḷḷi
15. yint-ī mūru hanneraḍu sthaḷamaṁ tribhōgyāṁ-āntaraṁ-āḷuttam-sukhadiṇ-ire ||..........
16. sadamaḷa-guṇa-maṇi bhūshaṇan-uditā-dita vaibhavaṁ bujā-bhīshṭhā phaḷaprada......
17. nenisi negardda-vibhu suṁkada Mādhavarāja-daṇḍanāthana besadiṁ || Parahita chari
18. taṁ-budha jana-parati pushṭha-vasantan-ūrjitōrjita vibhavaṁ narapati sabhāntarāḷa sphuri.....

19. tōn-māṇikya-dīpanibhan Ācharasṁ || Antu Chāmaṇḍa-śvarada Nārāyaṇa dēvar-aṁga bhō-
20. gakkaṁ snāna-naivedyakaṁ Dēvara-puradolirppa Bananjiga Sēnigara sagar-adityagi palarum
21. Kurmmāntaraṁgaḷaṁ māḍi jivisuvaroḷe laṁ taḷasari-Bīravaṇamaṁ Handaruvaṇam..dēvara-toṁṭada
22. keya Baṭṭe suṁkamumaṁ kuḷiya-suṁkamumaṁ || ka || bhūchakrim pogaḷutiral-Ācharasa-mukhya
23. māge Suṁkada sachiva prāchuryya yaśarttāv-āḷōchisi koṭṭar-mukuṁda pūjege satata
24. yama-niyama japa samādhi-krama-niratar-lōka pūjyar āgama [vē]dar uttamar-ene
25. negarda-sāṁyamar-Iśāntaśakti paṇḍita-dēvar || Avarag āgrima śiśyavargga...
26. tada-anupamar-sucharitra..............śvara.. brati
27. nāthar || Antu **Śaka-varshaṁ 1077 neya Dhātu saṁvatsanada pushya śuddha** || **Sōmarāra**
28. **mu-muttarāyaṇa Sankrāntiy-māge** tat-puṇya dinadoḷ ||ka|| prakaṭa yaśas-paṭahaṁ dik-
29. prakaramaneyadalke-sunkad-adhikārigaḷ-ī sakaḷa jagaṁ-nutar-ittar-ssakaḷāvanī chanda sū-
30. ryyar-uḷḷanevaraṁ || Sāmānyōyaṁ Dharma-sētur nnētaṇōm kālē kālē pālaniyō
31. bhavadbhiḥ sarvvā-nētān bhāvinaḥ pārthivēndrān bhūyo bhūyo-yā
32. chatē Rāmachandraḥ || Svadattāṁ paradattāṁ vāyō harēta vasundharāṁ shashṭhī-
33. rvvarsha sahasrāṇi vishṭhāyām jāyate krimiṇ @

XVIII

Mishrikoti, Kalghatgi taluk, Dharwad district
Slab set up in the Siva temple

Jayakēśi II – 1158 A.D.

While referring to the rule of Jayakēśi of the Kadamba family it mentions his wife Maiḷaladēvi, the daughter of Chalukya Vikramāditya VI, as administering Kundur-500 division. It mentions one Dāsirāja of Pulivara and his sons Soma, Mallidēva and Lakshma.

Further, the inscription says that Mallidēva, the *Urōḍeya* and Sōvarasa were attacked and were about to taken away by the men of Govindarasa, when one Bābiyanna of Barage appears to have come to the rescue of these persons.

The record also refers to a grant of wet-land, house-site by Bābiyanna for the worship and offerings to the god Māchēśvara of the place.

There are two dates given in the record (1) *Bhulōkamalla varsha 11, Naḷa, Śrāvana, ba.3, Monday* corresponding to 1136 A.D., July 18, which was Saturday.(2) Another date found in the record is *Śivachitta Vīra-Permāḍidēva varsha 12, Bahudhānya, A+śvayuja, su. Puṇṇami, Monday, Lunar eclipse.* Corresponding to 1158 A.D., October 9, Thursday. There was Lunar eclipse on that day.

There is a reference to *mahāprabhu-daṇḍanāyaka* Mallarasa and *prabhu* Mallidēva and also Bāchana, who has been described as the servant of the god Māchēśvara, appears to have made grant of land to the same deity.

Text

1. Ōm Namaśtunga śiras-chumbi chandra-chāmara chāravē-Trailōkya-nagar-āraṁbha mūla
2. ..... bhavē || Gaṇapatyāya namaḥ
3. Svasti samadhigata paṁcha-mahā-śabuda mahā-maṇḍaḷēśvaraṁ Banavāsi puravar-ādhīśvaraṁ Ma-
4. lege Bhairavaṁ Kādamba-kūrmma Kūrmm-āvatāraṁ mūrtti Nārāyaṇaṁ saṁkrā
5. nti dhavaḷa nissaṁka-Rāman-abhinava Pārtha subhaṭara-tīrthaṁ Nind-iṟev-ātaṁ Parādhi Parasurā
6. man-ubhaya dēsī-vallabhaṁ Tribhuvana-maṇḍaḷika sikhāmaṇi Kādaṁba Chūḍāmaṇi-
7. tyakhiḷa rājyāvaḷi-samāḷaṁkritar-appa-śrī-maj-Jayakēsi-dēvara Vijaya-rājyam-uttarōttaro-
8. ttar-ābhivriddhi pravardhamānam-ā-chandrārkka-tāraṁbaraṁ saluttaṁ-ire tatu
9. pāda-pādārādhakaṁ sakaḷa-guṇa gaṇ-āḷaṁkaraṇa bhūshaṇa parivāra-surabhi-kaṇeya-kaṁka
10. ṇa-barisa Jayakēśi-dēvana-arddānga-lakshmi Chālukya-kuḷa-pavitriyaruṁ-appa śrī Maiḷala-mahādēviya-
11. ru Kundūra nelevīḍindoḷu sukhadiṁ rājyaṁ-geyyuttaṁ-ire ||vri|| Toḷaguva kuṁ
12. taḷ-ānganeya Kuntaḷa-dēsaṁ-id-eṁbina karaṁ Palasige-nāḍu śōbhisutav-irpp-annegaṁ dhareg-iṁtu gōḍiya
13. baḷayisi Dēvarājan-Amarāvatiyaṁ naguvant iri-ppudī Pulivaravḍentu baṇṇipaḍaṁ-entu poga
14. ḷvaḍam-entu nōrppaḍā ||kaṁ|| Ā-grāma chakravartinnoḷ-aṁgriyan-abhimāni mānadhan-enisiḷva
15. vigraha kutūhaḷam-sujanāgraṇiyaṁ Dāsirājanaṁ pogaḷadarāru ||ka|| Ā-Dāsi

16. rājan-angane Mādhavana Pinākiya Jana-
vaniteyarggarbbī-pādhanege migil-enippaḷu mēdiniyo
17. ḷu Jakkaṇabbe lalanā-ratna ||kaṁ|| Ā mithunarkkaḷya
gaja-Hari-kāmāṁtakan- udayipaṁ
18. tirudi (da) yisi negardd-ā śrī Mallidēva lakshm
Sōmarssujanar-enipa mūvar-ttaneya
19. ru || Ā Lakkrasana kulavadhu bhū-lalane samāne
Sāntikabbege puṭṭiṟd-ī-lōkadoḷage guṇadoḷ mēle-
20. nisidan-adhika śaurya diṁ Poḷalarasa || Lakkarasangaṁ
guṇadoḷu mikki sati-Muddikabbegaṁ puṭṭi jagak-
akkuṁ
21. ṁivar-enisi negarddita kūrmmeya Sōma Mallanuṁ-
Mādhavanu || Svasti śrīmad-ūroḍeya Mallapadēvarasa
22. raṁ Sōvarasaraṁ Gōvindarasana mānasaru baḍidu kuṭṭi
peḍi-geyyaṁ kaṭṭi ūr-indaṁ poramaṭṭu
23. pōgiv-enalu Baragiyava Bābiyaṇṇan-aḍḍaṁ bandu
tividu-bīḷal-emma jatiyiṁ-vritti
24. yalu melesidane(ṁ)dūriṁ mūḍaṇa Piriya-keṟeya modal-
ēriya keḷage tamma-mānya
25. da sthaḷad-oḷage sarva-bādhā-parihāram-āgi-koṭṭa gadde
kammaṁ 450 magim teṁkalu padinaydu-ka
26. yya-maneya nivēśaṇamaṁ salisuvaru || Svasti samasta-
praṣasti sahitaṁ śri
27. matu **Bhūlōka-varishada 11 neya Naḷa-saṁvatsarada
Śrāvaṇa Baḷuh (Bahuḷa)a 3 Sōmavārad-andu Bāram-**
28. giyara Bāchaṇa śrī Māchēsvara-dēvargge taṁna
mānyada kayyaṁ nivēdyakkaṁ Nandā-dīvigegaṁ biṭṭa
gardde kammaṁ
29. 450 **Svasti śrī Kādaṁba Śivachitta śrī vīra-permāḍi-
dēvara 12 neya Bahudhānya-saṃva-**
30. **tsarada Āśvayuja-Suddha-Puṇṇami Sōmavāraṁ
devasa-Sōma-grahaṇadalu**

31. Śrīmatu Pūlivarada mahāprabhu-daṇḍa-nāyakaṁ Mallarasaruṁ Prabhu Malli-
32. dēvanuṁ ūriṁ mūḍa Hiriya-keṟeya-modal-ēriya-keḷage Kammatēśvara Nakharēśvara dēva-
33. ra keyiṁ baḍagalu śrī Māchēśvara dēvargge sarvva-namasya-māgi biṭṭa saṁvu Kammaṁ
34. nūṟu 100 śrī Pūliya Bāraygara Bāchaṇṇa śrī Māchēśva-
35. ra dēvara tottu @ Svadattāṁ paradattāṁ vāyō-(h)arvti vasundharā-shashṭhir-vvarsha saha
36. srāṇi vishṭhāyāṁ jāyatē krimiḥ @@@

XIX

Tambur,Kalghatgi taluk, Dharwad district
Hidden in a field belonging to Sri Nandikatti saheb,Tambur

1214 A.D.

It is a lengthy record, broken at both the ends. As the beginning also is broken, the name of the ruler and other details are not available.

The record, while making reference to the Mallapa-*dandanāyaka*, gives the genealogy of a *Samanta* named Kagga, who has been described as brave as well as very generous. He appears to have constructed a temple called Permēśvara, in the name of his over-lord Vīra Permāḍidēva and made grants for worship in the temple and for education purpose, after laving the feet of Śiva Śakti-Bratināṭha. Further it says thar the *gāvuṇḍas, prabhus, ainūrvaru, nakaras, telligās* of the place made grant of land, money and oil for the worship in the temple.

There is a reference to a Maṭha at Dāravāḍa and also the list, probably Kalamukha ascetics of the *Maṭha* are find a mention in the record. Some of the villages, are mentioned such as Kāragōḍataḷa, Balagadde, Heggere are still in existence today. The divisions like Māvaḷḷi-12, Huligōḍu-12, Tammiyūru-12 are also find a mention in the record.

The record is dated in chronogram and it can be equated to 1214 A.D. There are two more dates [1] 16th regnal year of Śivachitta Vīra Permāḍi, *Chitrabānu, Chaitra Su,Panchami, Sōmavāra,* equated to 1153 A.D. *Śrīmukha*, April 1, Wednesday. [2] *Śaka* 1019, *Virodhi, Pushya Su*.5, corresponding to 1097 A.D. December 12, Saturday , *Īśvara Samvatsara.*

Text

Broken

1. .... kaḷā santatiya......... su.......... sadata......
2. ....reṁ baṇṇisalke santatiyali Mallarasana .... nāgi-barisirivaṁ sirivaṁbuja vriksha dalli sāmanta
3. ....Mādhava-rājana santatige tadiya...bagini...... gatmajana branti sajanutim budha-saṅtati-pogaḷalke Malla-nripanaṁ-Kagga @Janm......
4. ...ṁ-pina tayasadguṇi Muddiyaka(na)sura-pradvaṁsidd.... tanajeyamkaḍu gūrmeyaṁ prakaṭisirpp-ātmānujaṁ Mādhavaṁ tanag-endaṁḍe.........
5. paṁ Mallapaṁ @ Antu-Mallarasa-daṇḍanāyakaṁ Prabhutvaṁ.... nire @ ārpu-sura-drumake sale koṇḍidutirppudu kūrppunādeyuṁ sarbba.....

6. du mānyatevetta mūti(rti)-kandarppana-
neḷisirppu(du).... pōdarppa..... prati daksva
vrittiyimdirppalad-enutu māvaḷa-suvappudu kīrtti-
Jagake Kaggana @..........
7. janasēvyanudātta-vārdhiyant-anupama dinga-
bhīran-uragādhipanantire bhōgiyōdhīśana teṟadiṁ
kaḷādharanamartya-gaj-ādhipan-ante dāni endanu-
naya........
8. dharaṇi taḷamoldu baṇṇikuṁ @ Himagiriyante khaḍgi-
gaṇa-sevyan-iḷā-taladante sasthira tuṁb-rukhiyaṁdadi
kuvaḷaya priyan-aṁbuja-mitran-ante peṁpa ma(sha)
bu(bhū)ja
9. dgirīśanante virājita rājabhūshaṇaṁ-samanoḷare
vicharipade Kagganoḷurvvīyoḷ-anya mānavar @ āgāraṁ
nija-khaḍga-yashthiiyoḷ-arāti-brātamaṁtu....
10. ninnā rāranji śaranbuṇgal-karuṇadiṁ kāyaṁ-
mahaudāryadiṁ-dārārbba. ḍi-daḍa setirvena-gami-
eṁbāppu vikhyāta Lakshmī-rāmāpati Kaggaṇaṁ
samada sā.
11. maṁta.. kaṇthīrava karavaḷ-sūlige tōmaraṁ parasu-
bilkontaṁ Katāraṁ-mahachhu-charikā bhallaya
sellamullasita-chakraṁ baṇḍivāḷadi dustara...
śastraṁgaḷavā....
12. vādaḍamavakuṁ kaige-vandadu tāne ripushṇaṁ
bagevāga Kaggaṇaṁ nanārāmpar maho-grājiyoḷ @
Janakaṁ śrī Śāntivarmaṁ jananī-bhuvana vikhyāte
Tippavve Vidvajjaṇa vandaṁ
13. di-rājaṁ poreda-pati-dharādhīśvaraṁ Vira-Permmādi
nripaēndraṁ śri mad-ardhamkulavadhu vilasadrūpe
lakshmavve-yeṁdintu nitānta khyātige nōntanō-nikhiḷa
jagannuta Sōma(ṁ)

14. Kagga @ pariyaṇṇaṁ padavaḷa Barmmananujaṁ sandarbhataṁ peṁbi Nāgaramāgiḷdi Sarbevveyakkan-aḷiyaṁ tāṁ Barmma-chamūpa vistara bhāgyādhike bōsi tanna sōse-bhāvaṁ munjaṇaṁ ma
15. nādaradiṁ śāntan-enalkritārthar-oḷare Sāmanta Kaggaṁbaram @ Ā Samāntōragaru.... ḍaṁ sāmanta kujātā khaṇḍanaika kūṭhāra sāmaṁṭakkudhara vajrama Sāmantadinēsha ssaimhikeyaṁ Kagga
16. Svasti-samadhigata paṁcha-mahā-śabda-mahā-sāmantā vīra śrī dharmella-mallikā latānt | ati-chapaḷa vāchāḷa sāmanta dāra-dhara samīraṇa | Kādaṁba rājy-ābhyudaya kāraṇa | maṁ..
17. vadadaṭaṁ samudaya kari-karaṭa-vidaḷana mrigēṁdra| bhō gōpa bhōgyatā surēndra-dushṭha-nishsṭhura turagam-ārūḍha proudha rēvanta | nikhiḷa vibudha mākaṇdha nandana vasantha | vishama sam | grā
18. ma vijaya-bhēri ghana ninadi harshatā mayūra | saujanya karuṇāpūra | subhaṭaripu kadaḷī shaṇḍa khaṇḍana-kuthārara|| Saṁgrāma sūtradhāra| samara samayārōpīta vīra
19. śrī bhrū vibhramōpama chāpadaṇḍam toṇḍaragaṇḍa | bahu-vidha śāstrō pachita kauśalya bāhu-daṇḍa | toḍarvvara-gaṇḍa | nāmādi praśasti sahitaṁ śrīmanmahā sāmanta Kaggayyaṁ sukha
20. sankaṭhā vinōdadiniḷḍu @ Mudadiṁ Permmāḍi bhūmīśvarana pesaroḷī dēvatāgāramam lōkadoḷ-intī chelvamattille-enal atiśayadiṁ śōbhe kaṇgoppe lakshmī sadanaṁ tāneṁbina māḍisidanama
21. ḷa vikhyāti kaigaṇmidhātri vidhitaṁ sāmanta khadaṃbiruda subhaṭa brindāṁghripachchēda khadga @ nirupamamid-enisal-aty-ādaradiṁ pati-bhakti-giduve taṁ kaḷaśamenal-karame-chelv-enisi Permmēśvara

22. maṁ sāmanta Kaggaṇaṁ māḍisida @ ādēvat-āgarada gurukuḷa @ iḷeyoḷesandudu Dāravāḍada maṭam tatthyanadiṁ parvvatāvaḷiyoḷ Nanni-munīndran udbhavisidaṁ Tachchishya Sōmēśvaraṁ kali-kāḷaṁ
23. tadīya śishyanesedaṁ śrī-Madvarēśma jagattiḷakaṁ tat-priya-śishyanīga Śivashakti-jñāni lōkōttamaṁ @ akutiḷa guṇa nilayaṁ Śābdika tiḷakaṁ pravara naishsṭhik-ābharaṇaṁ laukika śāstravēdi-bhaktaṁ |
24. prakar-āmbuja bhānu-negardda Śivaśaktibudhaṁ @ Śiva sidadhantayapa- yasva-yōnidhi himakri chāritra nīrēja.... vikāsa-dyumaṇi ...... rājahamsaṁ manōbhava-matta dvipasiṁ.
25. havan-uttama tapa śrī vallabhaṁ Yōga-vichhava-śakti brati-pungava sakaḷa-śāstra prauḍha-nīrējaṁ @ Yama-niyama sachhāritraṁ śama-dama-nishsṭhitaḷ prabhāvaṁ lōkōttaman-enisidapaṁ
26. sakaḷ-āgama Vichhava-śakti yōgi yati-pati tiḷakaṁ @ ṛutu śaiḷāṁbara Sōma-saṁkhye **Śaka-kālaṁ Bhāva-saṁvatsara kshitiyoḷ-varttise Pushya-māsa sitapaksh-ēkādaśi Bhānu-saṁyutavā**
27. **raṁ byatī-pāta-uttarāyaṇaṁ Sankrānti kūḍirda puṇya-tithi prābhavaṁā**galūrjita yaśa sāmanta vajrāyudha @ Śiva-śakti bratinātha pāda-kamaḷa prakshāḷanaṁ māḍi bhū
28. bhuvanaṁ baṇṇise mangalā-nakaravaṁ bhōr-eṃbinamtī digvivara prāntamanatyudātta Charitaṁ sāmanta Kaggaṁ-mahōtsavadiṁ viśrutam-āge puṇya-dinadoḷ-hastōdakaṁ māḍida @
29. @ antu hastōdakaṁ-māḍi śrīmat Hermmēśvara dēvara-dēvālayadiṁ saṁyitu haḍuvalu baḷḷi-gaddeya kerevoḷagāgi baḍagal-Kārugōḍa hola-sīmeyā

30. gi mūḍa-mogade Herggeṟeya nīrottu-gaḍiyāgirdi bhūmiya parisankhye piriya gaḷdeyā mūmiṁ mattargge....vi mattaru hakala hiriyakeya ba

31. ḍagaṇa tumbina modala maḍavāyoḷ-ainur(500)-mmarada toṇṭmumaṁ sarvva-bādhā parihāramāge @ jananū (nu) ta brahmacharyya brati pati nichayak anna dā

32. nakke nity ārchana naivēdyakke pūjārigam-atithige jīrṇṇōdhārak-endu chandrārka-nagēndraṁ dhātri nilvannegam-akhiḷa jaga baṇṇisal-bhūmiyaṁ sarvva-namasyaṁ māḍi-koṭṭaṁ śa

33. śi vishada yaśōd-bhāsi sāmanta-kagga @ mattaṁ Tammiyūru-hanneraḍdu Mavaḷḷ-hanneraḍu Hūligōdu-hanneradinnitaḷ-prabhu-gāvuṇḍuga

34. ḷū-rūvoḷ-ondu paṇamaṁ chandrārka-sthāyiy-āgi koṭṭaru @ mattam-ainūrvvar-mahānāḍāgi neredu sante-sahitaṁ nānā-bhaṇḍakraya-vikrayadoḷaṁ koṭṭa

35. lli pong-are-vīsaṁ koṇḍalli pong-are-vīsamaṁ koṭṭar @ mattaṁ eleya-gātrigar-ellaṁ hērige nūr-eleyaṁ horeg-aivatt-eleyaṁ santataṁ dēvargge naḍevanṭ-āgi koṭṭar @

36. @ Nakara-samūhaṁ saṭṭuga-vattamaṁ koṭṭar @ Telliga-samūhaṁ sadākālaṁ dēvargge nandā-dīvige naḍevant-āgi soṇṭige yeṇṇeyaṁ koṭṭar @ ankada kaladiṁ haḍuva-mogade hōda

37. bīdiyiṁ Hori kēṟi-muṭṭe baḍagalu Heggegaḍiy-āgirdda bhūmiyaṁ dēvara-puravargga nivēshaḥam-āgi koṭṭar @ mattaṁ @ Māvaḷḷiya mūraṁśada mūva prabhu Chaṭṭima-

38. yyanuṁ Mādhavanuṁ bhū-vidhitaṁ Kallaṇanuṁ pāvana charitarkkaḷ-achaḷa bhakti samētam @ Adent-endaḍe Mādirāja daṇḍanāyakaṅge Māvaḷḷi dānāhi-sindhu parichchēdam-āgiyuṇuttaṁ baral-āya

39. niṁ parōkshadoḷ Kaggaya sāmantanuṁ pala-kālvu-ṇuttirddu pūrvva-dūroḍeyargge punarbharaṇa māḍalvermmēśvara dēvar-anga-bhōgakkā.... mūvar-ūroḍeyaruṁ Māvaḷḷiyoḷē Kētaya-goḷada modal-ēriyiṁ

40. baḍagalu-munūṟu-marada tōṇṭamumaṁ baḍagēriya bayalal Chattimūṟ-odeyana gaddeyiṁ mūḍal baḍagal-āladamarada baṭṭeyoṇiyiṁ tenkal-piriya gaḷeyoḷ-ondu matter-ggaddeymaṁsiḍiya-bachchaliṁ

41. baḍagal Hūliya-guḍḍeyiṁ tenkal Gaḷagēśvarada hakkaliṁ hāḍuval mareyara hakkaliṁ mūḍal hiriyagaḷeyoḷ-eraḍu mattaru hakkalumaṁ Gaḷagēśvaradiṁ tenkal hadinaru-kayya-mane

42. ya-nivēshaṇamumaṁ sarvva-namasyam-sarvvabādhā parihāram-āgi mūvar-ūrodeyaruṁ koṭṭar @ Sadamaḷa guṇa-maṇi-bhūshaṇanudit-ōdita vaibhavaṁ-budha bhīshstha phaḷa-pradan-enisi

43. negaradirdda vibhu suṁkada Mādhavarāja daṇḍanāthana-besadiṁ @ Haridēvaṁ negarddbhirājan-amaḷaṁ Chāmaṇḍa-rayaṁ mahātmari varppermme nripēśvarakke piriduṁ sadbhaktiyiṁ bittar-ā-purado

44. ḷ Telligar-ādiyāgi palavuṁ vyāpāramaṁ māḍi bālyarig-ellaṁ Taḷasāri Bīravaṇamaṁ chandrārkka-tāraṁ-baraṁ @ mattaṁ Baḍagēriya mālagāṟa-dōṁtada mūḍaṇa bhāgaḍoḷainūṟu

45. hū-giḍuvina sṭhaḷamaṁ bittar @ Mattav Ammayana-bhāviya mānya-gēriya holadoḷ Tōḷana-moṟaḍiyiṁ

haḍaval | bāga nandiya holadiṁ baḍagal | Kaḍakuḷada baṭṭeyaṁ (yiṁ)

46. mūḍal kaggulige-tana-sthaḷadoḷu Kundūra-kōlal-ondu mattar-kkeyaṁ dēvara nandā-dīvigegūroḍeya Baladēvayya-nāyakaṁ sarvva-namasyam-āgi koṭṭaṁ @ intīśāsanastham-appa dharmmamaṁ

47. pratipālisidar Gangā-sāgara Kurukshētrādyārghya tīrthaṁgaḷol sāsira-kavilegaḷaṁ kōdu koḷagumam pancharatnagaḷiṁ kattisi sāsirvar-vvēda-pāragar-appa brāhmanarggu

48. bhaya-mukhiyaṁ koṭṭa phaḷaṁakku @ Ī-dharmmaman-aḷidavar-ā puṇya-tīrthaṃga-ḷoḷā-sāsira kavileyaṁ sāsirvva brāhma-narumaṁ konda mahā-patakaṁ-akku @ Sāmānyō-

49. yaṁ dharma-sētu nripāṇō kālē kālē pālaniyō-bhavadbhih sarvva-nētān.... bhāviṟppārthi-vēndrān-byūyō bhūyō yāchatē Rāmachandraḥ @ bahubhirvvasudhā bhuktā rāja

50. saṁsagar-ādibhiḥ yasya-yasya yadā-bhūmis-tasya-tasya tadā phaḷaṁ @ Svadattāṁ para-dattāṁ vāyō harēti vaṣundharāṁ shashsthir-vvarsha sahasrāṇi vishsṭhāyaṁ jāyatē krimiḥ @

51. idanininitī dharmmamanoldu pāḷisidavargg-akkuṁ mahataiśvarya saṁpadam-ārōgya-vaṁ-bhīsḥtha-siddhi bahu-santānaṁ yaśa śrī baḷik-adan-ullanghisi dharmmamaṁ kiḍipavarge-janmadoḷ nāyi bā

52. rada dukhaṁgaḷan-uṇḍu puṭṭugum-avar ppuḷāga-mōdyaṁgaḷōḷ @ Jātōjana makkaḷ Kētōja Muddōjar linga-pīṭhamaṁ besageyda śāsanad-akkaramaṁ khaṇḍirisidar mangaḷa-mahā śrī

53. @ udādyuchhaudu chāryāvaḷe pōdruta pubhaṭari subrata-sāmanta chētōmadyadga ndēbhaniṁ-hasukavi nikara dāridrȳa śaiḷēnḍra vajraṁ pradyumnālaṅkāra rūpaṁ Gunigana gaḷeyoḷ nālku matta pra

54. māṇaṁ vidyādānake koṭṭaṁ sadamaḷa charitōdbhāsi sāmanta Rudraṃ @ Baḍagēriya bayaloḷiroṁ... nervadanītaṁ śāstramanōduva chhātrargadiṁ-baliy-enisida garddeyaneḍe maḍagade rudra-nadi tarippa

55. mukha-mudram @ mattaṁ sadāśiva chittaṁ śrī Vīra-Permmaḍidēvar @ vri @ rviḷasaddīpakke sunkakk-adhipatiy-enipa ssruṅkadird-ādivāragaḷol-ondu hāgamaṁ neṭṭane kuḍuvudu dēvarggerttō-

56. ṭa sthaḷamūroḷvantā mūru tōṁtakkavaraṁ Kuḷiya-suṁkangaḷaṁ māṇbud-ī-bhū-vaḷayaṁ nilvannameṁdādaḍame niyamisidaṁ Vīra-Permmāḍī-dēvaṁ @ka @ Bhūtarasa Kēsirājarggōtukuḍa a

57. irl Permma-nripati sunka-sthaḷamaṁ khyātiyin-avar adhikāraṁ bhūtaḷadoḷ negaḷalaytu dharmmōdyōgaṁ @ mattaṁ dēvara-purada maduveya handaru-vaṇamaṁ koṭṭar @ Ā-puradoḷ maduveya honnabaḷi –

58. y-āyamumaṁ beḷgoḍe vaṇamumamūra-dātārar koṭṭar @ svasti **śrī Kādamba Śivachitta-Vīra-Permmādi dēva varshada 16 neya Chitrabhānu saṁvatsarada Chaitra-suddha paṁchami Sōmavāradaṁ**

59. **du** śrī-Vīra-Permmāḍi dēvaru śrī Permmēśvara dēvargge aivattu-honnaṁ chaṭṭiya-sāvantana-mēle hēḷalārppugange Baḍagēriya bayaloḷu mūdalmodeya baruhu sīmey-āgi tenkal-kuḷiya tōṃṭa-gaḍi

60. yāgi paḍuvalu Hermmēśvara Siddēśvarada tōṁṭa-gaḍiy-
āgi baḍagalu basadiya-tōṁta sīmeyagidda bhāviyaṁ
sarbba-namasya sarvva-bādhā-parihāravāgi koṭṭaru
Sakavarsha l019 neya Virōdhi saṁva

61. **tsarada pushya śuddha 5 Guruvāramuṁ**
Saṁkramaṇamappa puṇya-tithiyoḷu Śivaśakti-
dēvara pāda prakshāḷanaṁ-māḍi || vri || vilasan-mangaḷa
turyan-ādavakhiḷā-śā bhaktiyaṁ muṭṭaliṁ toḷu-dinda
janakā

62. yyanuṁ Padumanābhaṁ .... nāluku kuḷiya suṁka-
biṭṭa suṁkaṁgaḷa biṭṭa.... chandr-ārkkar-uḷḷannegaṁ||
piriduṁ khyātiya Permmēśvara kolviṁ mantri-
maṇḍanaṁ chā..... Hermmēsvararendud-biṭṭareseyalu
chandrārka

............broken ....

XX

Hasarambi,Kalghatgi taluk, Dharwad district Inscription lying in the premises of Śiva temple

Permāḍidēva - 1171 A.D.

The record mentions the rule of Jagadēkamalla of Kalyāṇa Chalukya dynasty, when Śiva-chitta-Vīra-Permāḍidēva of the Kadamba family was administering Konkaṇa-900, Palasige-12000 from the capital Gōve. It makes a reference to Maiḷaladēvi, the queen of Jayakēśi and her two sons viz., Permāḍidēva and Vijayāditya.

The grant, while describing Hasurage in Palasige-nāḍu mentions Dēva-gāvuṇḍa, his wife Chauḍiyakka and two sons viz., Chāva-gāvuṇḍa and Sōva-gāvuṇḍa.

Further it registers a grant of land and three houses made for the incense, offerings and worship of the god Sōmēśvara by Sōva-gāvuṇḍa and *aravattokkalu,* after laving the feet of Divya-śakti-paṇḍita of Baguḷagere. Grant of *okkaludeṛe* by *Sunkad-adhikāri* and oil by Sova-gāvuṇḍa is also mentioned in the record.

The date specified in the record is 24th regnal year of Śiva-chitta-Vīra-Permāḍidēva, Vikrama, Jyeshtha, su.Panchami, Thursday, Uttarayana Saṅkranti, corresponding to 1171 A.D., *Khara,* May 27th Thursday. Another date given in the record is 25th regnal year of Śiva-citta-Vīra-Permāḍidēva, Khara, Bhadrapada, Su.Tadige, Somavāra, Solar eclipse, corresponding to 1172 A.D. Nandana, August 24th, Thursday, No Solar eclipse on that day.

Text

1. Ōm namaḥ Śivāyaḥ | Namastunga-śirakumbi (schuṁbi) chandra chāmara-chāravē Trailōkya naga

2. [rā] raṁbha mūla-staṁbhāya śaṁbhavē || Esepa Pasurageyoḷorppare Vrishabha dhvaja
3. nelasi ninda Sōmeśvaraṇuṁ besakeyya taṁnna bhaktarigosed-īvanu-varaṁ-eṁdu
4. kāṇisidayayiṁ || Ghaḷigeya-grāmada baḷiyolu paḷiyillad-esedu
5. tōrppa Pasurageyoḷu tāṁ ghaḷa-ghaḷane baṁdu nelesida-Negaḷēśvara divija-haranu Sō
6. mēśvaranu ||Svasti|| Samasta bhuvan-āśraya śrī prithvī-vallabhaṁ Mahārājā-
7. dhirāja paramēśvaraṁ parama-bhaṭṭārakaṁ Satyaśaya kuḷa-tiḷakaṁ Chāḷu-
8. ky-ābharaṇaṁ Śrīmaj-Jagadēkamalla-dēva vijaya-rājyaṁ-uttar-ōttar-ābhi-
9. vriddhiḥ pravarddhamānaṁ-āchandr-ārkka-tāraṁbaraṁ saluttam-ire || Svasti samadhi-
10. gata paṁcha-mahā-śabda mahā-maṇḍaḷēśvaraṁ Banavāsī puravar-ādhīśvara samasta bhuvana saṁsthūyamāna hara-dhara-
11. ṇī prasūta Trilōchana Kadamba vaṁśa mahōdaya mahīdhara śikharābhyudaya-māna-mahā prachṁḍā marttaṇ-
12. ḍa Mārttaṇḍa karāti tībra nija-pratāpa-vaśīkrita saraḷa-maṇḍaḷanuttunga Simha lānchhanaṁ Vānara-mahā-dhavaja Permmaṭṭi-
13. tūryya nirghōśaṇaṁ chaturāsīti nagar ādhishṭhitā daś-āśva mēdha dīkshā-dikshita kuḷaprasūtaṁ Himavad-girīndra-
14. rundra śikhara sthāpita mahā-śakti prabhāvaṁ tyāga jaga-Jhaṁpaṇ-āchāryya niśśanka-rāma su-bhaṭara kanaka-nikaśōpaḷa-śaraṇā-

15. gata vajra-prākāra lōkaika kaḷpa-dhrumaṁ Sankrānti-dhavaḷa mūrtti-Nārāyana kīrtti-mārttaṇḍa maṇḍaḷika lalāṭa-paṭṭa
16. vairi-gharaṭṭa subhaṭa-rājaśikhāmaṇi Kādaṁba-chūḍāmaṇīty-akhiḷa nāmāvaḷi samāḷaṁkritar-appa śrī manu-mahā
17. māhēśvaraṁ **śrī Śivachitta Vīra-pammāḍi dēva Konkaṇa-voṁbhainūrumaṁ Halasige-pannichchāsiramaṁ samasta-dēśaman-āḷuttire ra-**
18. **jadhāni Gōveyoḷu** sukha-saṁkathā vinōdadiṁ rājyam geyuttamire || Arigabaḷājanakkera darandige vīradin-ātma-rūpa sunda
19. [ra] teyoḷ-ārppinan-idan-īṁ palavu kūrggaṇeyaṁ naney-aṁbinōḷiyaṁ sura(ru)chira Kanchana prakaramaṁ sale taṁnnaya hasta
20. [yugma] diṁ surida-pa .... rvvagedu baṇṇisarīnipa Permma-bhūpana || tad-anujaṁ|| Ārameyaṁ surada (dru) madin-oppa
21. [va-siddha] gōdadhi (di)ṁ gaṁbhīra taṭākamaṁ varusadiṁ Śiva-lingamanoppe māḍi tat-kshira nimittar-iṭṭu suradhēnuvanā paḷa
22. [diṁda-vī] mahōdārguṇāḍhyanaṁ paḍedol-aṁbike dig-Vijayādityana || Ā nirmmaḷa sangrāma-....vara Kuntaḷa-rāja
23. [putri-cha] chandr-ānane yāchaka-prakara kalpa lat-ōpameyamdri (adri) jātegaṁ Jānakigaṁ samānar-enip-unnata śīḷa-nīla
24. [sa] rūpaduddāṇi nagartteyaṁ paḍedaḷurvvige Maiḷala-dēvi permmeyiṁ || Ant-avargge tanayar-ādark Kuṁtaḷa
25. [dēśādhina] tha dauhrityar-bhū-kāntēśareṇisi bhuja vikrānta Permādi-dēva Vijayādityaru || Kaḍupiṁ

26. Permāḍidēvaṁ nija-vijaya gajārūḍhan-āgalke Lāḷam-
guḍugita ganḍa garvva Dravidan-aḍagidaṁ Mā
27. [ḷa vaṁ bhi] tan-ādaṁ seḍedaṁ Nēpāḷan-aṇṇa-(aṇṇaṁ)
Toṟedu kaḷedan ā Gūrjjaraṁ Pāriyātraṁ-miḍukal-tān-
aṁji-nindaṁ Malepa
28. [n-aḷakidaṁ] Maghadaṁ sēde-geṭṭa | ari bhūbhritpari-
daṇḍan-ārthi-jana kalp-ōrvvī janātyanta vistara kīrti
29. [pramu] dā [ma] nōrmmaḷan-udyat-bhūri-dhātri dura(ṁ)
dharana ūrjjitā-vairi-bhavaṁ vinuta dhātrī-pāḷa-chūḍā
30. maṇi sphrit-amghrī dvayugaṁ Jigīśu Vijayādityāvanī-
pālaka || Vāsugī-bani (ṇṇi) sal-aṟiye [dēśa]
31. [śikhāma]ṇiy-enipa Palasige-nāḍoḷ Hasurage
sōbhisutirkuṁ Vāsavan-Amarāvatiya-pura-
32. kkadhikaṁ-enal || Binkadin-esev-ī Hasurageya-
teṁkaṇa-deṣeyalli bandu nelasiye nindaṁ Śankara-sva
33. [yaṁ] bhuv-enisida kuṁkuma-lōḷaṁ kāpāḷi
Sōmeśvaranu || Sōma-gāvuṇḍavi anvaya ||
Ant-ā Hasurage
34. .... ye santōsa dind-irppa dēva-gāvuṇḍana peṁpaṁ
santatamey-annadānantuṁ kuḍutippanalte āśrī-
35. tajanake || Ant-enisida Dēvagavuṇḍana kāntey-enippa
Chauḍiyakkana sadguṇa niḷaya santatame dāna-śīle
36. yan-entu pagaḷuttamīpari vasumatiyoḷu || ant-avargge
taneyar-irbbaru | Śivapada-bhaktaṁ kēḷire Śivaleṁkaṁ
37. Śivana torttu Śiva-gaṇa mitraṁ Śiva pāda-padma
bhringaṁ Śivan-ālḍam Sōva-garudana pogaḷadar-ār-
oḷare || Tad-anuja | dā...
38. ..... rmaratane hitavan-āgipanella-kālao śrī-nāri patiy-
enna mānavaroḷu rāja-pūjita Chāva-gāvuṇḍa ||
39. Ant (enisida) Sōvagāvunḍana kānte guṇ-ōnnati-yoḷ-
anna-dāna kramadoḷ chintāmaṇi sura-bhū-ruhadant-
esedaḷu ....

40. ....kka vanitā-ratna || Ant-avar-irvvarge sale santati **śubha-lakshaṇānvitaṁ rūpinoḷu Kantunibhan-enipa putra ....**
41. ..... puṭṭidaru guṇa-niḷeyaru || [17] Svasti | śrī Kadamba **śrī Śivachitta Vīra-Permāḍi-dēva-varśada 24 neya Vikri saṃvatsara**
42. **da Jēshṭha Śuddha Panchami Brihavārad-ōttarāyaṇa Saṁkrānti-ā-vyatī pātada-ndu** Hasurageya Sōmēśvara dēva-
43. ra gandha-dhūpa nivēdya kantha(ḍa)sphuṭita-jīrnnōddhārake āchāryyara-grasakk-endu Sōvagavuḍanu-aṟuva-
44. ttokalum-iṟddu Baguḷageṟeya Divya-śakti paṇḍitara kālaṁ karchchi dhārā-pūruvakaṁ māḍi-biṭṭa keyya sī-
45. mā sammadhi (sammandhi)y-ent-endaḍe ūrimda mūḍaṇa Īśānyada deseya seḷḷa-keṟeyoḷagu-ādiy-āgi mumdaṇa kō-
46. ḷana ēri-mērey-āgi koḷanimda-teṁkaṇa basuriya-marada haḍavalu ā gaddey-inda tenkalu hakkalu
47. dēvara baḍaga-deseya maṭa-ondu [1] Bāgarigara mane-ondu [1] Telligara mane-ondu [1] int-iyuṁ mūru maneya
48. nelasaṇamumaṁ sarbha-nama śivāya-sarbba-bādhe parihārav-āgi.. biṭṭanu || Intī dharmmamaṁ prati-pālisidava-
49. rgge Gange-Vāraṇāsi Prayāge arghya-tīrtta Gurukshētradalu sāsira-kavileya sāsirbba-brāhmaṇarige-ubhaya-mu-
50. khi dāna-goṭṭa phalaṁ-akku || Int-ī dharmaman-aḷidavaru sāsira kavileya sāsirbba-brāhmaṇarumaṁ ēḷu-
51. kōṭi Tapōdhanarumaṁ konda mahā-pātakan-akku || sva-dattaṁ paradattaṁ vāyō-harēti-Vasundharāṁ sasṭhi-

52. varisha-sahasrāṇi-misṭhāya jāyatē krimi || [18] Svasti śri Kādaṁba śrī **Śivachitta-Vīra-Pemmāḍi-dēva va-**
53. **rshạda 25 neya Khara-saṁvatsarada-Bhādrapada Śuddha Tadige-Sōmavāra Saṁkramaṇa-vyati-pātad-andu Sunkạda-adhikāri**
54. Lakshmī-dēviyaruṁ maga-Madhuhayyaṁgaluṁ-irddu Hasurageya Sōmēśvara dēvarige nandā-dīvigeya-e-
55. ṇṇege Tēligar-okkalu-deṟeyumaṁ Kumbārad-okkala teṟeyuma int-ī-eraḍ-okkalateṟeyumaṁ dēvarige-bittar ||
56. Teligara-mān-eṇṇe dēvara nandā-dīvigege Kumbāṟada-āvagege maḍake chatrakkevuṁ dēvara-nivēdyakkaṁ Sōva-gāvuṇḍa biṭṭa ||

XXI

Mavalli, Kalghatgi taluk, Dharwad district
Slab lying in the field of Parasappa Kallappa Hasarambi

Chālukya Jagadēkamalla – 1125 A.D.

The record while mentioning the rule of Jagadēkamala, states that Jayakēśi of the Kadamba family was administering the divisions like Konkaṇa-900, Palasige-1200, Kavadi-dvīpa savalakka. It further refers to Padmaladēvi, the elder-sister of the king who was married to Hākiballadēva who was in charge of Banavāsi-12000 and also to his minister Barmachayya, a devotee of *Jina*, who constructed a *Jina* temple. The grant of land, wet-land, oil, garden etc. were made by him for the worship, offerings and feeding the *Jaina* ascetics in the Śantināth *basadi* after laving the feet of Varisēna-paṇḍita, belonging to *mūla-sangha* and *sēna-gaṇa.*

The date of the record is *Chalukya Vikrama* year, *Visvāvasu, Margasira, śu. E+kādasi*, Thursday, *Uttarāyaṇa, Sankramaṇa Vyatipāta* equated to 1125. A.D. November 12.

Text

1. Śrī ...... dē charitra ... śi...tana samadhikaṁ nelevīdi....kīrti-kante....... naya-chitta..... na guṇ-āgraṇi....bhū
2. ...... vimukta nima...... bhinava.......
3. vaṁ ..... nale........ guṇa-nidhi śirōmaṇi ye
4. .... Śrīmatparama gaṁbhīrasyāddvōd-āmōgha lānchchanaṁ jiyā trailōkya-śāsanam Jina-śāsanam || bhū yōdā vīra-sēna
5. sya Vīrasēnasya śāsanaṁ bhū yadā vīra-sēnasya vīrasēnasya śāsanaṁ[||] Svasti-samasta-bhuvan-āśraya
6. śri prithvī-vallabha mahā-rajādhirāja paramēśvara parama bhaṭṭaraka satyāśraya kuḷa-tiḷaka Chālukyābharana śrīma-Tribhuvanama
7. lla-dēvara vijaya-rājyam-uttarōttar-ābhivriddhi pravardhamānam-āchandrārkk tāraṁbaraṁ saluttam-ire tat=pāda padmōpajīvi...ma
8. sahāyan-enipa narchchinaḷiyaṁ || vritta || Aribhū-bhritkari-simhanarthi-jana bentā-ratnan-ā śrānta bhāsura kīrti pramōdapriya ripu-kira-vrātama.....
9. Konkaṇa-chakravartti tiḷakam śri mūrti-Nārāyaṇa nara-nāthaṁ || .. Jayakēśi dēvan esedaṁ Kādamba-kanṭhirava || . ..Konkaṇādhīsa Konkaṇa vombhainūrumaṁ Palasigepa
10. nnirchhāsimumaṁ Kavaḍi –dvīpa-savālakkamumaṁ ēka-chhatradind- āḷuttam sukhadin-ire tan-

mahīsvaraniṁ Piriyaḷu Padmala-dēviya manōvallabha Hākiballadēva Banavāsi pannirchhāsirama-

11. N-āḷuttaṁ Sukhadin-ire ||vri|| viditaṁ. . . . .
.vividha . . . .

12. Dadhīchi śrī-sutaṁ Tā-enal-atiśaya rēvantan-i-
Hākiballa||va|| Āmaṇḍaḷika trinetraṁ Manōvallabhe. . . .
. . tāḷdida sura-kunjam eṁbante vāranganā

13. . bant-eseva surabhi kāntāvataratvam-ādant-uditaṁ
śrī Hakiballa prasutara bridayāvāsi Kūttivaḷ-ānandade
Lakshmidēvivandi pratatige kanakā. . .

14. . . . .jana kalpakam jātege nirale sama subhānu-bhavana
vibhavege dhareyoḷ Padmaḷa-dēvige nirantaraṁ
Hākiballanasinge satiyaru Tat-tanūjāte-

15. Dēvige puṭṭdaḷu mahā-mānava-māninī taḷake neṭṭane
Padmaladēvi visva-vidyāniḷayaika māḷike yaśah
paripāḷike nī-Ratnakarbbe Kōtuka. . .ratnamāḷi.

16. Chandadim|| Tat-pradhānaṁ Manamaṁ S`rī Jinarājan
chāru charaṇāṁbōjāyanoḷ nishsṭheyiṁ Tanuvaṁ Jaina
viśuddha-mārgga charita vyāpāradoḷ-santataṁ ghana-

17. Teyam dig-bhittiyoḷ kūḍI sajjana-chintāmaṇI
Barammachayyan-esedaṁ Samyatva ratnākaraṁ
Jina-pādambhojz bhringaṁ Manu-charitan-apāra
śritāmbodhi samvarddhana chandraṁ nī. . . . .

18. rājyāmbujōnmīḷanatigma jyoti vistarita dhavaḷa yasaṁ
Gōtra vistāran-urvvinutaṁ s~rī Barmmachayyaṁ
Sukavisuka phaḷōpēta bhyūt-ōrvvī-jataṁ||vri||

19. jjakke. . . tatmāvitatvavidan-ēka su-dharmma. .
n-ānivahakke. . . . labhavyahara . māhyatva-vivēka. .
.drāḷa yōddhāra vaibhava. . .... ma . . . .

20. . . . . tat-putraṁ Jana-nutan-endu satya-yutan-endu. . .
. . naran-endu Jaina-pūjana su-charitran-endu ou. .·. pe
me. . . . .

21. Sutanaṁ Tachhaturvidha sudāna samanvitaṁ. . . . . . .mārggade sāntana-shadgunaṁ-gaḷa ||ka|| Śrī sa. . .mamanīśa. . . dhegi dānana. . . . . .

22. Ta sukrita-sthānaṁ Dēsige nād-adu. . . tāgi. . . . . sakaḷa jana-manah prīti karaṇa. . . . bhāva-bhuvana . . .rati-dēvige rati sukhakaraṁ Saṁ[jāta]. . . . . tāvaṇa

23. . . . . .yya nōḍalka-adēṁ vaṇṇisuveṁ|| Āmahī-bhūshaṇad[ante]. . . . .baṁ|| Dēva-kulagaliṁ Jina-grihaṁ Galin-unnata saudha-śāḷeyiṁ S`rī vanitā nivāsa. . . . . .

24. haṁgalim dēva-nadī-samānam-enipudghatara. . .bhū-vaḷayaṁ. .d-unnati. . . . . .nayan-ābhirāmaṁ Bhūnuta pūga.

25. Pārijāta santānavangalugapana sāmra. . . . . . bhūrjja. . . .nada māḷikā vakuḷa kānanadim-?nandanam tān-esedirppa Māvaḷḷiya. . . .

26. ḷu||vri|| Bhū-dēvānvaya vārddhi varddhana śaśānkar-ssajja. . . . .nri ya prādurbhāvara pāra paurusha gunarn-nānākalā kauśalar-vvēdōktādi purāna Dharmma-kathana. . . . .

27. ṇa Padmaṇah ||Vibhugaḷu sāmānyare. . . . . .chāgi . . . . . Lakshmīgriha maṇḍanaṁ Nijam-enippa. .

28. . . . .nidhi dharma-durandharan-endu dhatri nāna =guṇa. . . vistarade. . . . prabhu-Mādirājanaṁ. . . .tra|| Narasiṁhaṁ sakaḷa kaḷā paripūrṇṇaṁ Mādirāja daṇḍa. . . .guṇa. . . . .

29. . . . . .tya. . . . . . . || Tat-pradh=na|| Anaya-vagge. . . . . . . .ṭṭisa. . . . enirppa Mādirājana mandanna. . . . . . . .pa

30. Jagājjana-nuta nōḷouvettan-udita kirtti vadhū- vilāsa varddhana mahōtsava. .
. .bhāva-vibhavaṁ Sakaḷōrvvīḷ-nirantaram|| Śrī nij Jina-samaya. . . . .vyo. . . .
31. tinma kiraṇan-akhiḷa-jana pramōd-bhāsi mantri-sikhāmaṇi vikhyāta Lakshmīgārmmaṁ Barmma|| Antum-allade ||vri|| Jinanāptaṁ Ballirāja. . . . . .
32. tāyi Sāntivarma tanayaṁ S`rī Gōpaṇandi vrati-gurubsudhāyarsanda Jina. . . . .ni. . .ntam / Hākiballa-āvanipati patitaṁ Barr=mmachayyaṁ. . . .ttāṁ
33. . . . . . . .Bāgavve māgolk-esedire nere mū . bhūmi-pradēśa|| Jina-mandira Puruhūta mandiradoḷu chalvam tāḷdire saujanya nidhānam
34. Jina-vinuta Barmmachayyan-ā puravaradoḷu Jina. . . . . .rya. . . . . . pati . . guru-tāyi tanayaruṁ jaganmadaḷana Ayyadēva-dāsa prabhu ta . . . . .
35. tiya vaṁśa pradīpaṁ vinayāmbōrāsi parśvam. . . . . .yaśa śrī vanitāḷaṁkāranarhatvada yuga naḷinī dēvya sachharīkaṁ ||va|| asatyā
36. layācharyarvārisēṇa Muni-patigala jagat prasiddha Sēnagaṇāchārya-varma prabham-entedoḍe || śḷō|| Arhata Sa-sana-Mūḷābhyō sanghē
37. chārita nimmaḷa Pu. Sēna ganākhye-pagari . . nāmani Anaghaṁ Jaināga . . .vidhividu gupti vyāpti yuktam Jina svaranam chāritra. . . . .
38. kamaḷa . . . . bhavya padmākarō . . chāritra chakrēsvarana . . . .yaśōmaṇḍna dhanyan-ā sena Jainarāddhāntaka ni . . . ta . narghya māṇikya paṭṭa . .
39. ra || Śrauta siddhāntagabhasti . . . ḷi sakaḷeḷa pāḷa chūḍamaṇi-dyuti virajita pāda-padma yugaḷam . . . jyāṁ . . . palyakravājitanātmīyaṁ

40. . . . . .honnatiyiṁ Sambhavasēnadēvan-esedaṁ Rāddhānrikāgrēsaraṁ ||. . . . . .Guṇa-sampannana . . .. Padmasēna gunāvyā-vrittiyaṁ Yōgi bhūshaṇōnyatvada . . . . .

41. . . . . .tatvajn#ānāhār-āgama . . . .lakshaṇa śikshāvidan-udghavāgmarime . . . . Siddhānta vidyā-samarppaṇa . . . . yasamaṁ Jagaṁ-pogaḷguṁ Siddhānta Chakrēśanaṁ || Ta . . .

42. . . . . .pati . . . .mōham-eṁba . . . . toḍaraṁ Biḍe māna kāshāyam-eṁba . . . . . .keya-kamba . . . .muridud-indriyavargga visāḷi. . . .taḷidudu māyavene

43. Kāppora-gaṭṭa-meṭṭi sīḷdiridu Nāgasēna muniyemba varotkaṭa gandha sindhuram / || Tatra dharmmaru || . . . . śōdha sarvva sātva prakaradoḷ - enisal sandaḷdaānantadu manōbala-

44. . thya patindrāsuranalamadu gāmbhiryamad bōdhi . . . . .peṁ Chandra śailendra tunga tvaman-ā . demde kīḷmāḍuvud-ene

45. . . . . su-pūjya vratindraṁ [saka] ḷa karmārāti . . . . sakala tanu . . . bhadra kanthīravȧ-vendram viḷasachhri Jaina dhammāmbaradi vasakara kshira-vārā

46. . . . . . rāehīsat ārādhipaviśapa yaśōrājitaṁ Dhuti tilakaṁ ŚrīVāsupūjya vratipati negarddaṁ Viśva lōkaika-pūjyam || vri || kshiti pūjyaṁ Vāsupūjyam

47. . . . . . .guṇayutam Vāsupūjyaṁ Dharitripati chūcha chumbita . . Pra Krama Karmma-yugaṁ Vāsupūjyaṁ . . . . . . .nētra kshaṇa bānachhi

48. . . . . .dharitrīstutan-āda vidyavidan-enisida sēnānvaya Vāsupūjyaṁ || Tatrisyaru ||dhare pogaḷuvud-Āryasēna racha . . . .

49. . . . . .tvamaṁ tatva savistara vijnāna manatyādaradiṁ [Jina] muniparoḷu mahōnnatar-ādaru || Tatsadharmmaru || Chandra prabha siddhāntigarīndre-bhēndra du . . . .

50. . . . . dra prahara supamita munīndra .. . . . . .haḷdoḷu || Tatsadharmmaru || Bhūnutan-aśesha vidya-dānaṁ Vāchhalya niḷayō. . . . .

51. Śrī-nāri ramaṇiyantān-enisuva . . . . . .Sēna-munīndra|| Tatsadharmmaru || A+ . . kāthā prabandha kavanāvagu jāḷadoḷu silkaninta vormmaṭa vitaṇḍa chaṇḍa vachana. . .

52. dind-āvoṁ Korgguḷiggoḷḷananya samayōdyadvā(di) yandaṁdere. . . . . .vidyodgama. . n-eseda . vādībha panchānanaṁ ||Tatsadharmmaru || Harana vishāḷa . bhāla nayanārbbe mankdgha. . . . .

53. Tōddurapaviya payōdhi . gi mathanādbhuta jāta samasta lōka saṁhara . .. ṣamākritiyim Nayasēnadēva vistaratara jilpakalpa sivikalpaman-ī . . .

54. Ritriyoḷu || Tatsadharmmaru || Para vāchāḷa virodhi vā . . gaśā. . . . . ḷa . . . ḷi bhūdhara vajra para vādisatamana saṁghōdbhūta bhabhānu du . . . . vādi prati. . .

55. ni pam Māṇikyasēna digambara vistarita kīrtti Jaina mata. . . . . ||Tatsadharmmaru || sruta vidya Vāsupūjya suta . . . mma kaṇḍakēḷi virājita kira .

56. haṇanagaṁ Sāhitya vidyā samanvitana prārtita bhavya bandhu Jinadharmma. . . . drajanastutan-ādaṁ Muni Jinasamaya samuddharaṇa. .

57. gamāmbōnidhi niva . ndana vidhurtānjina pāda padma kaḷpa-janan-ene panḍita-dēvaru|| upakaraṇamgaḷam palavumaṁ Paḍedittu kritārthiyādaḷagga . . . . .

58. gatiyarā Jina –mandirakke dharma pareyaśōka Rōhiṇiya . . . ḍindaṃe || . .ṭa || . . .ṇa . . .vibhu Vārisēṇa munināthara . . . ti dhātri baṇṇisalu || gadya || Svasti Śrīmachhāḷu-

59. kya **Vikrama varshada Viśvāvasu samvatsarada Mārggaśira śuddha [Ēkādasi] Brihavāram-uttarāyaṇa śamkramaṇa vyatipatam kūḍida** puṇya tithiyoḷu Perggaḍe Barmma-

60. chayya-nāyaka tanna Basadiya Śāntināthadēvara-anga-bhōgakke . . gga .hāra-dānakke ā chandrārkka tāraṁ naḍe-vantāgi-ralalliya Mahāprabhu Mahādēvanāya-

61. kange Chiddanangaṁ Padmanaṁgaṁ pāda-pūjeyam koṭṭu sarvva-bādhā pariharamum namasyamum-āgi paḍedu Śrī man Mūlasanghada Sēnagaṇada Pogarigachchhada śrima

62. du Vārisēṇa-paṇḍita dēvara kālaṁ Karchhi dhārāpūrvvakaṁ māḍi biṭṭ adharmmam-entendaḍe ūriṁ-mūḍalu haṭṭageya bayalu Gaḷagēśvara-dēvara keyim Temka-

63. lu Hiriya kōlu gardde mattal-ondu mattam-adar<baḷiya hakkal-osadiya bachhalaṁ Haḍuvalu matta baḍagaḷeya harida tōṇṭa guṇiga matta 1 gāṇa

64. vondu @ || Ānegaḷda Bammachayyana mānini Jinakbegaḷu Rati-dēvige sanmāna-nidiya-Attimabbege tāne migil tāne vandye tāne pavitre || Gangege tāne nirmmaḷeye

65. nippa negaḷteyan-nt-ā Bāgiyakkaṁgara nūnadāna nidhi Jaina Śikhamani Barmmachayya nāthangavudāra vāridhi vivēka mahānidhi Śāntināthan-uttungayasaṁ samudbhavi

66. sida Jinadharmmamaṁ Puṭṭuvaṁ pa || Antu-puṭṭe || Sura taru śākhegaḷoḷ kēsari-kēsaradoḷ sudhaṁśu rasmigaḷoḷ nirbbarav-enipa guṇadoḷ-esedaṁ Dharagoḷ Śrī Śā -

67. ntināthanuchitasanātha || Enisida Śāntināthana sahōdarimannuta Rājiyakkanuṁ dharaṇige Jakkiyakkanu vaden-esedirddarō rūpinoḷ kalāparinate

68. yoḷ vivekadoḷ udārateyoḷ dhritiyoḷ mahatvadoḷu surachira kīrttiyoḷ vinayadoḷ nayadoḷ dharaṇī taḷagradoḷ

XXII

Tambur,Kalghatgi taluk, Dharwad district
Hero-stone set up near the Cholappa Basappa, Hora-oni of the village

12th Century

The record is engraved in 12th century characters. Further it states that a hero named Hiriya-Rāma Konati who laid his life in a boundary dispute, when Sāteyanahaḷḷi was besieged. Further, the record says that the stone, was set up in his memory by his elder sister named Malliyabbe-nāyakiti.

Text

1. ra tottu paranārī-sahōdaraṁ | [dē]vara hiriya Rāma-koṇati Sā

2. teyana-haḷḷiya muttidalli bīḍiṁ munniṅdu-kādi palaraṁ Kon

3. ndu geldu tann-āḷdana chōḷa-vāḷiya(ṁ) nī (gi) suralōkamaṁ sūṟegoṇḍu dēvalō-
4. kakke pōda || ātana akka Malliyabe nāyakiti kaḍasida-kallu ||

XXIII

Tambur,Kalghatgi taluk, Dharwad district
The slab lying near Basavaṇṇadēvara hoṇḍa

12th Century

This badly damaged record is in 12th century characters, refers to Permāḍinrpa and one Mallinātha. Further it tells that the *Tantris* and *Parigrahas*, led by *sāhani* Talava Nayaka made grants to Budha-chandra swami Other details are lost.

Text

Lines 1 to 8 are not clear

9. .... vajra arahārama......
10. sāmānya hajjagāṟara Permmaḍi nripaṁ
11. ..... Chāmavvegantu sanjasama
12. .... Tri-malla chūḍāratna || ad-ent-ene || muḷisiṁ vīra-ripu
13. .... dōr-vvaḷadiṁ tāgidar-ātiyaṁ taṟidu dig-deyvaṁgaḷa śākinī kuḷamaṁ bhū
14. gaṇa ..... ṇipuva vairi-sankaḷa ond-ādanarāge rakshisuvaṁ śrī Mallināthōttamam || Ant-ā.....
15. mahānubhāvaṁ Malli.... ā prakāradiṁ tantra parigrahaṁgaḷu Basadige-goṇḍu bari-
16. dharmamaṁ saṁbōdhise....... sāhaṇi mukhyav-āgi tantraṁgaḷalu pratyēka hāgamaṁ haḷiya

17. Talava-nāyaka mukhyav-āgi samasta **parigrahaṁgaḷalu** pratyēka hāgamaṁ Budha chandraswāmig
18. gaḷige dhārāpūrvakaṁ māḍi chandr-ārkkavāgi koṭṭaru || paripāḷiśadolla-davarnarak-ābdhiyoḷaddu
19. biddu dukhavettāntaradoḷati ghōra-taradiṁ nirantaraṁ namage pautra-petra-samtēaṁ||

XXIV

Tambur,Kalghatgi taluk, Dharwad district
A slab lying inn the Backyard of Basavannayya Hiremath

12th Century

The record refers to a Jaina-devotee named Padmavati and mentions grants for worship and feeding the Jaina ascetics in the *Nakara Jainālaya Basadi.* Further it records the grants made by *Nakaras, Sandhi-vigrahi* Basavaṇṇa and *sunkadadikāri* Vāmayya to the basadi.

Text

Broken

1. ……la…ke…saṭṭaga-vatta..
2. jatanakara Jinālayakke..Sūrya Śaśi…..
3. ……jajjege kai-mugidu bhaktiyiṁ Telligar-ellā-neredu…..
4. ……im ….. hēṟiṁge santataṁ nūṟeleyaṁ [ku]lagiri daritri nilpinam-olaviṁ……..
5. …….. neyade... ....mu heṟuvaraṁ Chaitrakka-hāgamaṁ Jōgina-puṇṇameyandu hāgamaṁtā……

6. .... taḷam-uḷḷinegam || @ Tat-puṇya-dinadọl ||ka|| vāravadū tiḷake Jina-pāda nirēja-vinaṁnaṁ bhangi-chāri

7. .. kara śishṣthēshtha jan-ādhāre manōjāta-rāga padmaṁ padmaṁ ||vri|| Jinan-āptaṁ guru Nāgachandra-munipaṁ muttā....

8. .... bana chāritrada dharmmad-unnatiya-chāmaṁtāyvara strī-jānā śōbhā mukurunda satyadruśe Sōma.....

9. ....tāṇāndadiṁbine Padmāvatiy-antur nōntaroḷare vārāṅganā sankuḷaṁ ||ka|| Smarana sakaralangajātana-kara-chakraṁ chitta....

10. nalatike manōhara nripana kusuma-chāpaṁ dorey-enipudu rūpin-ēḷge Padmāvatiya ||vri|| manamaṁ śrī Jī......

11. nātha pāda-kamaḷa dvandvangaḷoḷ-vittamaṁ manam-oldādaradiṁ viśishṭha janargoḷetta-kūrmmevaṁ mikka māntanamaṁ mānyaroḷ-udva...

12. .namaṁ svātmāngadoḷ kūḍe neṭṭane Padmāvati tāḷdidaḷ guṇa-gaṇaprōttuṁga vikhyātiyiṁ || antu Padmāvati Nakara Jīna-

13. nālayadoḷ-irppa rishiyar-āhāra-dānakkendu Mādirājayya-daṇḍa-nāyakangaṁ Narasiṁha-daṇḍnāyakaṁgaṁ pāda-pū

14. jeya koṭṭu Tuyyala Boppa basadige koṭṭa garddeya tenkaṇ-ombattu goḷi mēreyāgaḍu vaḷageṟeya nīrottu-mēreyāgi

15. haḍuva mogadirddarmma-guṇṭina Kiṟumoṟadi-gaḍiy-āgirdda garddeyann-adaṟa baḍagaṇa hattidarppordirldage mērey-āgo matta-rbbe

16. .... yalumaṁ paḍedu ||kam|| paḍeddrtha-nivahamaṁ pūḷdidaḍe-yaśōvaḷi-nayade pallavise manaṁ biḷe dānaradharma

17. maṁ nūrmmaḍisidaḷēm satiyaroḷ kritārtharpayō padmaṁ || Jina-muni-janad-āhāra dānakk-anunayadiṁ rāgamodave

18. Padmāvati sandanupamam-enisuva bhūmiyan-anavarataṁ koṭṭalavanī-taḷaṁ muḷḷinegaṁ || Sāmānyōyaṁ dharma.

19. sētu nripaṇārṁ kāle-kāle pālaniyō-bhavadbhiḥ sarvvā nētān-bhāvinaḥ pārthivēndrān-bhūyō bhūyō yāchatē

20. Rāmachandraḥ || Svadattāṁ-paradattāṁ vāyō hareti vasundharām shashṭhirvvarsha sahasrāṇi-vishṭtayāṁ jāyatē krimiḥ @

21. lasadiya Teṁkaṇa kēriyaneseyalkumaṁ Tribhūshaṇaṁ Basavaṇṇaṁ Vasudhe Śaśi-Sūryya-kuḷagiriy-esed-irppina koṭṭanu

22. ḷdu sadbhaktiyoḷaṁ || aṁtu sandhi-vigrahi Basavaṇṇaṁ Nakara-jinālayakke Nakara-jinālayada tenkal-eṁbhattu keyi-nīḷada nela

23. numaṁ dāna-śālegaṁ kavitegaḷigaṁ-sarvvabā-dha-—parihāram-āgiy-āchandrākaṁbaraṁ biṭṭa || akaḷaṁka-chāru-charitaṁ

24. prakaṭa-ya śaṁ mantri-makuṭa-ratnaṁ Basavaṁ Nakara-jinālaya basadige sukarateyiṁ-biṭṭan-ondu teliga-maneyaṁ-antu

25. sandhi-vigrahi Basavayyan-aṟuveya Tippaṇa-maneyiṁ haḍaval-ippattu kayi-nīḷada Teliga-maneyaṁ Nakara-jinā

26. layada dēvara nandā-dīvige naḍevant-āgi biṭṭa-da telliga-maneya taḷasārige-bīravaṇavaṁ sunkādhikāri Vāmayyaṁ

27. chandrārkkaṁbaraṁ sarva bādhā parihāravāgi-biṭṭa ||

XXV

Tambur,Kalghatgi taluk, Dharwad district
A slab lying near the Basavanna temple

Gūvaladēva - 12th Century

It is a damaged record. It refers to the rule of Tribhuvanamalla of Chālukya dynasty. Further it mentions Gūvaladēva as ruling over Konkaṇa-900 from his capital Gōve and gives the genealogy of Mādirāja and Jayakēśi. There are references to some officers named Mādirāja and Hiṭṭimayya . As the record is damaged, the details can not be made out.

Text

1. * Namas-tasmai Varāhāya līlayāchatē bhavi bur-āntara-gatō yasya mēruḥ khaṇa-khaṇāyatē || ja
2. gra.viśrānta bhuvanaṁ vapuḥ || Svasti samasta bhuvan-āśraya śrī pṛithvī-vallabha mahārāj-ādhirāja paramēśvara
3. **Tribhuvanamalla-dēvara.**vijaya-rājyam-uttarōttar-ābhivriddhi pravardhamānam-āchandrārkka tāraṁ [salu] ttam-ire

4. samasta bhuvana saṁsthūyamāna hara dharaṇī prasūta Triḷōchana-Kadamba vaṁśa mahimābhirāma..
5. bra nija praṭāpa-vaśikrita sakaḷa mahī [ma]ṇḍaḷaṅ uttuṁga Simha-lānchhanaṁ | Vānara-mahā-dhvajaṁ | Permaṭṭi......
6. prasūtaṁ | Himavad-girīndra śikhara-sthāpita mahā-śakti prabhāvaṁ | tyāga-jaga-jhaṁ [paḷā]...
7. kaika-kaḷpa-dhrumaṁ | saṁkrānti dhavaḷaṁ | mūrti-Nārayaṇaṁ | kīrtti-mārttaṇḍaṁ | maṇḍaḷika lalāṭa-paṭṭaṁ | vairi....
8. jjita śrīman-mahā-maṇḍaḷēśvaraṁ | **Gūvala-dēvan-nija-rājadhāni Gōveyoḷ Konkaṇa-voṁbhainu[ṟu]..**
9. pratipāḷaney-ind-uttar-ōttar-ābhivriddhi-pravarddamānaṁ-ā- chandrārkka-tāraṁ sukha saṁkathā-vinōda [diṁ] vijaya rā....
10. ...yūroḍeya || vritta || naya samvnnanudagra vikrama dhanaṃ samkruddha vidvishtha.durjjaya...., tta virōdhi..
11. jitaṁ-śri_mad-akshaya-puṇyaṃ guṇi Hiṭṭimayyan-esedaṁ Viśvaṁbharā-chakradoḷ || [ba] ḷa vatsa....
[ddha] vaivaśvata ni..
12. piṁchhāta pratāṁ doḷakētu brātah śankhānana kachaya jaya-ghaṭāvaḷi kāhaḷā-saṁkuḷa.... tritaḷa manu
13. chāritra-guṇadoḷu śīḷadoḷam Sīteg-Arundhatige Kubajjātege dore Māychikabbey-eṁba.... prakaṭaya...
14. Māychāṁbike sakaḷa mahī-bhāgadoḷ raṃjisidaḷ ||vachana|| Iṁtu samasta guṇa.... meyenisi.....
15. gitaṁ dāmōdarātmajaṁg-uddāma yaśōrājitange Bīchige mudadiṁ || Yāchaka-kuḷa .... marīchiya...
16. nakhiḷōrbbar-ātaḷaṁ baṇṇisuguṁ ||vritta|| nrita-sad-vākyan-anūna-dāna janatā santarppi.... gannvita.. shṭha....

17. Bīchirājaṁ virājita-tējaṁ Jamadagni-gōtra tiḷakaṁ lōkaika kaḷpa drumaṁ || ||vachana|| i....gaḷdi Bīchirāja....
18. ranukūḷa prabhāvadiṁ [ne] gaḷuttum-iral ā-daṁpatigaḷge ||kanda|| naya-vidar aśēsha lō..... r-amaḷa charitra....
19. bar-eṁba-tanūjar || ā satīratadoḷu mōhaṁ musiyoḷt-advāṇi... gurugaḷol .. desakaṁ poṭṭi
20. manutadyumaṇi vibudha Māgadha-jana-Chintāmaṇi śaraṇāgata rakshāmaṇi... si negaḷda....
21. vīrānganā-sādhankan-udyut śrī... va dhūṭī-kuchakaḷaśa samālinganōdbhūtarar-ādti....chintāmaṇi
22. bhū-nutaṁ Madirājaṁ || avaroḷage || kanda || śrīmat-samasta guṇa-gaṇā ..... dīn-ārtha kumu....
23. vaniyoḷ ||vritta|| Kanakādr-indradavol-samasta vibhudhā-dhāraṁ phaṇi-dhvaṁsivo..... dāyakaṁ..
24. l-padvinitan-enal śrī Jayakēśi-yeyde-taḷedirdda sadguṇānīkamaṁ ||sa.... gi negaḷda..
25. sanda kāḷima-kaṇṭha priyan-āgiyuṁ sakaḷa-lōka khyātam-āgirddu Mārapa...bhivisalke..
26. sūnu bhānujaṁ mura-ripu-kāyaluṁ pirida.. mānalu... dha...
27. kēsiyeyed taḷedaṁ vibudhāvaḷi-kūrttu baṇṇisalu ||kanda|| ī-janōda [vū] .. na keḷe [yā]....
28. yaśa śrī virājitaṁ Jayadēva ||vritta|| Sura-taruvaṁ ma.. Kanaka śai... dri paya....
29. dantiyaṁ kari-khaga-rājanaṁ vihagaṁaidada mārggajan-entu nōrppaḍaṁ do.. milla jaya...
30. puṇyānganōtkrushṭheya-Yāychāṁbike tāyi. sand-agrajaṁ [ma] mmigan-eseva.... rājaṁ.... natō.
31. vayō-graṇi guṇi Jayadēvaṁ yaśa Śrīnivāsaṁ|| dharaṇītaḷakkaḷaṁkara.... gartteya-da[ksha]...

32. bana māṭa-kūṭa taleyiṁ neṟed-oppuva Tammiyūroḷ-
oppire Jayakēśi... da Vishnu-grihaṁ...
33. nta bāṁbara baḷedu Surēndra-Rudra-niḷayākaleyaṁ
taḷed-abja-nābha.. da sannidhā...
34. daṁ Jayakēsiy-idēṁ kritarthano ||kanda|| Sakaḷa-dvijai
[hi] kāmyaṁ trika.... lke satra..
35. daṁ Jayadēvaṁ ||vritta|| Akshayam-āva-dānadoḷalu
śruta-dāna [da].... muṁ mōksha....
36. m-ōtsavadiṁdame-māḍi-śishṭha saṁrakshaṇa
dakshan-ā.... daḷavu [bhuṁbukavā] ... dhātriye....
37. m-anēka ratna-niḷayaṁ-pōlkuṁ Gunāṁbōdhiyoḷ dorey-
āgalu Jaya.. dud-illaṁ bhō....
38. yiṁ ||gadya|| Svasti samadhigata paṁcha-mahā-śabda-
mahā-prachaṇḍ-ḍa....... janābhīshṭha [pha]
39. Kaukshēya kavigaḷita muktāphaḷ-āḷaṁkrita vijaya-śrī-
kāntā.... ta Jimū ...
40. bara-samara-samaya-rudra | naparāhna daridraṁ Kali-
kamaḷa kaḷaṁ.... raṇa-vi.....
41. nija-bhuja mada-madir-ōnmatta duranta-durdhar-ā-rāti
chakra-vikrama... prasanna...
42. shat-karmma-dharmma-samanvitōttama-chāritra pavitra
dhar-āmar-ānvaya..kasitā..
43. chāpōpama-bhū-vibhrama dēvānganāpānga
jyōtsnāmrita bha... vaibhavā....
44. pāssūchakā-sahanādi-baḷa samiti hritkanṭaṁ |
berppa..... dōrd-aaḍa..
45. sāra pūra-praśamita kōp-ānaḷaṁ virōdhi-vipina
dāvā......
46. surabhi sura-chira jangama latōpama [llaṁ] Ji...........
47. pa gana Gangā-jaḷaughā bakīrtyaṁgan-ā.....
48. bhaṭa bhaṭa chētō vibhīshaṇaṁ........
49. virājitaṁ śrīman-mahā........

50. Kārttika-māsa sita..triti.........
51. su-ruchirataraṁ-enisu [va].......
52. prakara khachita māṇi........
53. sarbba bhōgānvitaṁ | sarbha na........
54. ḍeya.... māṁ-ddha vo........
55. gaṇa niḷayara pari.........
56. yā pāyakara heda.........
57. tārtha-prada Śri-chintāma........
58. Jayate- dēva-dēvasya-dāna........
59. prasiddha ...

XXVI

Tambur,Kalghatgi taluk, Dharwad district
Slab lying in the premises of Cholappa Basappa, Hora Oni

12th century

The record mentions the hero named Maileya-nāyaka who, with the permission of his master Permāḍi opposed the soldiers and horses of one Māyidēva and laid his life in the battle.

The date given in the record is....Sarvạdhāri, Chaitra, Śu. Chaturdashi, Mangalawāra. The date portion is incomplete.

Text

1. vi matsara ma himda...... parisaṁ .... bbakē- **Sarrvadhārimanvayadoḷ Chaitra śudhada Chaturddaśi**
2. **Mangaḷavārad-aṁdu tannaya** patiya.... besaṁ baḍedu Maileya Nāyaka Māyi-dēvanaṁ bhaṁvam
3. toḷdisamarānganạdoḷ suralōkave-yididaṁ || esev-ī-Permmāḍi-rāyaṁ besase

4. ..bila…me nātaṁdagaṁ besanaṁ kaikoṇḍu-māṟ-āntarī-kuḷa bhaṭaraṁ… basa… kaikoṇḍu vāji..
5. ……. yalu saṁgrāma-dhīraṁ Javana-parākramamaṁ tāḷdu śauryatvadiṁdaṁ pesariṁ ranjirppa
6. dēva-vadhu ku. rāvagaṁ prāptan-ādaṁ || [ka]li mechchayidade, bāyaṁ biḍalu pati [su] ta stutyadiṁ baṇṇisa[lke] sa
7. lladēvāniyoḷōkisidanu [japa] manna [l-adariṁ manābhra bhrī] bhra…yindaṁ nīle….. pūrvvada nikaramu [maṁ]
8. ….muṁ-koṇḍu tannondaḷavaṁ sangrāma-doḷu mechhisi sura-vadhu-manada.. diṁ koṇḍu . pōdaru || .. ri..
9. de [nipa] Māyidēvana tura[gā]-nīkaṁgaḷa padāti taleyaṁ… radolu [vāḷisu] tamaileyan-ura….si…
10. [ye] koṇḍu sura-vadhū-priya[nā]… Jitēna-labhyatē Lakshmī mritēn-āpi sur-āmganā kshaṇa-vidhvaṁ-
11. sinī kāye kā chintā maranē raṇe @ Jaga-mechhe haḷeya [ta] dima maga vailaṁ pūrvva saṁpadaṁ toḷdi…..

XXVII

Tambur,Kalghatgi taluk, Dharwad district
Slab in the compound of Basavanna temple

Tribhuvanamalla(Vikramaditya VI) – 12th century

While referring to the rule of Chalukya Trubhuvanamalla, it mentions, Gūvaladēva of Goa Kadamba family, as ruling over Konkaṇa-900, Halasige-12000, and Kāvaḍidvīpa Samālakka from his capital Gōvage. It refers to one Mādirājayya *Daṇḍanāyaka* as administering Tammiyūru and twelve villages. As the record is badly damaged, the purport of the record cannot be made out.

Text

1. ....ṁbi chandra-chāmara-chārave | Trailōkya nagarā-rambha mūla-stambhā........
2. @ Svasti samasta bhuvan-āśraya śrī prithvī-vallabha mahā-rājādhirāja paramēśvara parama bha-
3. ṭṭāraka Satyaśraya kuḷa-tiḷaka chāḷukyābharaṇa śrī Tribhuvanamalla dēva vi
4. jaya-rājyam-uttar-ōttar-ābhivriddhi pravarddha-mānam-ā-chandrārkka tāraṁ saluttam-ire @ Tat-pāda
5. padmōpajīvi @ samadhigata paṁcha-mahā-śabda mahāmaṇḍalēśvaraṁ Banavāsī puravar-ādhīśvara samasta
6. [bhuvanasaṁsthū]yamāna Hara-dharaṇī prasūta (Tri) lōchana Kadaṁba vamśa mahōdaya mahī-dharēndra
7. [śikharābhyuda]........ ya māna mahāprachṇḍa ārttaṇḍaṁ-mā...karāśītibra nija-pratāpa vaśīkrita sa
8. kaḷa mahī mandaḷan-uttuṁga Simha-Lanehhanaṁ vōnara mahādvaja yan-ī permattitūrya nirghōshaṇaṁ chatu-
9. rāsiti naga rādhitāshṭhā-daśāśva mēdhā dikshita kula prasūta Himavad girindra rundra śikhara sthā-
10. pita mahūśakti prabhāvam ...... bhataka kanakanika......
11. .... saranagata vajra pra ....saṁkrānti dhavaḷuṅs mūrtti Narāyaṇa kīrtti-mārttaṇḍa maṇḍaḷika
12. latāṭa paṭṭaṁ vairigharaṭṭa subhata rajāsikha maṇi kādamba chuḍamaṇī.tyākhila rājāvalī virā jitarappa
13. śrīman mahā-maṇḍalēśvaraṁ Gūhalladēvar nnija **rājadhāni Gōvageyoḷ Konkaṇa-vombhaynūṟumaṁ Pala-**

14. **sige-pannichhāsiramuṁ Kavaḍi-dvīpa savālakkamumaṁ** ... dushṭha nigraha viśishṭha pratipāḷaneyind-uttar-ōttarō-
15. ttar-ābhivriddhi pravarddhamānam-ā-chandr-ārkkatāram sukha saṁkathā-vinōdadiṁ vijaya-rājyaṁ geyuttam-ire @ Tat-simhāsanā
16. āśraya...... y-āsannavaṟa Māvale nāḍ-āgrahāraṁ Tammṃiyūr-oḍeya @ [śrī mat sama] guṇaagaṇa dhāmaṁ dīnārthi-
17. kumudavana.... lasatsoman vārānganā najinakamda Jayakēśi negaṟdārnn akhiḷ āvaniyoḷ || Akaḷaṁka Bīchirājam
18. .... janakanakhiḷa puraṇa puṇyāgaṇōtkristha Yaychāṁbike-tāyi-sand-agrajan Mammigaṇaṁ eseva nujaṁ Mādirājan-tōrvvīśa Kadaṁba Gū-
19. halorvīpati....... pari...... dayda.... vipra vaṁśāgraṇi guṇi Jayadēvaṁ yaśa Śrī nivāsaṁ tad-ānuja ||
20. Svasti samadhigata paṁchamahā sabda-mahā sāmant-ādhipati mahā-prachaṇḍa daṇḍa-nāyaka vairibhayadāyaka |
21. samara-sāgar.taraṇḍa ....ripu kōladaṇḍa chaturaṁga baḷa sūtradhāri mōnege-murāri vijayāṁganā -bhujaṁga-chatu-
22. raṁga simgaīkriti guṇa krityaī Kaliyuga Vikramāditya | vīra lakshmī grihā-tōraṇanaṇṇana gandhāvaraṇan-asama-sāhasa
23. Vainatēya durdanka [jēyaī bahu] bala [bava] nna vīravipra kēdāra | parārtha Paraśurāma | subhaṭaṁka-bhīma
24. vandi brindā chintāmaṇi |........ Chakravarti śrī Tribhuvanamalladēva rājya-lakshmī-viḷāsaṁ sakaḷa

25. lakshmi nivasaṁ.................. śrīman-mahā-prachaṇḍa-daṇḍa-nāyakaṁ Mādirājayyaṁ .... Tammiyūruṁ
26. hānnirppaḷḷiyumaṁ sāmya ..... diṁ-dushṭha-nigraha viśishṭha-prati-pāḷaneyin-āḷdu sukhadin-ire || @
27. tatpāda padmōpa-jīvi Sēṇiga-Chāvuṇḍayana-vaṁśāvatārav-ent endoḍe @@ Śrīge Hariyoḷ-vivāhārpyogaṁgeyva
28. ṁ mangaḷanaka .... meseyalu-begaṁ kaṭṭida gudigereraga dinosedōppe-puṭṭid-ūrb-Baṇṭayana || śri Guḍigeṟe
29. ....sa le nile.......... yagiratatkkula vibhūshaṇaṁ Baṇṭayanoḷ-bāgiyab.... bandu kūḍire-ragadinan-ant-avargge puṭṭidaṁ Chāvuṇḍa @
30. Hara charaṇa-kamaḷai-śringa Hari-charaṇ-āṁbuja' śīḷama.... Brahma pād-āmbūruha-nava-padmahamsa-charitaṁ Chāvuṇḍan-eseye tāṁ bhā
31. suradoḷ | ant-eseye bā .... ḷidaṁtna-pūrbba-puṇyōdayadoḷ-antāgaratido... Koṇḍada...ntiyumaṁ
32. .... Chandiyabbe negaḷdaḷu || Ramaṇi sati Chandiyabbegadumaḷa guṇīndrāṁ siva-maṇḍayagaṁ mudadiṁ sumana
33. .... rggame piriyaṁ Jaganātanindaṁ-baraṃ || Bīrange sakaḷa guṇa-gaṇadāranga manōja-rāja..... da hāra .... va
34. .... dāraṁge negaḷda tammaṁ dhāriṇiyoḷ dāni Sāsigaṁ guṇi subhaṭaṁ || Intu guṇamanar-enisidavan-taḷedu sa..........
35. kuladipakariṁ saṁtōsaman-eydi haṇādinint-odavida chāmaṇḍanan-tirantarananaru || vādi ... pa vataṁda ... sanda ......

36. ḷe raṇādi balva-galada saṁsāra phalaṁ Māvaḷe-nāḍūrugaḷoḷ-Tammiyūru sogayisuguṁ ...... Harihara ka........
37. ma...... hālayamaṁ sabhāgrihaṁ Śatra-grihaṁ Piriyakeṟe bhāviya.... verasegiḷạ puṭṭi-nandana
38. sagaḍad-angaḍige * beḍaṁgiḍidi sūḷegērive... ni ... ppagada pālve.... kirimanmgo... kalige geriyo.......
39. raṁyam-eṇisippar-akkarigayyaṁ-gaḷasa śrī jīvigaḷa jīyarajiyy-eṁba bhaṭṭa gāyaṇayya grihaṁgaḷo........
40. sūsuṁ || Harihara vimāna mantra-dirō Vishṇu-dēvarājaṁ tann-ishṭharavina-vimānaduṁ-tamḍiriyaniḍane...Chāvuṇḍa.......
41. phaṇirāja niḷayamaṁ dhāriṇig-iralidu pūjyam-ene tad-irisidana phaṇi-rājanen endonnidaneṇisma rābba
42. va grihamaṁ | sahājaṁ śiva-padayugalam-ivahā patada sukhārtḥa he.... vendaṟidu mahāmahigiru permme
43. maneṇigara Chāvuṇḍayaṁ dēgulamaṁ || Tāṇḍavaraṁ śrī khaṇḍa-mani-maṇḍana maṇḍita bhōga bhūpaṇa cha...
44. yanaṁ vibudhātramananta mūrthi kaikoṇḍu nirantaraṁ nalage Tāmbrapura kritayā....... seyalli...... Chāvuṇḍa-nade
45. sedattā samasta dhātriyoḷ || Samadhigata paṁcha-mahā-śabda mahā-maṇḍlēśvara | nahita maṇḍaḷi.......
46. śvara nija-kuḷa kuvaḷaya sudhāraka | vineya-ratnākara .... su-maṇḍaḷika taleya......
47. da.... nuḍḍugaṇa sutaṁ baḷasurva.... maṇḍaḷikaravā-nvayane [ke...] yaṟem-āge kāva | vishama tuṁga
48. rēvantan-ahitā-kritānta... Mallikārjunadēva-labda-vara-prasādan-ubhaya-baḷa raṇāchāri.........
49. .... śrī mat Tribhuvanamalla..... ḍanāmādi samasta praśasti sahitaṁ śriman mahā....

50. …….. Bamayyarasaṁ śrī…… genāḍa dushtha nigra sishṭha prati-pāḷane……..
51. ………. baresva prata….. Bhādra-suda……..
52. ………….. gaṁ-nira………la
53. ………… ṇa ponnako……. sya sarvabādhā parihāraṁ….
54. ….. vu viśaṃhāraṁ nābhi paṁ visha muchyate vishama
55. ttaṁ vāyō harēti vasundhara shashṭhirvvarsha śahaśrāni mishṭhā…….
56. ……….. vm̄a sangamadoḷ Vāṇarāsi Gayey-eṁb-ī tīrthaṁgaḷo
57. ………. di dēvagaḷ ||

XXVIII

Tambur, Kalaghatagi Taluk, Dharwad distric
Slab lying in the Backyard of Būdayya Hiremath

Permmāḍidēva: 12th century A.D.

The record speaks about Jayakēśi and Mailaḷadēvi and also their sons Permāḍi and his younger brother Vijayāditya. Further it states that Permmāḍi as ruling over Konkaṇa-900, Palasige-12000 and Kāvaḍi-dvīpa-Samālakka. While describing Tāmbrapura, it also describes a *daṇḍanayaka* Mādhavarāja and *Sāmanta* Kagga. It is said that an officer named Mallidēva was in-charge of Tammiyūr, Māvaḷḷi, Huligōḍa, Kōte-kiruvatti, Nelkunda and Hasurage. It refers to the conastruction of *Jina Bhavana* by *Kuruṁba Sēṇiga Samūha* and also grants made by *Sāmanta* Kagga to this *Kuruṁba Sēniga Jinālaya* after laving the feet of Mēghachandra Munipa.

Text

1. @ Śrimat-parama-gaṁbhīra syādadvāmōgha lāṁchhanaṁ jiyā-Trailōkya-nāthasya śāsanaṁ Jina [śāsaraṁ]
2. @Svasti samasta bhuvan-āśraya śrī-prithvīvallabha mahārājādhirāja paramēśvara parama
3. bhaṭṭarakaṁ Satyāśraya kuḷa-tilakaṁ Chāḷukyābharaṇaṁ śrīma-Jjagadēkamalla-dēvara vijaya
4. rajyam-uttarōttar-ābhivriddhi pravarddhamānam-ā-chandrārkka-tāraṁ saluttam-ire @ Tachhakrava
5. rtti vikrama sahāyaṁ @vri @ Jana-nāthaṁ Jayakēśidēvanakhiḷ-ōrvvināthan-ā-puṇya bhājana
6. narddhāngi Chalukya-Chakriyamagaḷ lōkaika-vikhyāta māninі tāṁ Maiḷaladēvi tat-priya tanuja-Vī
7. ra Permmāḍiy-ātana tammaṁ Vijayāvanīśan-enaliṁ mat-anyarēṁ dhanyarē @ Svasti samadhigata pañcha
8. mahā-śabda mahā-maṇḍalēśvaraṁ Banavasi-puravarādhīśvaraṁ samasta bhuvana saṁsthūyamāna ha-
9. ra dharaṇī prasūtaṁ Triḷōchana-Kadamba vaṁśa-mahōdaya śikhar-ābhyudaya-mānamahā prachaṇ
10. ḍa mārthaṇḍa mārttaṇḍa karāti-tībra prabhāva vaśīkrita sakaḷa mahī-maṇḍaḷanuttungana Simha-
11. lānchchanaṁ Vānara-mahā dhvajaṁ Permmaṭṭi-tūryya-nirghōshaṇaṁ chaturāsīti-nagar-ādhīśhatāshsṭhā-
12. ḍaś-āśvamēdha-dīkshā-dịkshita kuḷa-prasūtaṁ himavad-girīndra rundra śikhara-sthāpita śiḷā…..
13. sthaṁbhaṁ tyāga Jaga-jhampa-Jhaṁpaḷāchāryyaṁ niśśankarāmaṁ subhaṭa-kanaka nikashōpaḷaṁ śaraṇāgata-vajra

14. prākāraṁ saṃkrānti dhavaḷam mūrtti-Nārāyaṇaṁ kīrtti marttaṇḍaṁ maṇḍaḷika lalātapattaṁ vairi-gharaṭṭa
15. su-bhaṭa rāja-śikhāmaṇi maṇḍaḷika chūḍāmanī-tyakhiḷa nāmāvaḷi virājitar-appa śrīman-mahā
16. maṇḍlēśvarṁ **śrī Vira-permmāḍi dēvar Konkaṇa-voṁbhainūṟumaṁ Palasige-pannichchāsira-mumaṁ Kavaḍadvī**
17. **pa samā lakshayuman**-ēka chchatradiṁ sukhadin-āḷuttam-ire @ ka @ Palasige vishayāntaradoḷu phala-bha @
18. rita vinamna-chūtavallī kuḷadiṁ malevīrahita Jina-niḷayadi-naḷipudu **Tāmbrāpura**-purandhara-puramaṁ @
19. adan-āḷvanamaḷa guṇa-gaṇa sadana sishsṭhē-sḥtha vandi kallōrviruham kadana prachanḍan-abhinava-madanaṁ daṇḍēśamau-
20. ḷi-Mādhavarāja @ Ā Mādirājaṇ-aṇugiṁ. [gaṁ] sāmaja-vairi pratāpanaṁ kaggaṇanaṁ Sāmanyan-allanivanedīmendu mahi pō
21. galalke-poredan-utsāhadindaṁ @ Antu pati-kūrttu pareyal-ananta-gunakkōlida balada Mārmmale-vadaṭargantakane-
22. ne Kaggaṁ sāmanta śirōvajradandan-ene pesarvvaḍedaṁ @ Antu sāmanta Kaggayyaṁ Mādirāja daṇḍanāyakaniṁ parōksha
23. diṁ tat-santānadoḷ Mallidēva-daṇḍanāyakanaṁ nilisi Tammiyūr-Māvaḷḷi-Huligōda Kōṭe-Kiṟuvatti Nelkuṁ-
24. daṁ Hāvasageṟey-ent-initumaṁ Tribhōgyābhyaṁtaraṁ sukhadin-āḷuttam-ire @ Tadīya-dauhitraṁ @vri@
25. antu virōdhi-maṇḍaḷikanana havarangadol ugra-kōpa vikrāntadinaṭṭikolva javanaṁje śaraṇbuge va

26. jra gēha mēranṭiraniva dāna-guṇadindamarōrvvī-ruhaṁ virōdhi sāmanta manōja-Rudranene mechcha-
27. daḍāre ssamaraika Rudranaṁ @ Nava-Chandrābharaṇaṁ Vibhūti-nirataṁ darppishṭha vidvishṭhaddānava saṁhārā-nara
28. māramend-ī budha... brinda stutyan-ārādhya-bhū bhuvana viśva-mahīśvara priyanenala-Rudraṁ-gaḍeṁ Rudra-
29. nāmāvadenōrppaḍe bērppadaṁ kuḍuvanō-naudāryyadiṁ śauryadiṁ @ antu Sāmanta Rudrayyaṁ tadi
30. ya santānadoḷ tatprati pattiyaṁ vrittiyaṁ Sukhadin-āḷuttam-ire @vri @ Jina-pādāṁbuja bhriṁga
31. rūrjjita yaśaschhāritra-śiḷānvita vinayōpēta rudrā tā vikra-yutar Sadhamma... shtha-parar manado
32. ḷ-nishkaṭṭarchitassamaya bhaktar satya-saṃpannar-eṁbine-sandiḷdi Kuṟuṁba-Sēṇigara nāvam baṇṇa..... sabballavaṁ @
33. Jaga-vidita Kuṟum bitiga maggada.... bīran-enipaṁ..... chavau jjagavatāram-āgi pesaru-vettudu kāraṇadiṁ Kuṟuṁ
34. ba-Sēṇiga kulav-ādud ā kula-sampadavadaroḷ daye dāna-dharmmaṁ negardda charitramaṁ vinaya saṁpadamaṁ pogaḷvange santa-
35. taṁ @ Dhareyoḷe-sanda Kuṟumba Sēṇiga-samūhaṁ bhaktiyiṁ Jaina-mandiramaṁ mādisalakokum-endu pirid-ōtsāha
36. diṁ pūṇdu nirbbharadiṁ vistāram-āgi chelveseye puṇya-punjamādante bhāsura vikhyāti podaḷdurvvare-Jinēndrāvāsa

37. vaṁ mādidar @ ka @ Dharaṇēndra niḷayamaṁ kinnara-bhavanamanudita . [si] da kūṭada chelviṁ
38. dore saripāsaṭiyenal-ī-dhareyoḷ karamesetu tōṟuguṁ Jina-bhavanaṁ @ Ā Jinēndra bhavana sambandhad-āchārya @ vri @ chaṭuḷate
39. yiṁ chatussamaya nāmada patramanaide nālkumaṁ ghaṭadoḷ- gikkimaṁdideḍe tuḍumki..... keyge-vandu
40. daṁ sudatara-vākyadiṁ nuḍidu nirvahikuṁ ' sirinadiyandade kuṭiḷa-kumārga kutsita-ku-vādi-gelvare @
41. cha-chhiśyar @ ka @ Siddhānta-trayam-eṁbudu.... yēnisidudu Vāsupūjymam .... chakravarti Jaga-
42. davaḷita-kīrttiy-eṁbudondachhariye......... śishṭar @ vri@ dhareyoḷsaṁ ....sthagaṇ parivri
43. ḍha chhatrakūṭānvay-ēkābharanar bhavya.... Bhāskararamaḷina Jaināgamāṁ-bōdhi....... bhēndra simharjjaga-
44. vinuta-pada-viśva-siddhānta-chakrēśvara sishṭhā-kīrtti kānta pravidita Guṇanandi-brati...... r @ ka @ viḷasat-ku-
45. ṟuṁba Sēṇigad kuḷa-bhūshaṇa-namaḷa dharmmatatpara marddivararvīvara vaḷaya prasiddhan-ati-nirmmaḷa chittaṁ Kagga...... nedeteya vaṁ
46. śa lalāmaṁ @vri @ Māḷaya-muttayaneḷpu-vettaḷiyaṁ Kētaṁ dēvaṁ Jinaṁ śīḷa-prastute Kāḷikabbeṁ-janani
47. ... khyāte su-strī lasa.....saṁyate peṁpiniṁ Kanakiyakkaṁ lokamar....tamman-end-ī-lōkaṁ pogaḷalke-nōnta-narara...........
48. mānavar @ka @ guru mēgha-chandra-munipaṁ dharaṇī-jana stutyanātma-saṁbhūtar kaḷḷaramese

49. .... putraṁ Māḷa ..... ya Kaggaṇaṁ Kuṟuṁba Sēṇiga-Jinālayakke dēvara da

50. ..... geyaṁ baḍagaṇa nīrvvariya bachhal-mērey-āgite....

51. ..... gaḍiyāgi haḍuduvaluṁdi

52. .... basadiya hakkaliṁ haḍu

53. l-mattaru-hakkalmaṁ @vri @

54. .... nūnaṁ Koṭṭamā

XXIX

Junjarabailu, Kalaghatagi Taluk, Dharwad district
Slab lying in the field of Dyavanna Adiveppa Durgappanavar

Permmāḍidēva : 12th Century

It is a damaged record which refers to Mailaḷadēvi, and her son Permmāḍi and also to his rule over Konkaṇa-900 and Palasige-12000. *Ūroḍeya* Chadimayya finds a mention in this record. As the record is damaged, details are not available.

Text

1. Namas-tunga-śiras-chumbi chaṇdra-chāmara-chāravē Trailōkya nagar ....
2. Svasti samasta bhuvan-āśraya śrī prithvi vallabha ṁahārājā.............
3. parama bhaṭṭārakaṁ Satyāśraya kuḷa-tiḷakaṁ Chālukyābharanaṁ.......
4. dēvara vijaya-rājyam-uttar-ōttar-ābhivriddhi pravardhamānamā-chandr-ārkka tāram-sa
5. luttaṁ-ire ||@ Tat-chchakravarti vikrama-sahāya || Jaganātha

6. ....nāthan-ā puṇya bhājanan-ardhāngi Chaḷukya-Chakriya-magaḷu Lō-
7. ta... Maiḷaladēvi tat-priya tanūja Vīra-permmāḍiyāta
8. nenaliṁ mattan-anyareṁbanyare || Svasti samadhigata-paṁcha-mahā-śabda.....
9. vāśi puravar-ādhīśvaraṁ samasta bhuvana saṁsthūyamāna pa....
10. Triḷōchana Kadaṁba-vaṁśa mahārāya śikhar-ābhyudaya māna....
11. ... mātra... karātī-tībra nija pratāpa vaśikrita sakaḷa digvanne....
12. .... Vānara mahā-dhvaja permmāḍi-tūryya-nirmāpṇam chaturā
13. ...... śāśva-mēdha| dikvadikvita kuḷa-prasūtaṁ himavad-girindraru...
14. Śakti prabhāvaṁ | Tyāga-jaga-Jhaṁparuṁ Jaṁpaḷāchārya || Nissaṁkarā....
15. vaḷuṁ saraṇāgata vajra-prākāraṁ | Lōkaika-kaḷpa drumaṁ saṁkrā.
16. ..... yaṇa kīrtti-mārttaṇḍam | maṇḍalīka lalāṭa padam | vairi gharaṭṭaṁ
17. ... kā ....būdāma... nityakhiḷa-nāmangi virājitar-appa....
18. **Vīrapermādi-dēvaru Koṁkaṇa-voṁbhainūṟuṁ Palasige-pannichchā...**
19. .. sukhadiṁ rājyaṁ geyuttaṁ-ire @ tat-pāda padmōpajīvi @ Svasti

20. .... prabhugaḷuṁ Vidvajjanābhīshṭha phaḷadāyakaruṁ | paṭṭama.....

21. .. bhaya .... ledu [ha]bharuṁ dinartti jana samu sa...

22. .. tarappa śrīmad-ūroḍeya Chadimayya-nāyakaru....

23. neraḍu prabhu-sāṁyadin-āḷdu dushṭha-nigraha śis...

24. tat-pāda padmōpajīvi || Nidhiyenisidana.........

25. ḷu nelasirdda lakshmī gēṇa ....

26. dēvaṁ pāpaṁ tana-gā ....

27. yoḷu || ā ....

28. dativlri ....

XXX

Kāvalavāḍa, Haliyal taluk. North Kanara District

Kavalavāḍa, Haliyal taluk. North Kanara District

Hero-stone kept out-side Somēśvara temple

12th century A.D.

The hero-stone refers to the death of a hero while rescuing the cows from the hands of thieves. The date given in the record is 11th year of Chālukya Jagadēkamala, *Manmatha, Pushya Su.....* In the absence of details not mentioned in the record, the exact date not ascertained.

Text

Ist Panel

1. @ Svasti śrī **Chāḷukya Pratāpa-chakravartti [Jagadē]kamalla varshada 11 neya Mamatha Saṁvatsarada]**
2. **Pushya suddha śrīma**t-Kāhalavāḍada-baḷiya bāda tō. mana.

II panel

1. ḷiya .. va danamaṁ Kaḷḷaruyvalli Kētayaṁ hiṇḍa-hatti taḷutiṟidu halaraṁ koṇḍu tuṟuvaṁ
2. …. suralōka prāptanāda

XXXI

Muttage, Kalaghatagi Taluk, Dharwad District
Slab setup infront of Kalmēśvara temple

Jayakesi-III : 1223 A.D.

It menions the rule of Jayakēśi over Konkaṇa-900 and Palasige-12000 and Kāvaḍi-dvīpa-Savalakka from his capital Gōve. It records a gift of land to the *āchārya* Śambhudēva, for the worship, offerings, renovation and also for feeding of ascetics in the temple of Suḷḷēśvara by Bonta-gāvuṇḍa, Chāva-gauṇḍa, *adhikāris* and *aruvattokkalu* of the place. It also mentions grants made by *Tambūliga seṭṭi sāsīrvvaru* ,*sunkada adhikāri* Dinakara-nāyaka and *aruvattokkalu* to the same temple.

It is dated in the 42nd regnal year of Śivachitta-Vīra-Jayakēśidēva, *Chitrabhānu, Māgha, Puṇṇame, A+diwāra, Vyatipāta* correaponding to probably 1223 A.D., *Māgha Puṇṇame* is January 18, which was Wednesday.

Text

1. * Namas-tunga śiras-chuṁbi chandra-chāmara charavē Trailōkya nagar-ārambha mūla-stambhāya sa(śa) ṁbave || Jayatyā-vishkri-taṁ
2. Vishṇōr-Vvarāh(haṁ) kshōbhitārṇṇavaṁ dakshiṇōnnata daṁstargra viśraṁta bhuvanaṁ vapuḥ || Samadhigata paṁcha mā(ma) hā
3. mā(ma)hā-śabda Mā(Ma) hāmaṇḍaḷēśvaraṁ | Banavāsī puravarādhīśvaran-anēka saṁara jayōpārjjita vīra Śrīnivāsa da-
4. kshiṇa dōrddaṇḍa(m) | Paurādhirāja tyāga-vinōdaṁ | Kanduka sahasra kaḷa vidagda .... Pāṇḍu-na-
5. ndanaṁ | bhujabala mallaṁ | maṇḍaḷika śikhāmaṇi Kādamba chūḍāmaṇītyakhiḷa rājāvaḷi [samāḷaṁkrita] śrimatu
6. **Jayakēśi-dēvarasaru** nija rājadhāni Gōveyoḷy **Koṁkaṇa-Ombhainūṟumaṁ Palasige-pannichchāsiramumaṁ** dushṭha-nigraha śishtha-prati-
7. pāḷaneyiṁ sukha-samkha(ka)thā vinōdadiṁ rājyaṁ geyyuttam-ire || Ari-bhūpḷaran-āhavaj-iraṇadoṭārdde baṭṭi-beṁkoṁḍu tan-nara-
8. pāḷarkkaḷa-vastu-vāhana patākā-tūryya śubhāta-pātra ra[ṇa] chchaṁka-nikāyamaṁ kavarddu koṇḍāschairyyadiṁ Vikramābharaṇaṁ tāṁ

9. Jayakēśi-dēvan-esedaṁ Kādaṁba-kanṭhīrava || Svasti [sa]masta praśasti-sahitaṁ Kādamba-chakravarti **Śivachitta-Vira-Jayakēśi dēva-varshada nā-**
10. **lvatterad(ḍa)neya Chitrabhānu-saṁvachharada Māgha-Puṇṇame-Ādivāra byatīpāta-Saṁkramaṇa Sōmagrahaṇad-aṁdu** Muttageya
11. Boṅta-gāvuṇḍa Chāva-gāvuṇḍa alliya-adhikāri-aṟuvattokkalaṁ-irdu śrī Suḷḷēśvara-dēvara māṭa-kūṭa bhinnarādhārakka-nitya
12. [ni]vēdyak-āchāryyana .... Siṁgeya-gaṭṭeya keṟe-ottina baḍaga-deseya garddeyumaṁ adaṟa mundottina pakkalumaṁ-ūriṁ mū-
13. ḍa deseya Baḷḷigaṭṭeya modal-ēriya maṁjjiya-dōṇṭada mūḍa-deseya-garddeyumaṁ-Sullēśvara-dēvara-sthānāchārya Saṁbhudēva-
14. rige dhārā-pūrvvakaṁ-māḍi koṭṭaru || Sunkada-ȧdhikāri [Di] nakara nāyakaru śrī Suḷḷēśvara dēvarige baḍagiya taḷasāri-
15. geyaṁ dhāra-pūrvvakaṁ māḍi-bittaru || Ā-sthaḷada aṟuvattokkalu śrī Suḷḷēśvara dēvarige sauṭige-ẏaṇṇeya dhārā
16. pūrvvakaṁ māḍi-bittaru || Taṁbuliga **Seṭṭi-sāsirvvaru** śrī-Suḷḷēśvara-dēvarige hēriṁge-vīsamaṁ-dhāra-pūrvvakaṁ māḍi-bi
17. ṭṭaru || Horagindaṁ-bandu arihavaṁ māḍida-hēṟiṁge aravīsamaṁ-biṭṭaru || Sōmachandra daṁnnāyakaṁ baḍagiya-bāyi
18. veṇṇeya śrī Suḷḷēśvara-dēvarige dhārā-pūrvvakaṁ māḍi-biṭṭaru ||

XXXII

Tambur: Kalghatgi taluk, Dharwad district
Slab lying in thr premises of Basananna Temple

Jagadekamalla : 12th century A.D.

The record while referring to the rule of Jagadēkamalla of the Chālukya dynasty, mentions Jayakēśi of the Kadamba family as administering the divisions viz., Konkaṇa-900, Palasige-12000 and Kavaḍi-dvīpa-Savalakka from his capital Gōve. It also mentions his senior queen Maiḷaladēvi and their sons Permāḍi and Vijayāditya. Savitri, their daughter, given in marriage to Gangidēva son of Tailanrpa also find a mention in this record. Further the record refers to *daṇḍanāyaka* named Mādirājayya as in charge of Tammiyūru-12 near Māvaḷenāḍu division. As the record is damaged, the purport of it is not clear.

Text

1st piece broken

1. Namastunga śiraschumbi chaṁdra-chāmara chāravē trailōkya-nagar-āraṁbha-mūḷa-stambhāya Śaṁbhavē
2. Svasti samsta bhuvan-āśraya śrī prithvī-vallabha mahā-rājādhirāja paramēśvara parama-bha-
3. ṭṭāraka Satyāśraya Kuḷa-tiḷaka Chāḷuky-ābharaṇa śrī mat-Jagadēka-malla-dēvara vijaya-rājyamuttarō-

2nd piece

1. ttarābhivriddhi pravaddhamāna....... @ tat-pāda........ ya lakshmī-niḷayaṁ samasta vana..... vaṭṭa-

2. ṇādhīśan-udgha-yaśa-śrīyuta Vādirāja charita kā........ rājaṁ hara bhū-prasūtan-akhiḷa
3. kshāpāḷa Jaitra dhvajaṁ Jayakēśi kshiti-pāḷakaṁ negaḷdan-ī viśvaṁbharā chakrapāḷa || Svasti........ sahitaṁ Śrī man-ma-
4. hā maṇḍaḷēśvaraṁ **Jayakēśi dēvar-nnija-rāja-dhāni Gōveyoḷ Konkaṇa-voṁbhainu-rumaṁ-Palasige paṇṇichchāsira mumaṁ [Kavadi dvīpa]**
5. **Savā-lakkamumaṁ** dushṭha nigraha-viśishṭha pratipāḷaneyinduttar-ōttarābhivriddhi pravardhamānam-ā-chandr-ārkka tāraṁ suka-sankaṭhā-vinōdadiṁ...
6. ya rājyaṁ saluttam-ire || tad-anuja || yibha-vairi-parākramadiṁ-sva-bhuja-baḷōrdhru-tan-enippa maṇḍaḷikaṁ śrī[ma] Tribhuvana-mallam...vi...
7. taraṇa vibhava purandharanuṁ-enisi negarddaṁ dhạreyoḷ || Śrīge Hariyoḷ vivāhādyo-gaṁ geyavnte chakri tanujeya kott-anurā-
8. gade Jayakēśige Traibhōgābhyantarav-enittu Palasige-nāḍaṁ || karighaṭeyaṁ turaga-vajra-vara-vastu samasta kānçha
9. ṇābharaṇaṁgaḷ-veras-intu chakri narchchi-navara kanneyan-ittu parasidaṁ padepindaṁ || Kālaṁ karchchida-niraṁ-melenipattyuttamāngadoḷ dhari
10. yisidambhu lalanādhīśan-enal mēl-enisidarroḷare konkaṇōrvviśaniṁ || śrī man-mahā-maṇḍaḷēśvara Jayakēśidē-
11. vaṅgaṁ piriy-arasi Maiḷaladēviyarigaṁ puṭṭida tanūbhavar-entappar-endeḍe || Kādaṁba-vaṁśa-tiḷakar-Kādaṁba-Kuḷāssarō-
12. ja-rājita mitra Kādaṁba vaṁśavardhanar-ādarp-Permmāḍirvvijaya-dēvanuṁ-eṁbar || tad-agraje || śrī vanitey-enipa suteyaṁ Sāvitri

13. ya[m]Tailanripa-tanūjaṁg .. śāvidhita-kīrtiy-āgiral-ī vasumati pogaḷe Gangidēvang-ittar || tat-pāda padmōpajīvi ||
14. @ Svasti samadhigata paṁcha-mahāśabda-mahā-prachaṇḍa daṇḍa-nāyakaṁ vairi-bhaya-dāyakaṁ | samara-sāgara-taraṇ-ripu
15. kāḷa-daṇḍa chaturanga-baḷa sūtradhāri manege murāri vijayānganā bhujanga | chaturanga siṁga | krita guṇa-kritya ka-
16. .... liyuga....Vikramāditya | Vīra-lakshmī-griha tōraṇa | aṇṇana-gandhavāraṇa | asamasāhasa vainatēya duradankajiy
17. bāhubaḷa bāvannavīra | vipra-kēdāra | par-ārtha Paraśurāma | subhaṭ-aṅkabhīma | vandi-brunda-chintāmaṇi | Śaraṇāgata ra-
18. kshāmaṇi Konkaṇa-chakravarti śri_ma-Jayakēśi-dēva rājya-lakshmī-viḷāsaṁ | sakaḷa Lakshmī-nivāsa | nityākhiḷa nāmāvaḷi-vi
19. rājitar-appa śrī man-mahā prachaṇḍa-daṇḍa-nāyakaṁ Mādirājayyaṁ Māvaḷe-nāḍa baḷiya-bāḍa Tammiyūruṁ Pa-
20. nnirppaḷḷiyuṁ-aneka prabhu-sāmyadinda dushṭha-nigraha visishsṭha prati-pāḷaneyin-āḷdu sukhadin-ire || Baḷasida nandanā-va-
21. ḷigaḷim palamaṁ Kamaḷākara-gaḷiṁ toḷaguva-Śāta kumbha kaḷasōjjvalaṁappa-marāḷayṁagaḷiṁ miḷivaṁ Vrushandrasiṁ
22. ha vihāgēndra patākegaḷinde nāḍē-kaṇgoḷisi basantmaṁ meṟedu tōrppudu Tāṁbra puraṁ-nirantaraṁ || ā purakkādhīśa

23. nuṁ Kāśyapa-gōtra sarōjakara mitran-appa śrī Mādirāja daṇḍa-nāyakan-ent-appan-endaḍe || Dharmada mēru dānada
24. tavarmmane satyadabīḍu sauchadiṁ permmeyanānta mānasikegālayavoḷ-guṇad-unnatikeyiṁ Dharmajan-endu baṇṇiṁ
25. pudu santatā Mādhava-daṇḍanāthana kūrmmeyoḷintu sajjana su-hrūjjana sēvya-nijag A-jjanaṁ || antāviro-
26. dhigaḷge para-nārige vadhū-janakke kaiantanarange kolvi-peṟapinguva-kūrisuvi vaba keyind-anta kunembu
27. dā pavana-nandanageṁbudutkantu-veṁbud-āhāntu madalta kalpa-taruv-eṁbudu Mādhava daṇḍanāthanaṁ || Janakaṁ Chaṅga Chamū-
28. pa Rāma-ramaṇī vaidēhiyēnt-ante sajjanē tāy-Achaḷādēvi.... sa-chharitadoḷ saubhāgyadoḷ peṁ-pinolvi-nutaṁ śrī
29. Jayakēśi kūrppanenipaṇṇam-Nārasimgaṁgaṁ magaṁtanag endaṇdu... kritārthar-enduṁ-enisiṟdaṁ Mādhavaṁ-dhātriyoḷ || śrīge...
30. neleyenisi sukha.... mā... mudadiṁ chāgada chāgiya marmmaṁ Bhōga-purandharan-e-
31. nisida dhāriṇiyo........ ninde cha.....de-negardda-itin Viśvēśvarāgāramaṁ tanniṁd-ātana.....
32. Boppana........ ṇa siḷākarma..... dyādi-dig dēvariṁdinniṁt-āge....
33. .... d .. ja kaḷā ....surachiraṁ-udāra-chāru charitam bhū-jātey-ena ...
34. .... ḷaṁto.......rmanana...... nunibha kū

Damaged

XXXIII

Tambur, Kalghatgi taluk, Dharwad district
Slab lying infront of Uttarakumara temple

Chaṭṭayya : 12th century A.D.

The record refers to an endowment of land and houses made by Kētapayya, the Heggaḍe of Māvaḷenāḍu, for the maintenance of dancing girls in the temple of Uttarēśvara, after laving the feet of Lakulīśa pandita The Ūroḍeya Hiṭṭimayya also received two gadyānās from the donor. The record was composed by *paramakavi* Kannapayya and the engraver was Udayaṇṇa. It is in 12th century characters.

Text

1. Svasti-samadhigata paṁcha-mahā-śabda mahā-maṇḍḷēśvaraṁ Śrīmat-**Chaṭṭayya-dēvara** vijaya-rājya saluttaṁ-ire | Tammi
2. yūroḍeya Hiṭṭimayyaṁge Māvaḷe-nāḍa herggade Kētapayyaṁ pāda-pūjeyaṁ-koṭṭu Lakuḷīśvara-paṇḍitara kālaṁ-karchchi Uttarēśvara-dēvara bhō-
3. gada sūḷeyargge pāvuḷakkaṁ bā[ḷu] bbeya kaṭṭiṁ baḍagalaṟuvattaidu kay-nīḷada padināṟu kayyagalada bhūmiyindoḷagaṇa sūḷegēṟiyiṁ
4. mane panneraḍakke mattaṁ-avargge Ālakoḷadiṁ-keḷage teṁka-mogad-ā-nīrvvariyale Pārvva-gōla gaddeya mattarippattēḷakkaṁ Uroḍeyargge kāṇikey-eraḍu-gadyā

5. ṇamaṁ tettu sarbba-namasyaṁ sarvva-bādhā-parihāram-āge paḍedu dēvaśvamāge bittar || Int-ī-dharmmamaṁ kād-ātange Gange-Gangā-sāgara Vāraṇāsi Kuru

6. kshētragal-eṁba puṇya-tīrthaṁgaḷoḷ sāsira kavileya koṇḍum koḷagumaṁ paṅcharatnadi kaṭṭisi Vēdapāragarappa-sa-brāhmanargg-ubhaya-mukhi-goṭṭa phaḷa-

7. ṁ-akkuvidan-aḷidātan-inituman-alida paṅcha-mahā pātakan-akkuṁ sāmānyōyaṁ dharma sē-tu-nṛipāṇāṁ kāḷe-kāḷe-pāḷaniyō bhava-

8. dbhiḥ sarbbanētān bhāvinaṟppārthi-vēndrān bhūyō bhūyō yāchate Rāma-chandraḥ || Sva-dattaṁ para-dattāṁ vāyō-harēti vasundharā shashṭhir-vvarsha sahasrā

9. ṇi vishsṭhāyāṁ-jāyatē-krimiḥ || Parama kavi-Kannapayyaṁ virachisidaṁ su-ruchir-ātmadiṁd-akkaramaṁ baredaṁ palargge … yaḷk-ādaradind Udayaṇṇan-ī-śiḷā-śāsanaṁ [vaṁ]

XXXIV

Tambur, Kalghatgi taluk, Dharwad district
Slab lying infront of Uttarakumara temple outside the village

Permāḍidēva – 12th Century

The date given in the record is Kaliyuga Samvatsara 4248. It registers a grant of land by Chaṭṭayadēva, for the offerings to god Chaṭṭēśvaradēva after laving the feet of *sthanāchārya* (name lost) of the temple.

date given in the record is *Śivachitta-vīra Permāḍidēva varsha..... Visvāvasu, Pushya, ba. 2, Monday. Uttarāyana Sankrānti.* The regnal year is not given.

Text

1. Svasti **Kaliyuga saṁvatsara 4248 sandad-ādiy-ā**
2. gi **Śivachi[tta permmāna]ḍi-dēva varshada Viśvāvasu [saṁva]tsarada Paúsya bbhuḷa 2 Sōmavāradand-Uttarāyaṇaṭ saṁkrāti vyatipatamāge** tatpunya dina
3. doḷu śrī [machchaṭṭaya] dēvaru śrī Chaṭṭēśvara dēvara naivēdya naḍevant-ā-keṟeya muḍadiṁ [mū]ḍalu ḫiṁḷeya-geṟeya teṅkaṇa [haṁ]di guḷi gaṭṭi gaddeya ko-
4. ṭṭaru .... ā sthaḷadalli .... ya hāsugeya bhūmiya nīunōḍi ... [ru]v-endu-besasalu śrī[vai]dīśvaraya daṇḍanā
5. yakar-ā...... ydu Nāgavvagaḷa-keyya vāsugeyiṁ mūḍalu Hiṟe-haḷḷige srī [kē]d-Īśvarayya daṇḍanā..hōda baṭṭeyiṁ [mu]....
6. [ḍa]ṇdigeya..... hāsugeyim paḍavalu Tenkal aḍḍaḷigereya bachchalu mēṟey-āgiyu-dēvara sthānāchārya ....
7. Śrī .... bhēśvara-paṇḍitara kālaṁ-karchchi dhārāpūrvvakaṁ māḍi sarvva-namaśyaṁ sarvva-bādhā parihārav-āgi koṭṭa
8. .... ḷipidaṁ pañcha-mahā-pātakan-akku ||

BIBLIOGRAPHY

1. Epigraphia Indica (EI)
2. Epigraphia Carnatica (EC)
3. South Indian Inscriptions(SII)
4. Karnataka Inscriptions (KI)
5. Goa Gazetteer (GG)
6. Dharwad District Gazetteer
7. Belgaum District Gazetteer
8. Gazetteer of India – Maharashtra State – History, Part-I Ancient Period
9. Maharashtra State Gazetteer
10. Journal of the Bombay Branch of Royal Asiatic Society (JBBRAS), Old series
11. Karnataka Bharati, Karnatak University, Dharwad
12. Annual Report on Indian Epigraphy (ARIE)
13. Progress Report on Kannada Research Institute (1941-44)
14. Summaries of Inscriptions 1943-44 to 1949-50
15. Buhler G. Vikramankadeva Charitam of Bilhana (Ed.)

16. Coelho W. The Hoysala Vamsa, Indian Historical Research Institute, St. Xavier's College, Bombay, 1950

17. Desai Dinakara, Mahamandalesvaras under the Chalukyas of Kalyani, Indian Historical Research Institute, St. Xavier's College, Bombay,1951.

18. Desai P.B., Ritti S.H. & Gopal B.R., A History of Karnataka, Kannada Research Institute, Karnatak University, Dharwad, 1981.

19. Desai P.B., Studies in Epigraphy, Karnatak Historical Research Society, Dharwad, 1946

20. Dikshit M.G., Select Inscriptions from Maharashtra, (SIM) Deccan College Research Institute, Poona, 1947.

21. Fleet J.F., Dynasties of Kanarese Districts in Bombay Gazetteer , Vol.I, part-II, Bombay Government, Bombay, 1896.

22. Gadre A.S., Important Inscriptions from Baroda State (IIBS), Pratapasimha Maharaya Rajyabhisheka Grantha-mala, Baroda, 1943.

23. Gopal B.R., Minor Dynasties of South India; Karnataka, New Era Publications, P.B. No.2459, Raja Annamalaipuram, Madras.

24. Gopal B.R., The Chalukyas of Kalyāṇa and the Kalachuris, Prasaranga, Karnatak University, Dharwad, 1981.

25. Moraes G.M., Kalama Kula, Indian Historical Research Institute, Bombay, 1931.

26. Narasimha Murthy A.V., Coins of Karnataka, Directorate of Archaeology and Museums, Mysore.

27. Ritti S.H., The Seunas, Department of Ancient Indian History & Epigraphy, Karnatak University, Dharwad, 1973.

28. Thosar H.S., Historical Geography of Maharashtra and Goa, Epigraphical Society of India, Mysore, 2004.

29. Zakia Khanum Ansari, Some Feudatory Families of Medieval Karnataka – A Study, Sri Hari Prakashana, Dharwad, 1998.

Journals

30. Journals of the Bombay Branch of Royal Asiatic Society (Old series)

31. Journals of the Karnatka University, Dhrawad

32. Karṇataka Bharati, Karnatka University, Dhrawad

33. Quarterly Journals of the Mythic Society, Bangalore

34. Indian Antiquary.

ABBREVIATIONS

EI.	-	Epigraphia Indica
EC.	-	Epigraphia Carnatica
IA.	-	Indian Antiquary
ARIE.	-	Annual Reports on Indian Epigraphy
SII.	-	South Indian Epigraphy
KI.	-	Karnataka Inscriptions
SIM.	-	Selected Inscriptions from Maharashtra
KK.	-	Kadamba Kula
IIBS.	-	Important Inscriptions from Baroda State
GG.	-	Goa Gazetteer

INDEX

[*ag.*, *agrahāra; arch.*, *architecture; au.*, *author; cap.*, *capital; ch.*, *chief; co.*, *country; de.*, *deity; di.*, *division; dy.*, *dynasty; f.*, *family; fe.*, *female; h.tax.*, *house tax; k.*, *king; p.*, *prince, princes; l.m.*, *land measure; n.*, *name; off.*, *office, officer; pl.*, *place; re.*, *region; ri.*, *river; s.a.. same as; te.*, *temple; t.d.*, *territorial division; tit.*, *title; vi.*, *village; wk.*, *work.*]

H

I

R

T

U

V

PLATES

Hero stone, Archaeological Museum, Goa, (Courtesy A.S.I.)

Hero stone, Archaeological Museum, Goa, (Courtesy A.S.I.)

Hero stone, Archaeological Museum, Goa, (Courtesy A.S.I.)

Hero stone, Archaeological Museum, Goa, (Courtesy A.S.I.)

Hero stone, Archaeological Museum, Goa, (Courtesy A.S.I.)

Siva Temple,Tambadi Surla, Goa

Gold coin of Shivachitta Permmadi deva CH.5 Ref. 189

Mugad Inscriptions

Origin of River Shalmala CH.IX, Ref. 24

Phione

Tank at Mugunda CH. 8 Ref.18 (2)